image comics presents

THE WALKING DEAD™

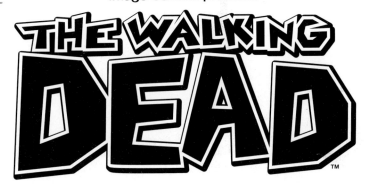

ROBERT KIRKMAN
CREATOR, WRITER

CHARLIE ADLARD
PENCILER

STEFANO GAUDIANO
INKER

CLIFF RATHBURN
GRAY TONES

RUS WOOTON
LETTERER

CHARLIE ADLARD
& DAVE STEWART
COVER

SEAN MACKIEWICZ
EDITOR

For SKYBOUND ENTERTAINMENT
Robert Kirkman - Chairman
David Alpert - CEO
Sean Mackiewicz - SVP Editor-in-Chief
Shawn Kirkham - SVP Business Development
Brian Huntington - Online Editorial Director
June Alian - Publicity Director
Andres Juarez - Art Director
Jon Moisan - Editor
Arielle Basich - Associate Editor
Carina Taylor - Production Artist
Paul Shin - Business Development Assistant
Johnny O'Dell - Social Media Manager
Sally Jacka - Online Editorial Assistant
Dan Petersen - Director of Operations & Events
Nick Palmer - Operations Coordinator
International inquiries: ag@sequentialrights.com
Licensing inquiries: contact@skybound.com
WWW.SKYBOUND.COM

® **IMAGE COMICS, INC.**
Robert Kirkman—Chief Operating Officer
Erik Larsen—Chief Financial Officer
Todd McFarlane—President
Marc Silvestri—Chief Executive Officer
Jim Valentino—Vice President

Eric Stephenson—Publisher
Corey Hart—Director of Sales
Jeff Boison—Director of Publishing Planning
& Book Trade Sales
Chris Ross—Director of Digital Sales
Jeff Stang—Director of Specialty Sales
Kat Salazar—Director of PR & Marketing
Drew Gill—Art Director
Heather Doornink—Production Director
Branwyn Bigglestone—Controller
IMAGECOMICS.COM

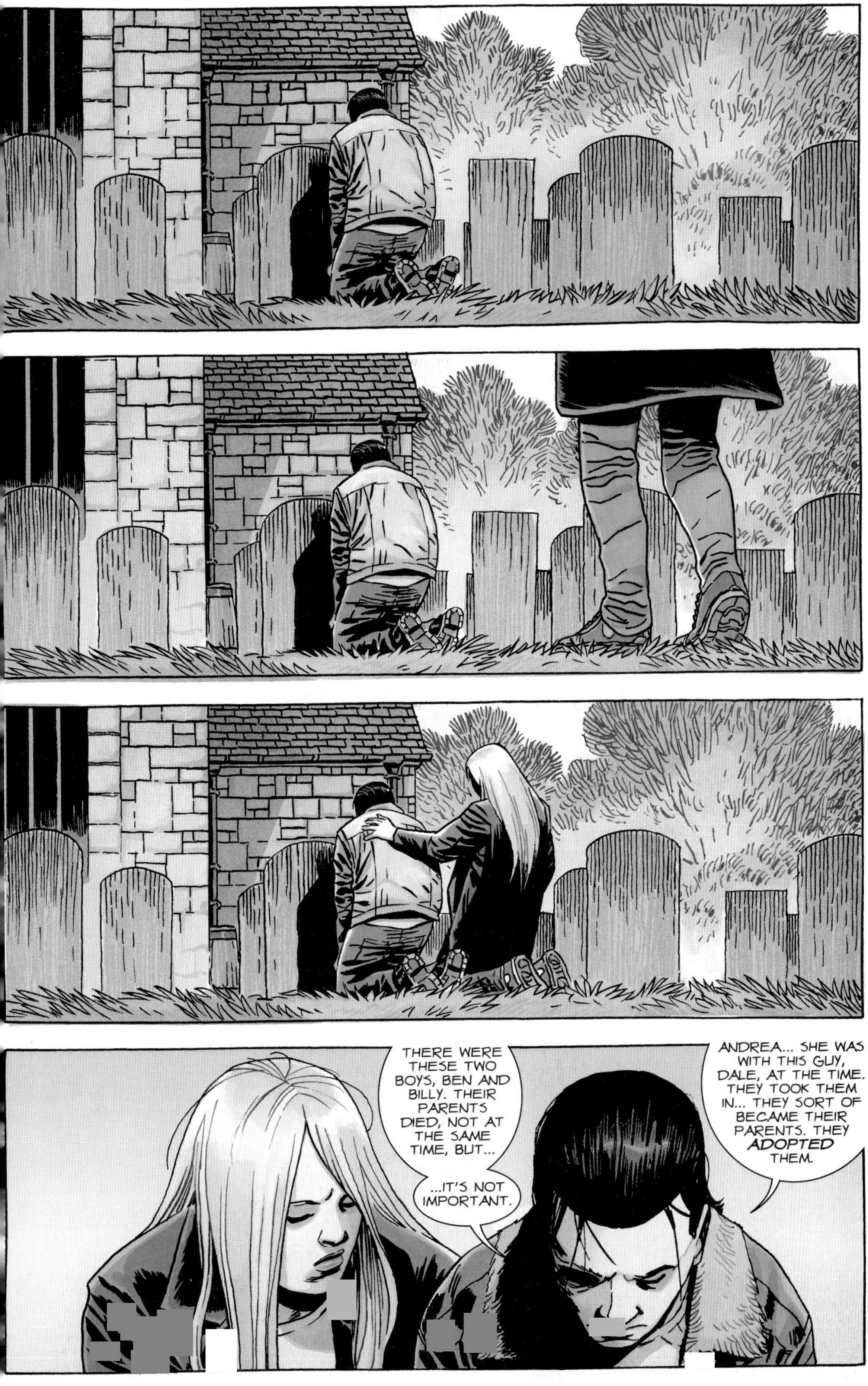
THERE WERE THESE TWO BOYS, BEN AND BILLY. THEIR PARENTS DIED, NOT AT THE SAME TIME, BUT...
...IT'S NOT IMPORTANT.
ANDREA... SHE WAS WITH THIS GUY, DALE, AT THE TIME. THEY TOOK THEM IN... THEY SORT OF BECAME THEIR PARENTS. THEY *ADOPTED* THEM.

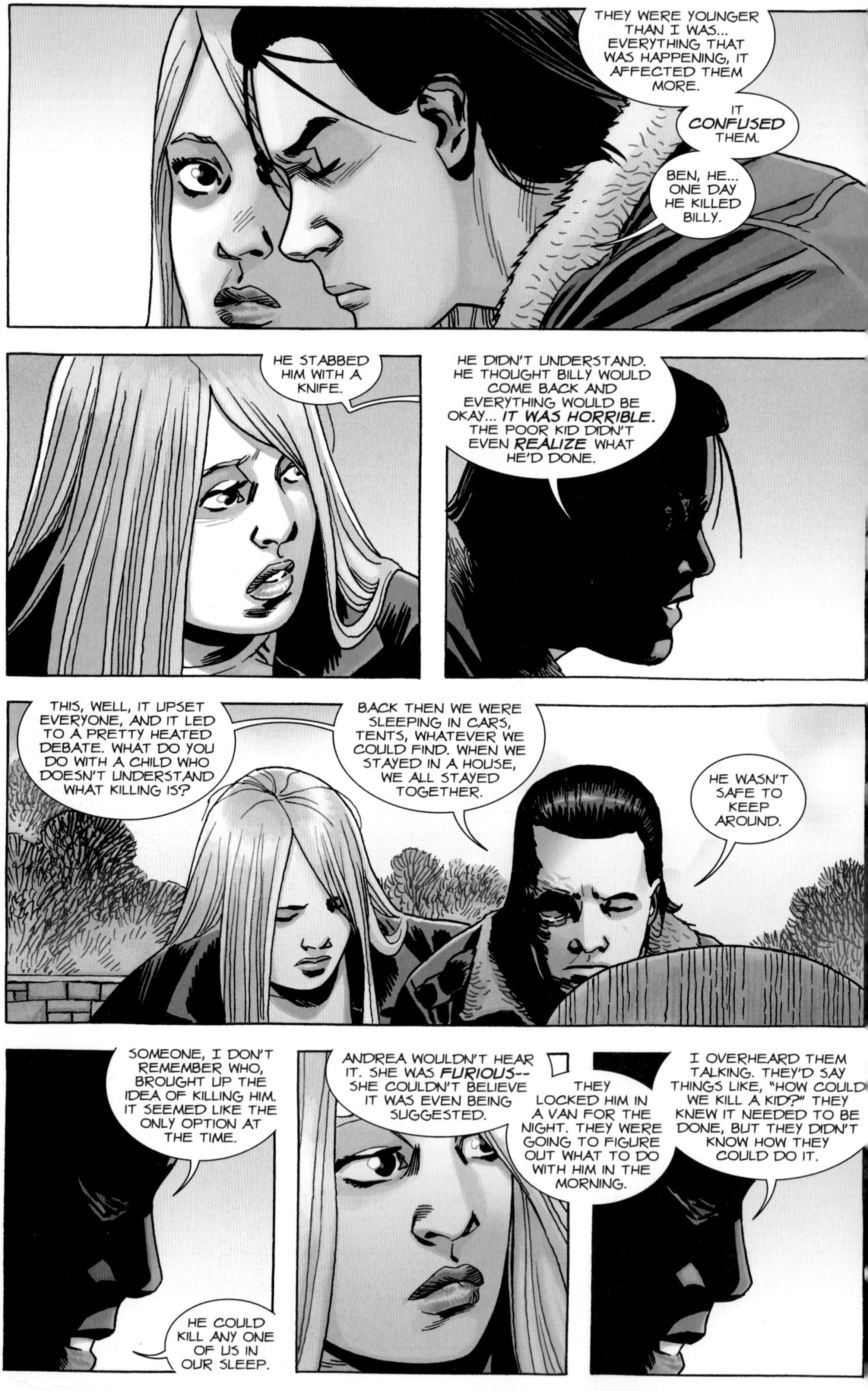

THEY WERE YOUNGER THAN I WAS... EVERYTHING THAT WAS HAPPENING, IT AFFECTED THEM MORE.
IT CONFUSED THEM.
BEN, HE... ONE DAY HE KILLED BILLY.
HE STABBED HIM WITH A KNIFE.
HE DIDN'T UNDERSTAND. HE THOUGHT BILLY WOULD COME BACK AND EVERYTHING WOULD BE OKAY... IT WAS HORRIBLE. THE POOR KID DIDN'T EVEN REALIZE WHAT HE'D DONE.
THIS, WELL, IT UPSET EVERYONE, AND IT LED TO A PRETTY HEATED DEBATE. WHAT DO YOU DO WITH A CHILD WHO DOESN'T UNDERSTAND WHAT KILLING IS?
BACK THEN WE WERE SLEEPING IN CARS, TENTS, WHATEVER WE COULD FIND. WHEN WE STAYED IN A HOUSE, WE ALL STAYED TOGETHER.
HE WASN'T SAFE TO KEEP AROUND.
SOMEONE, I DON'T REMEMBER WHO, BROUGHT UP THE IDEA OF KILLING HIM. IT SEEMED LIKE THE ONLY OPTION AT THE TIME.
HE COULD KILL ANY ONE OF US IN OUR SLEEP.
ANDREA WOULDN'T HEAR IT. SHE WAS FURIOUS-- SHE COULDN'T BELIEVE IT WAS EVEN BEING SUGGESTED.
THEY LOCKED HIM IN A VAN FOR THE NIGHT. THEY WERE GOING TO FIGURE OUT WHAT TO DO WITH HIM IN THE MORNING.
I OVERHEARD THEM TALKING. THEY'D SAY THINGS LIKE, "HOW COULD WE KILL A KID?" THEY KNEW IT NEEDED TO BE DONE, BUT THEY DIDN'T KNOW HOW THEY COULD DO IT.

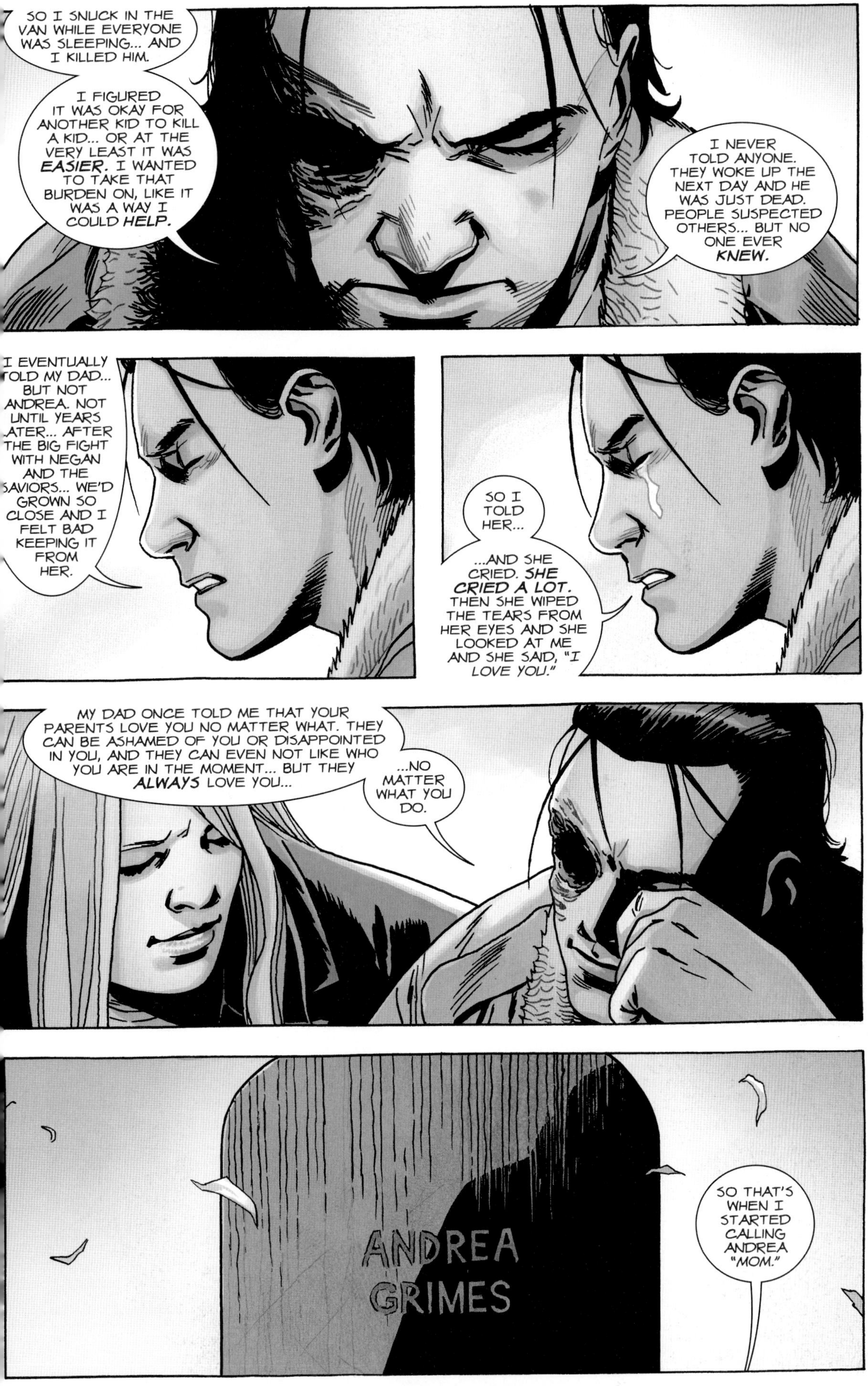
SO I SNUCK IN THE VAN WHILE EVERYONE WAS SLEEPING... AND I KILLED HIM.
I FIGURED IT WAS OKAY FOR ANOTHER KID TO KILL A KID... OR AT THE VERY LEAST IT WAS EASIER. I WANTED TO TAKE THAT BURDEN ON, LIKE IT WAS A WAY I COULD HELP.
I NEVER TOLD ANYONE. THEY WOKE UP THE NEXT DAY AND HE WAS JUST DEAD. PEOPLE SUSPECTED OTHERS... BUT NO ONE EVER KNEW.
I EVENTUALLY TOLD MY DAD... BUT NOT ANDREA. NOT UNTIL YEARS LATER... AFTER THE BIG FIGHT WITH NEGAN AND THE SAVIORS... WE'D GROWN SO CLOSE AND I FELT BAD KEEPING IT FROM HER.
SO I TOLD HER...
...AND SHE CRIED. SHE CRIED A LOT. THEN SHE WIPED THE TEARS FROM HER EYES AND SHE LOOKED AT ME AND SHE SAID, "I LOVE YOU."
MY DAD ONCE TOLD ME THAT YOUR PARENTS LOVE YOU NO MATTER WHAT. THEY CAN BE ASHAMED OF YOU OR DISAPPOINTED IN YOU, AND THEY CAN EVEN NOT LIKE WHO YOU ARE IN THE MOMENT... BUT THEY ALWAYS LOVE YOU...
...NO MATTER WHAT YOU DO.
ANDREA GRIMES
SO THAT'S WHEN I STARTED CALLING ANDREA "MOM."

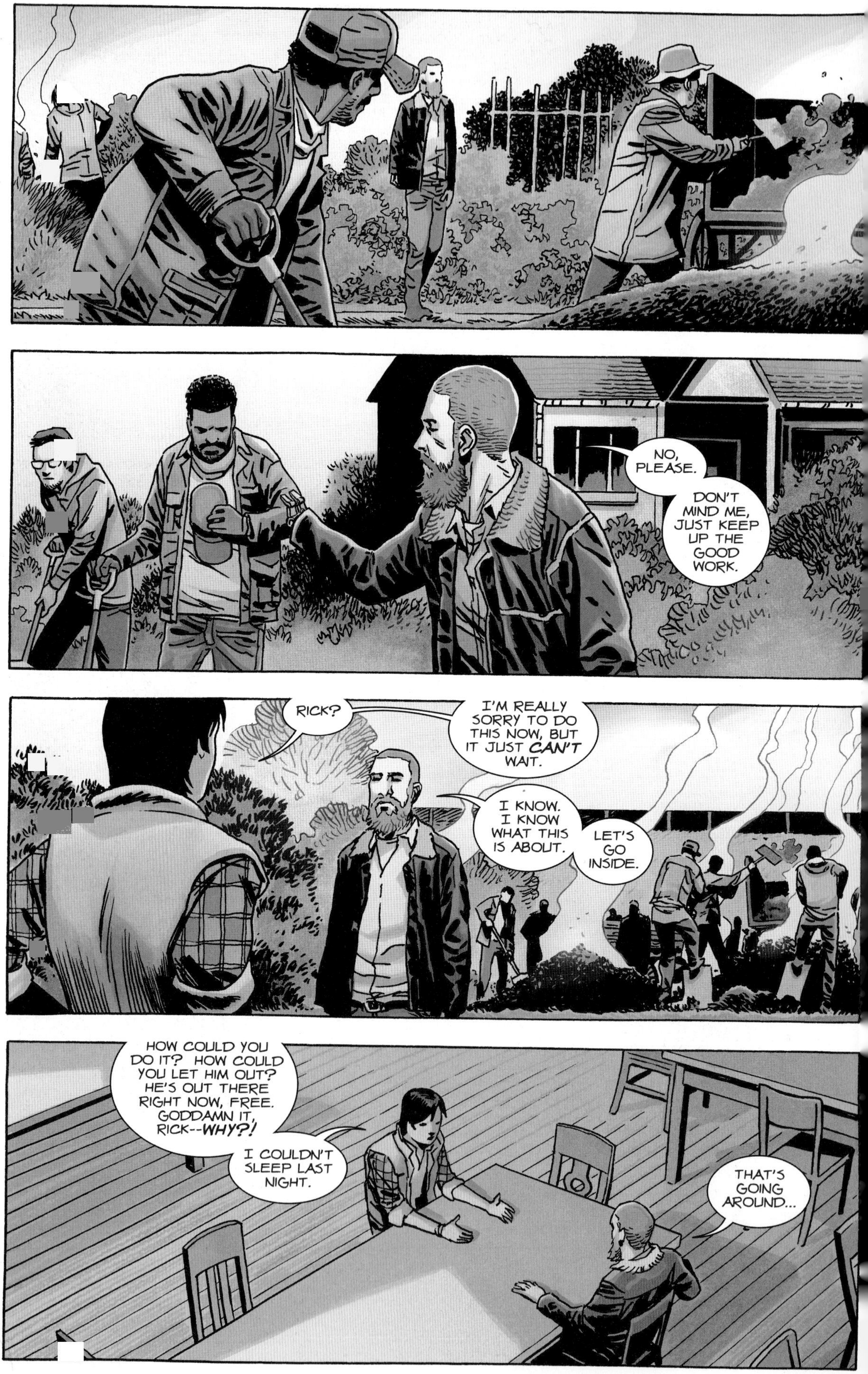
NO, PLEASE.
DON'T MIND ME, JUST KEEP UP THE GOOD WORK.
RICK?
I'M REALLY SORRY TO DO THIS NOW, BUT IT JUST CAN'T WAIT.
I KNOW. I KNOW WHAT THIS IS ABOUT.
LET'S GO INSIDE.
HOW COULD YOU DO IT? HOW COULD YOU LET HIM OUT? HE'S OUT THERE RIGHT NOW, FREE. GODDAMN IT, RICK--WHY?!
I COULDN'T SLEEP LAST NIGHT.
THAT'S GOING AROUND...

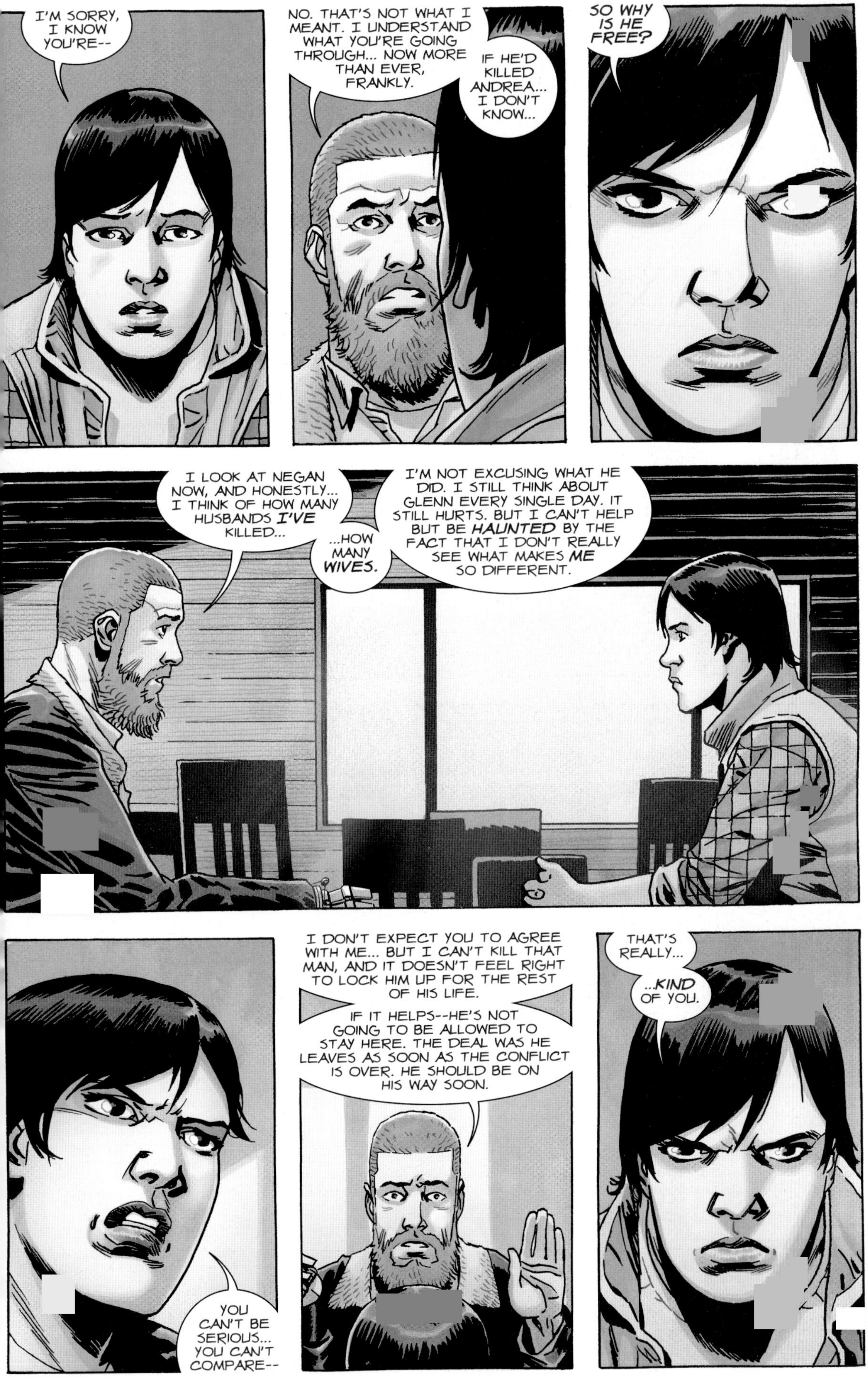
I'M SORRY, I KNOW YOU'RE--
NO. THAT'S NOT WHAT I MEANT. I UNDERSTAND WHAT YOU'RE GOING THROUGH... NOW MORE THAN EVER, FRANKLY.
IF HE'D KILLED ANDREA... I DON'T KNOW...
SO WHY IS HE FREE?
I LOOK AT NEGAN NOW, AND HONESTLY... I THINK OF HOW MANY HUSBANDS I'VE KILLED...
...HOW MANY WIVES.
I'M NOT EXCUSING WHAT HE DID. I STILL THINK ABOUT GLENN EVERY SINGLE DAY. IT STILL HURTS. BUT I CAN'T HELP BUT BE HAUNTED BY THE FACT THAT I DON'T REALLY SEE WHAT MAKES ME SO DIFFERENT.
YOU CAN'T BE SERIOUS... YOU CAN'T COMPARE--
I DON'T EXPECT YOU TO AGREE WITH ME... BUT I CAN'T KILL THAT MAN, AND IT DOESN'T FEEL RIGHT TO LOCK HIM UP FOR THE REST OF HIS LIFE.
IF IT HELPS--HE'S NOT GOING TO BE ALLOWED TO STAY HERE. THE DEAL WAS HE LEAVES AS SOON AS THE CONFLICT IS OVER. HE SHOULD BE ON HIS WAY SOON.
THAT'S REALLY...
...KIND OF YOU.

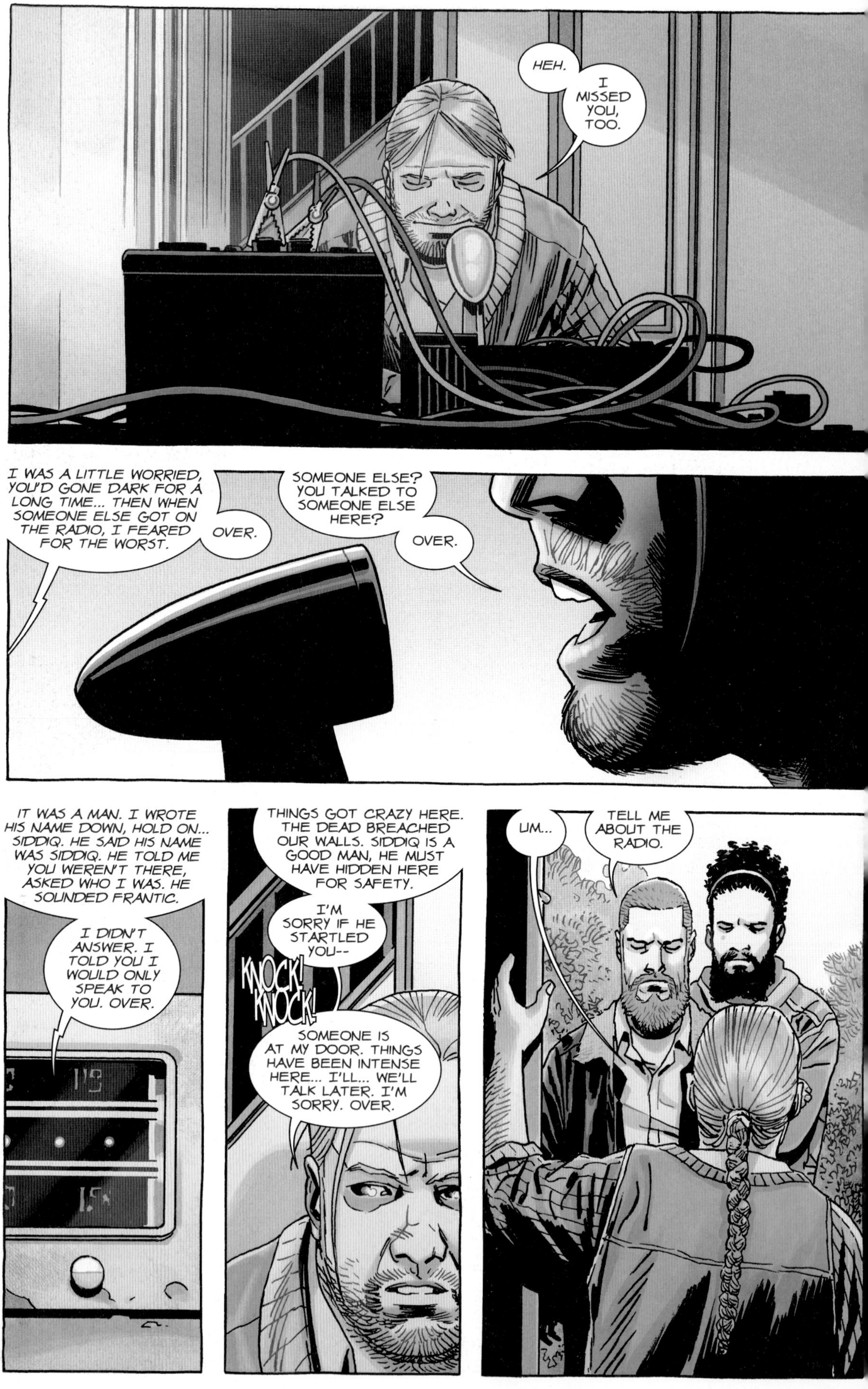
HEH.
I MISSED YOU, TOO.
I WAS A LITTLE WORRIED, YOU'D GONE DARK FOR A LONG TIME... THEN WHEN SOMEONE ELSE GOT ON THE RADIO, I FEARED FOR THE WORST.
OVER.
SOMEONE ELSE? YOU TALKED TO SOMEONE ELSE HERE?
OVER.
IT WAS A MAN. I WROTE HIS NAME DOWN, HOLD ON... SIDDIQ. HE SAID HIS NAME WAS SIDDIQ. HE TOLD ME YOU WEREN'T THERE, ASKED WHO I WAS. HE SOUNDED FRANTIC.
I DIDN'T ANSWER. I TOLD YOU I WOULD ONLY SPEAK TO YOU. OVER.
THINGS GOT CRAZY HERE. THE DEAD BREACHED OUR WALLS. SIDDIQ IS A GOOD MAN, HE MUST HAVE HIDDEN HERE FOR SAFETY.
I'M SORRY IF HE STARTLED YOU--
KNOCK! KNOCK!
SOMEONE IS AT MY DOOR. THINGS HAVE BEEN INTENSE HERE... I'LL... WE'LL TALK LATER. I'M SORRY. OVER.
UM...
TELL ME ABOUT THE RADIO.

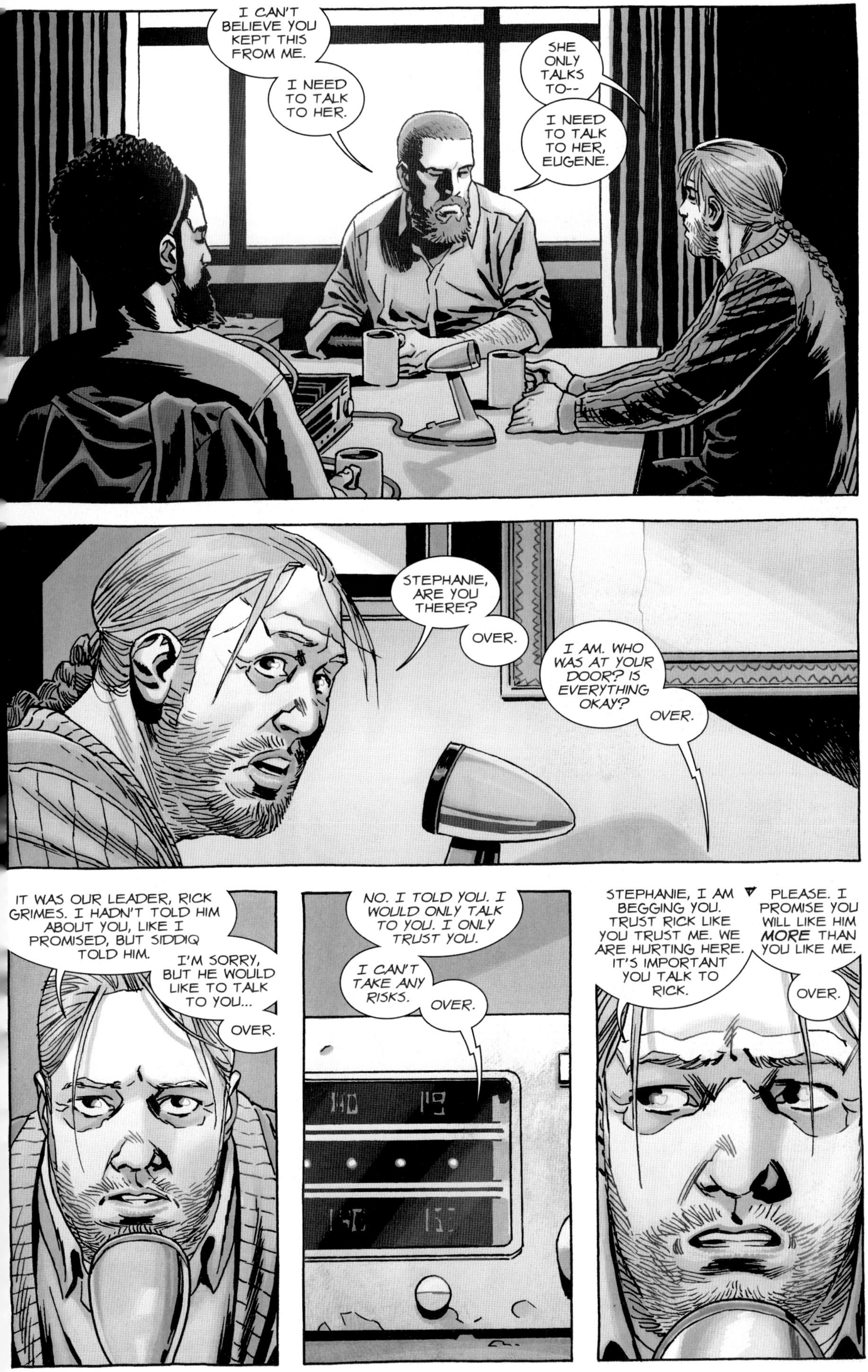
I CAN'T BELIEVE YOU KEPT THIS FROM ME.
I NEED TO TALK TO HER.
SHE ONLY TALKS TO--
I NEED TO TALK TO HER, EUGENE.
STEPHANIE, ARE YOU THERE?
OVER.
I AM. WHO WAS AT YOUR DOOR? IS EVERYTHING OKAY?
OVER.
IT WAS OUR LEADER, RICK GRIMES. I HADN'T TOLD HIM ABOUT YOU, LIKE I PROMISED, BUT SIDDIQ TOLD HIM.
I'M SORRY, BUT HE WOULD LIKE TO TALK TO YOU...
OVER.
NO. I TOLD YOU. I WOULD ONLY TALK TO YOU. I ONLY TRUST YOU.
I CAN'T TAKE ANY RISKS.
OVER.
STEPHANIE, I AM BEGGING YOU. TRUST RICK LIKE YOU TRUST ME. WE ARE HURTING HERE. IT'S IMPORTANT YOU TALK TO RICK.
PLEASE. I PROMISE YOU WILL LIKE HIM MORE THAN YOU LIKE ME.
OVER.

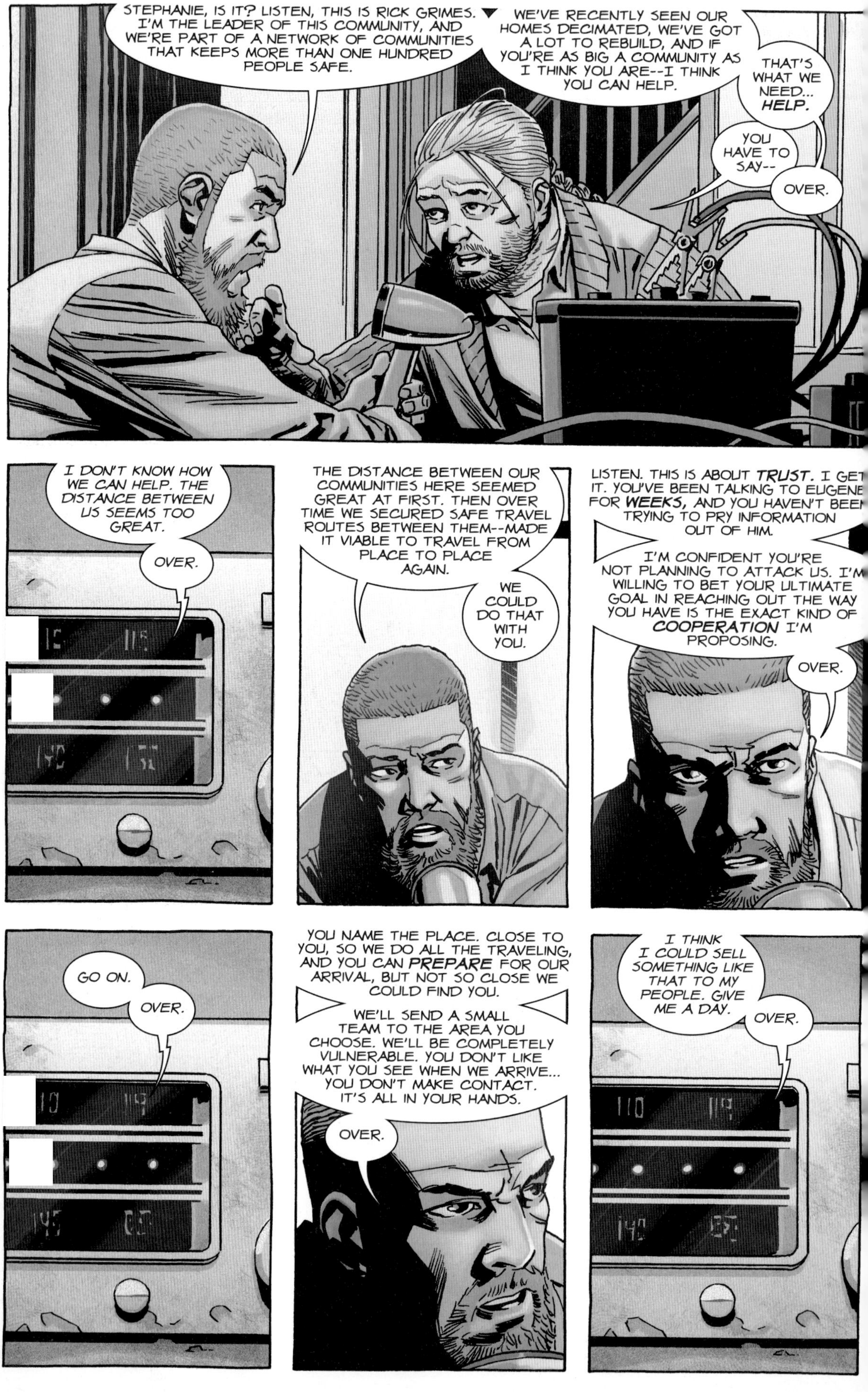
STEPHANIE, IS IT? LISTEN, THIS IS RICK GRIMES. I'M THE LEADER OF THIS COMMUNITY, AND WE'RE PART OF A NETWORK OF COMMUNITIES THAT KEEPS MORE THAN ONE HUNDRED PEOPLE SAFE.
WE'VE RECENTLY SEEN OUR HOMES DECIMATED, WE'VE GOT A LOT TO REBUILD, AND IF YOU'RE AS BIG A COMMUNITY AS I THINK YOU ARE--I THINK YOU CAN HELP.
THAT'S WHAT WE NEED... HELP.
YOU HAVE TO SAY--
OVER.
I DON'T KNOW HOW WE CAN HELP. THE DISTANCE BETWEEN US SEEMS TOO GREAT.
OVER.
THE DISTANCE BETWEEN OUR COMMUNITIES HERE SEEMED GREAT AT FIRST. THEN OVER TIME WE SECURED SAFE TRAVEL ROUTES BETWEEN THEM--MADE IT VIABLE TO TRAVEL FROM PLACE TO PLACE AGAIN.
WE COULD DO THAT WITH YOU.
LISTEN. THIS IS ABOUT TRUST. I GET IT. YOU'VE BEEN TALKING TO EUGENE FOR WEEKS, AND YOU HAVEN'T BEEN TRYING TO PRY INFORMATION OUT OF HIM.
I'M CONFIDENT YOU'RE NOT PLANNING TO ATTACK US. I'M WILLING TO BET YOUR ULTIMATE GOAL IN REACHING OUT THE WAY YOU HAVE IS THE EXACT KIND OF COOPERATION I'M PROPOSING.
OVER.
GO ON.
OVER.
YOU NAME THE PLACE. CLOSE TO YOU, SO WE DO ALL THE TRAVELING, AND YOU CAN PREPARE FOR OUR ARRIVAL, BUT NOT SO CLOSE WE COULD FIND YOU.
WE'LL SEND A SMALL TEAM TO THE AREA YOU CHOOSE. WE'LL BE COMPLETELY VULNERABLE. YOU DON'T LIKE WHAT YOU SEE WHEN WE ARRIVE... YOU DON'T MAKE CONTACT. IT'S ALL IN YOUR HANDS.
OVER.
I THINK I COULD SELL SOMETHING LIKE THAT TO MY PEOPLE. GIVE ME A DAY.
OVER.

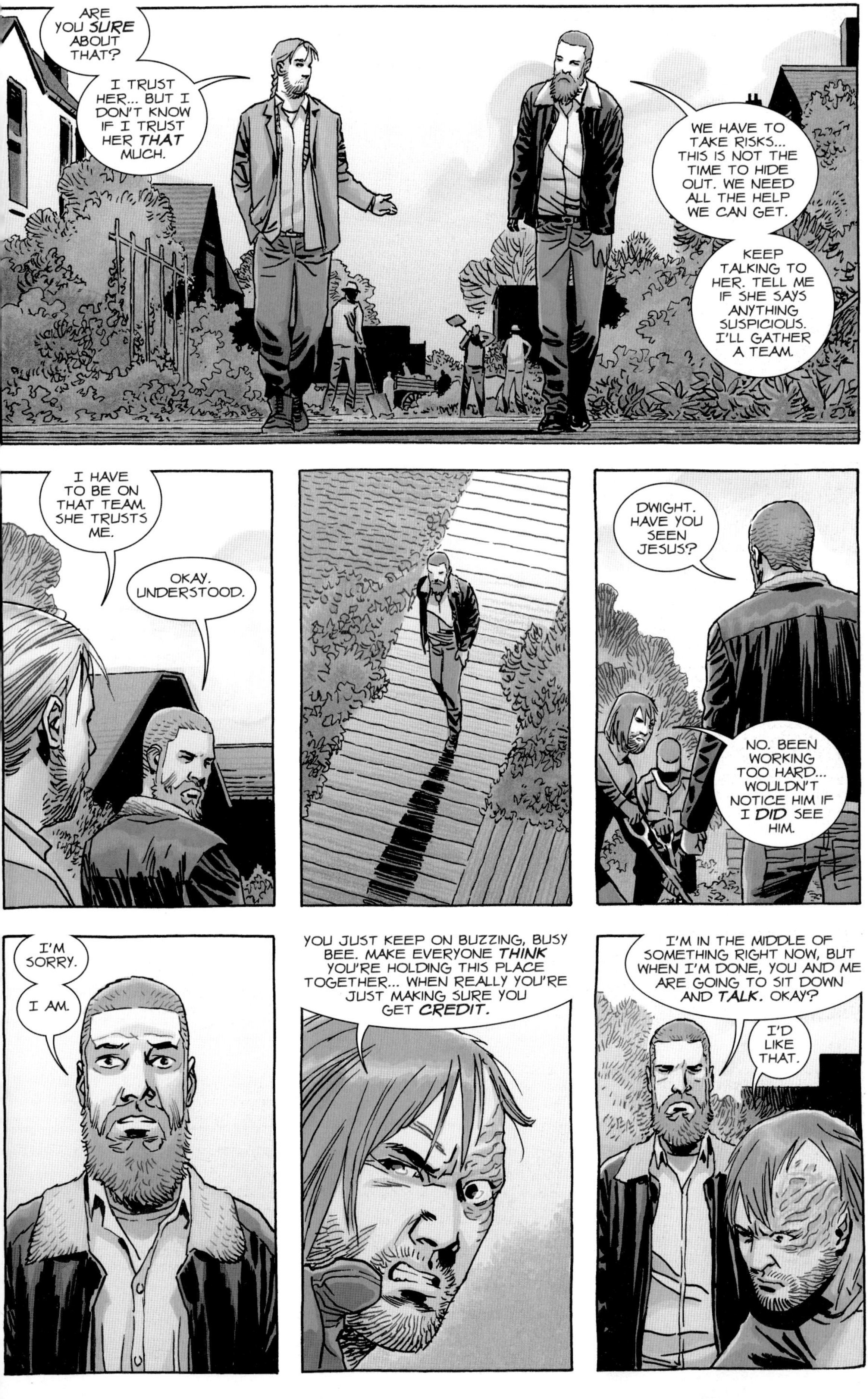
ARE YOU SURE ABOUT THAT?
I TRUST HER... BUT I DON'T KNOW IF I TRUST HER THAT MUCH.
WE HAVE TO TAKE RISKS... THIS IS NOT THE TIME TO HIDE OUT. WE NEED ALL THE HELP WE CAN GET.
KEEP TALKING TO HER. TELL ME IF SHE SAYS ANYTHING SUSPICIOUS. I'LL GATHER A TEAM.
I HAVE TO BE ON THAT TEAM. SHE TRUSTS ME.
OKAY. UNDERSTOOD.
DWIGHT. HAVE YOU SEEN JESUS?
NO. BEEN WORKING TOO HARD... WOULDN'T NOTICE HIM IF I DID SEE HIM.
I'M SORRY.
I AM.
YOU JUST KEEP ON BUZZING, BUSY BEE. MAKE EVERYONE THINK YOU'RE HOLDING THIS PLACE TOGETHER... WHEN REALLY YOU'RE JUST MAKING SURE YOU GET CREDIT.
I'M IN THE MIDDLE OF SOMETHING RIGHT NOW, BUT WHEN I'M DONE, YOU AND ME ARE GOING TO SIT DOWN AND TALK. OKAY?
I'D LIKE THAT.

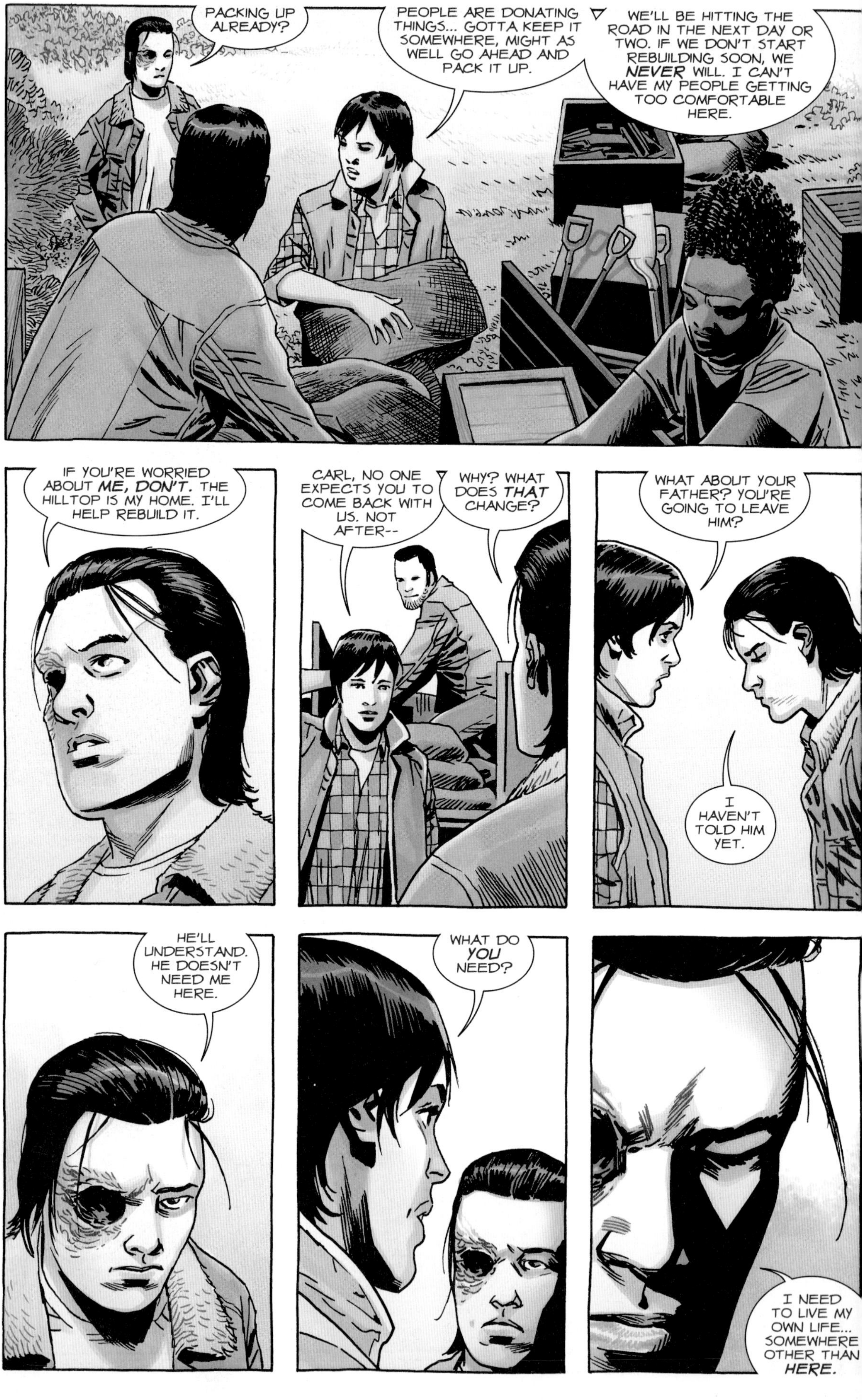
PACKING UP ALREADY?
PEOPLE ARE DONATING THINGS... GOTTA KEEP IT SOMEWHERE, MIGHT AS WELL GO AHEAD AND PACK IT UP.
WE'LL BE HITTING THE ROAD IN THE NEXT DAY OR TWO. IF WE DON'T START REBUILDING SOON, WE NEVER WILL. I CAN'T HAVE MY PEOPLE GETTING TOO COMFORTABLE HERE.
IF YOU'RE WORRIED ABOUT ME, DON'T. THE HILLTOP IS MY HOME. I'LL HELP REBUILD IT.
CARL, NO ONE EXPECTS YOU TO COME BACK WITH US. NOT AFTER--
WHY? WHAT DOES THAT CHANGE?
WHAT ABOUT YOUR FATHER? YOU'RE GOING TO LEAVE HIM?
I HAVEN'T TOLD HIM YET.
HE'LL UNDERSTAND. HE DOESN'T NEED ME HERE.
WHAT DO YOU NEED?
I NEED TO LIVE MY OWN LIFE... SOMEWHERE OTHER THAN HERE.

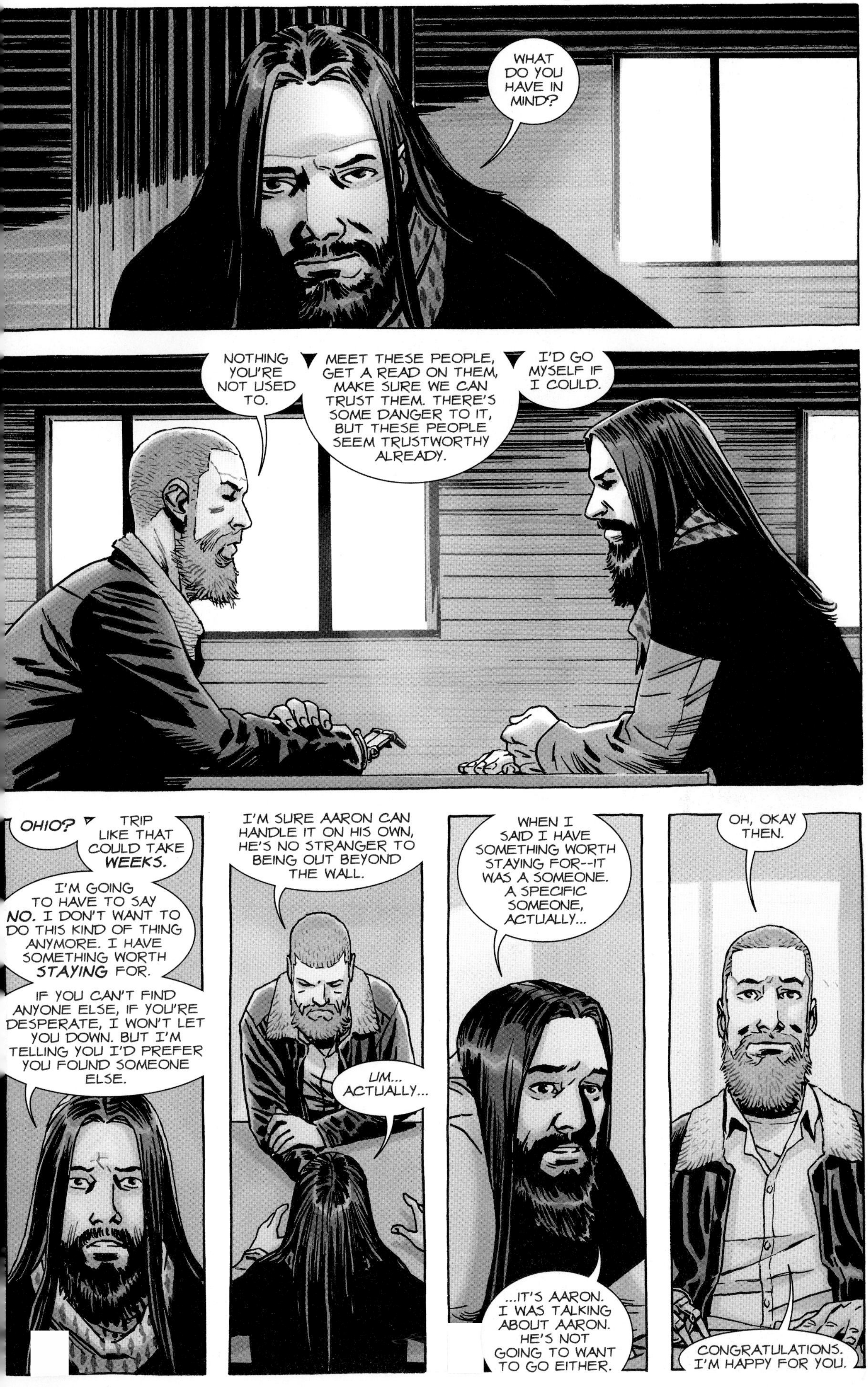
WHAT DO YOU HAVE IN MIND?
NOTHING YOU'RE NOT USED TO.
MEET THESE PEOPLE, GET A READ ON THEM, MAKE SURE WE CAN TRUST THEM. THERE'S SOME DANGER TO IT, BUT THESE PEOPLE SEEM TRUSTWORTHY ALREADY.
I'D GO MYSELF IF I COULD.
OHIO?
TRIP LIKE THAT COULD TAKE WEEKS.
I'M GOING TO HAVE TO SAY NO. I DON'T WANT TO DO THIS KIND OF THING ANYMORE. I HAVE SOMETHING WORTH STAYING FOR.
IF YOU CAN'T FIND ANYONE ELSE, IF YOU'RE DESPERATE, I WON'T LET YOU DOWN. BUT I'M TELLING YOU I'D PREFER YOU FOUND SOMEONE ELSE.
I'M SURE AARON CAN HANDLE IT ON HIS OWN, HE'S NO STRANGER TO BEING OUT BEYOND THE WALL.
UM... ACTUALLY...
WHEN I SAID I HAVE SOMETHING WORTH STAYING FOR--IT WAS A SOMEONE. A SPECIFIC SOMEONE, ACTUALLY...
...IT'S AARON. I WAS TALKING ABOUT AARON. HE'S NOT GOING TO WANT TO GO EITHER.
OH, OKAY THEN.
CONGRATULATIONS. I'M HAPPY FOR YOU.

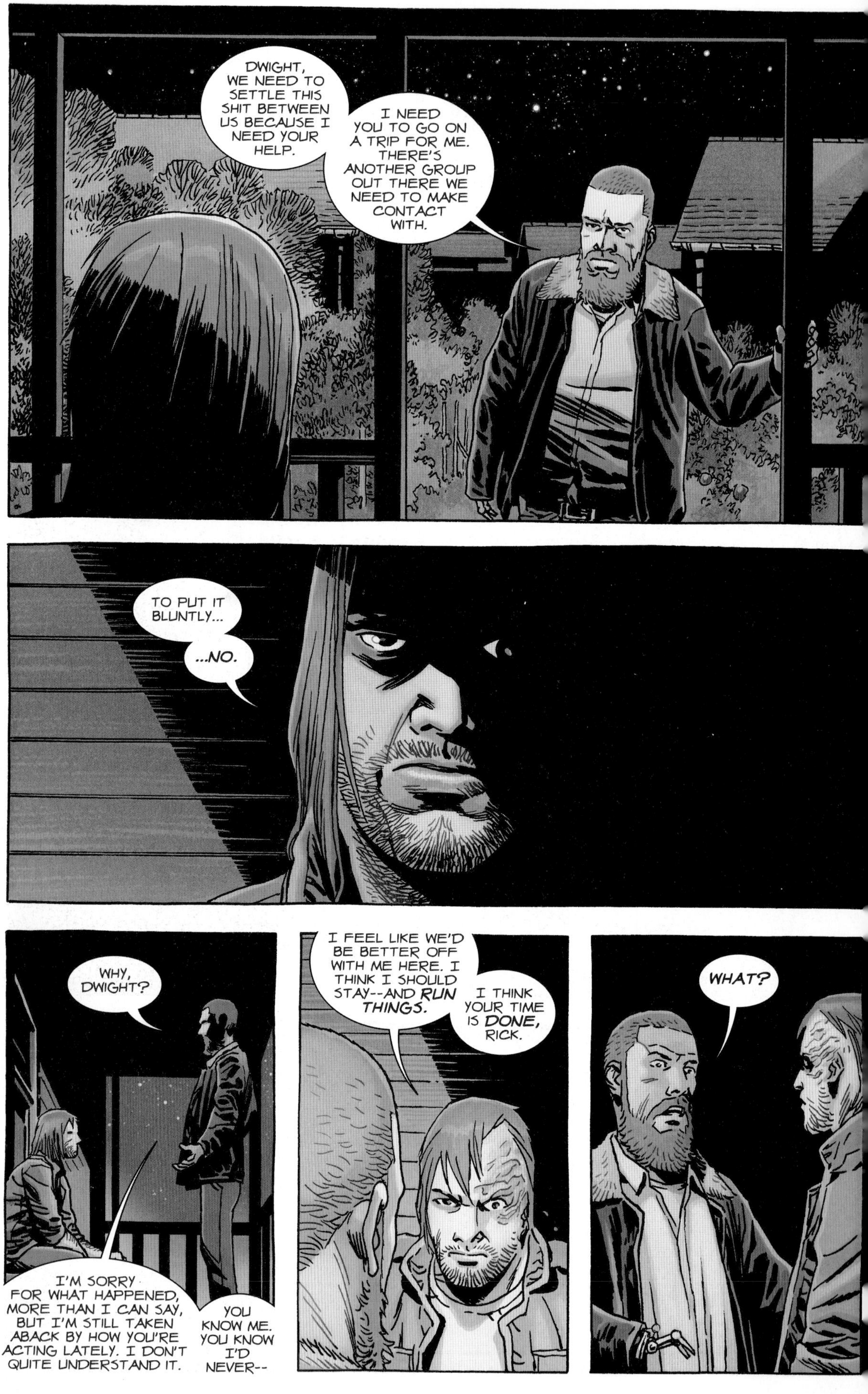
DWIGHT, WE NEED TO SETTLE THIS SHIT BETWEEN US BECAUSE I NEED YOUR HELP.
I NEED YOU TO GO ON A TRIP FOR ME. THERE'S ANOTHER GROUP OUT THERE WE NEED TO MAKE CONTACT WITH.
TO PUT IT BLUNTLY...
...NO.
WHY, DWIGHT?
I'M SORRY FOR WHAT HAPPENED, MORE THAN I CAN SAY, BUT I'M STILL TAKEN ABACK BY HOW YOU'RE ACTING LATELY. I DON'T QUITE UNDERSTAND IT.
YOU KNOW ME. YOU KNOW I'D NEVER--
I FEEL LIKE WE'D BE BETTER OFF WITH ME HERE. I THINK I SHOULD STAY--AND RUN THINGS.
I THINK YOUR TIME IS DONE, RICK.
WHAT?

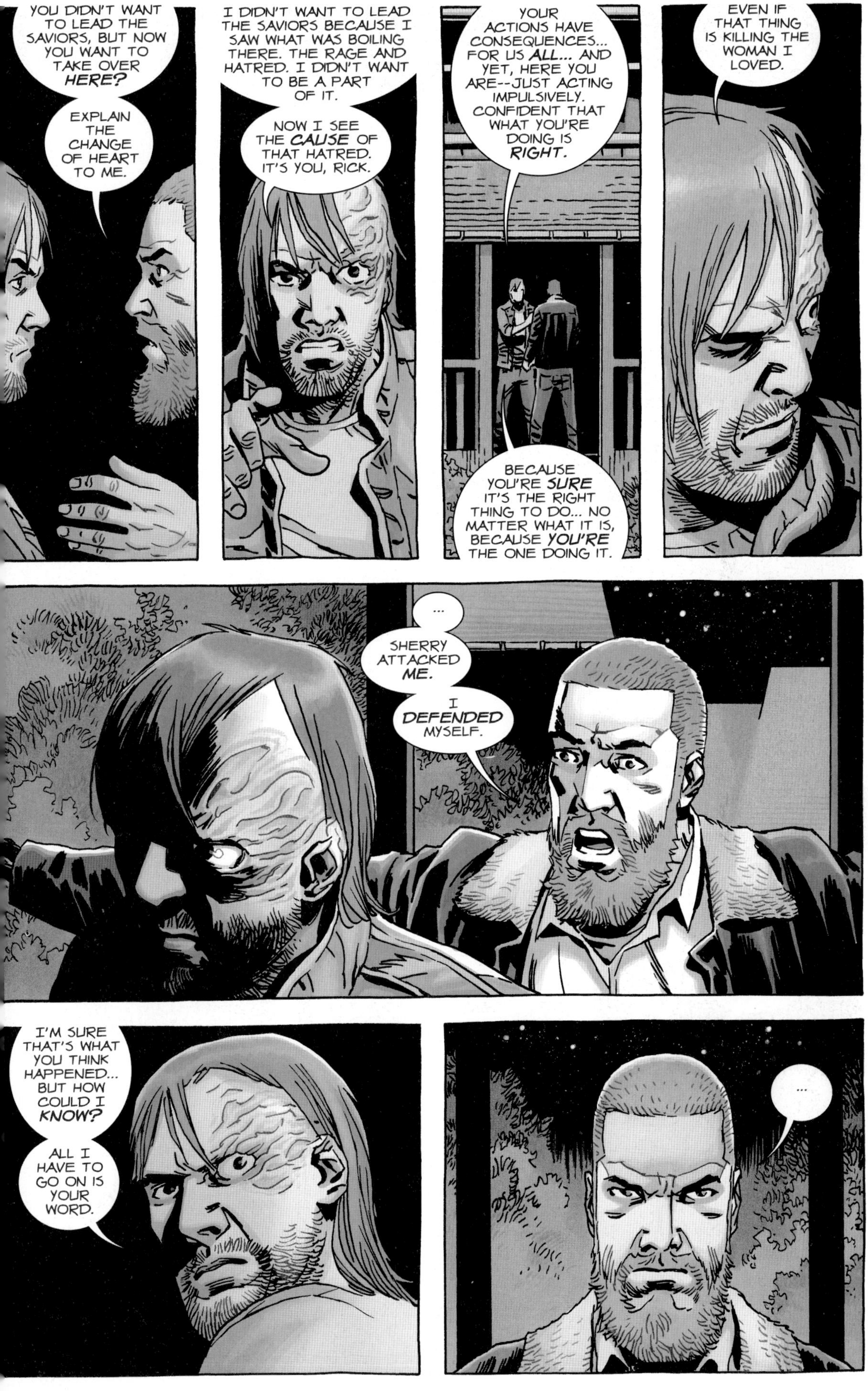
YOU DIDN'T WANT TO LEAD THE SAVIORS, BUT NOW YOU WANT TO TAKE OVER HERE?
EXPLAIN THE CHANGE OF HEART TO ME.
I DIDN'T WANT TO LEAD THE SAVIORS BECAUSE I SAW WHAT WAS BOILING THERE. THE RAGE AND HATRED. I DIDN'T WANT TO BE A PART OF IT.
NOW I SEE THE CAUSE OF THAT HATRED. IT'S YOU, RICK.
YOUR ACTIONS HAVE CONSEQUENCES... FOR US ALL... AND YET, HERE YOU ARE--JUST ACTING IMPULSIVELY. CONFIDENT THAT WHAT YOU'RE DOING IS RIGHT.
BECAUSE YOU'RE SURE IT'S THE RIGHT THING TO DO... NO MATTER WHAT IT IS, BECAUSE YOU'RE THE ONE DOING IT.
EVEN IF THAT THING IS KILLING THE WOMAN I LOVED.
...
SHERRY ATTACKED ME.
I DEFENDED MYSELF.
I'M SURE THAT'S WHAT YOU THINK HAPPENED... BUT HOW COULD I KNOW?
ALL I HAVE TO GO ON IS YOUR WORD.
...

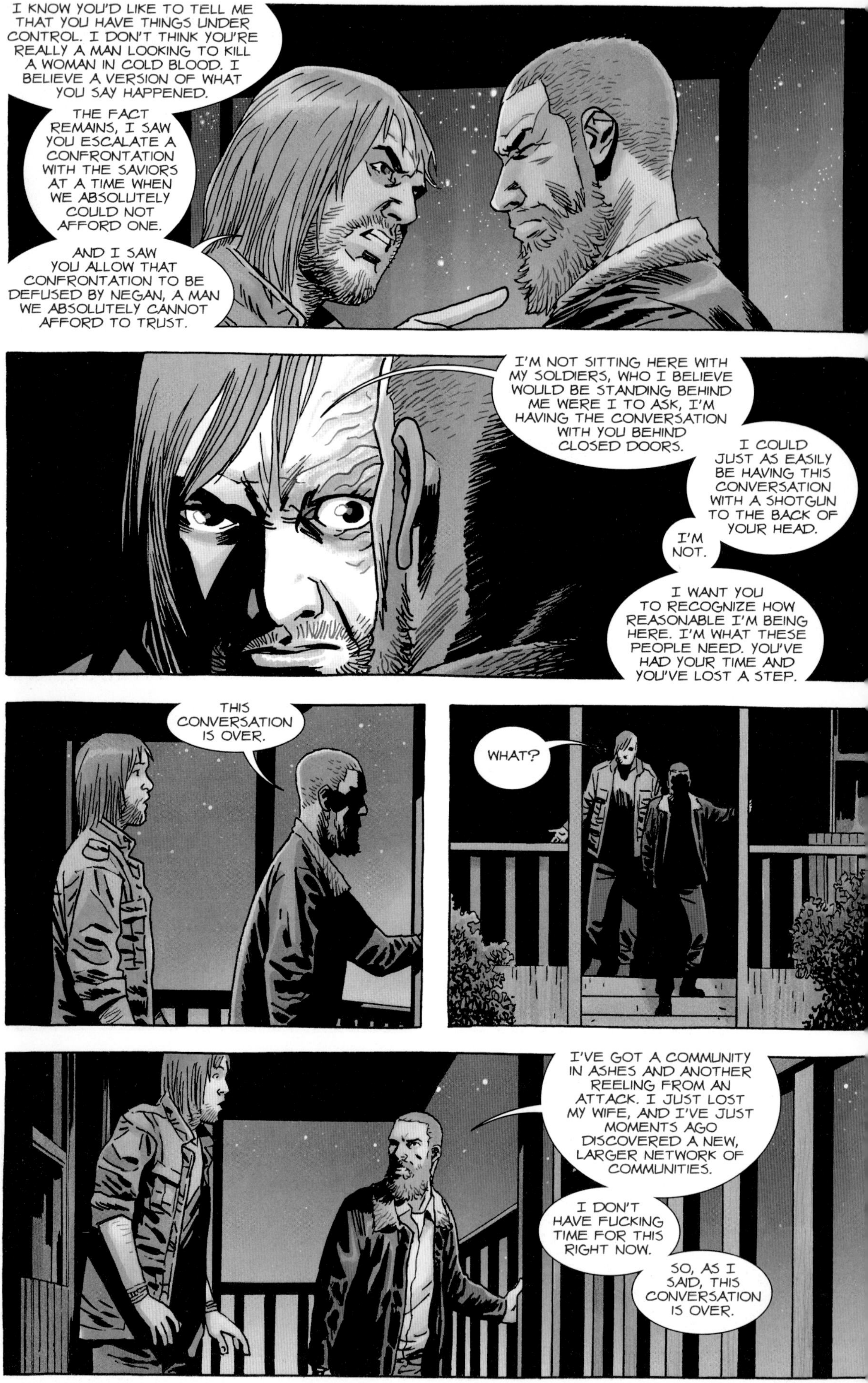
I KNOW YOU'D LIKE TO TELL ME THAT YOU HAVE THINGS UNDER CONTROL. I DON'T THINK YOU'RE REALLY A MAN LOOKING TO KILL A WOMAN IN COLD BLOOD. I BELIEVE A VERSION OF WHAT YOU SAY HAPPENED.
THE FACT REMAINS, I SAW YOU ESCALATE A CONFRONTATION WITH THE SAVIORS AT A TIME WHEN WE ABSOLUTELY COULD NOT AFFORD ONE.
AND I SAW YOU ALLOW THAT CONFRONTATION TO BE DEFUSED BY NEGAN, A MAN WE ABSOLUTELY CANNOT AFFORD TO TRUST.
I'M NOT SITTING HERE WITH MY SOLDIERS, WHO I BELIEVE WOULD BE STANDING BEHIND ME WERE I TO ASK, I'M HAVING THE CONVERSATION WITH YOU BEHIND CLOSED DOORS.
I COULD JUST AS EASILY BE HAVING THIS CONVERSATION WITH A SHOTGUN TO THE BACK OF YOUR HEAD.
I'M NOT.
I WANT YOU TO RECOGNIZE HOW REASONABLE I'M BEING HERE. I'M WHAT THESE PEOPLE NEED. YOU'VE HAD YOUR TIME AND YOU'VE LOST A STEP.
THIS CONVERSATION IS OVER.
WHAT?
I'VE GOT A COMMUNITY IN ASHES AND ANOTHER REELING FROM AN ATTACK. I JUST LOST MY WIFE, AND I'VE JUST MOMENTS AGO DISCOVERED A NEW, LARGER NETWORK OF COMMUNITIES.
I DON'T HAVE FUCKING TIME FOR THIS RIGHT NOW.
SO, AS I SAID, THIS CONVERSATION IS OVER.

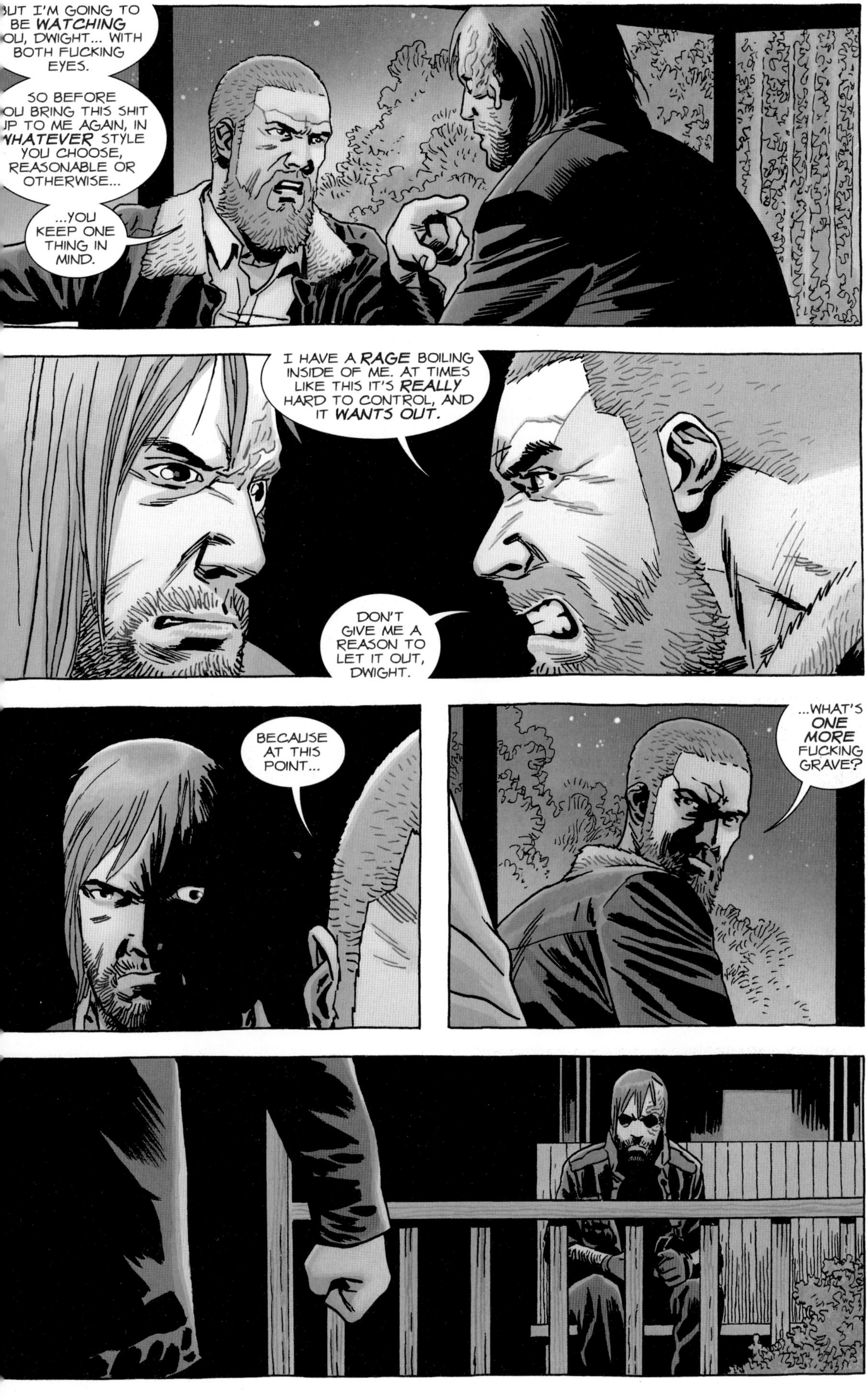
UT I'M GOING TO BE WATCHING OU, DWIGHT... WITH BOTH FUCKING EYES.
SO BEFORE OU BRING THIS SHIT UP TO ME AGAIN, IN WHATEVER STYLE YOU CHOOSE, REASONABLE OR OTHERWISE...
...YOU KEEP ONE THING IN MIND.
I HAVE A RAGE BOILING INSIDE OF ME. AT TIMES LIKE THIS IT'S REALLY HARD TO CONTROL, AND IT WANTS OUT.
DON'T GIVE ME A REASON TO LET IT OUT, DWIGHT.
BECAUSE AT THIS POINT...
...WHAT'S ONE MORE FUCKING GRAVE?

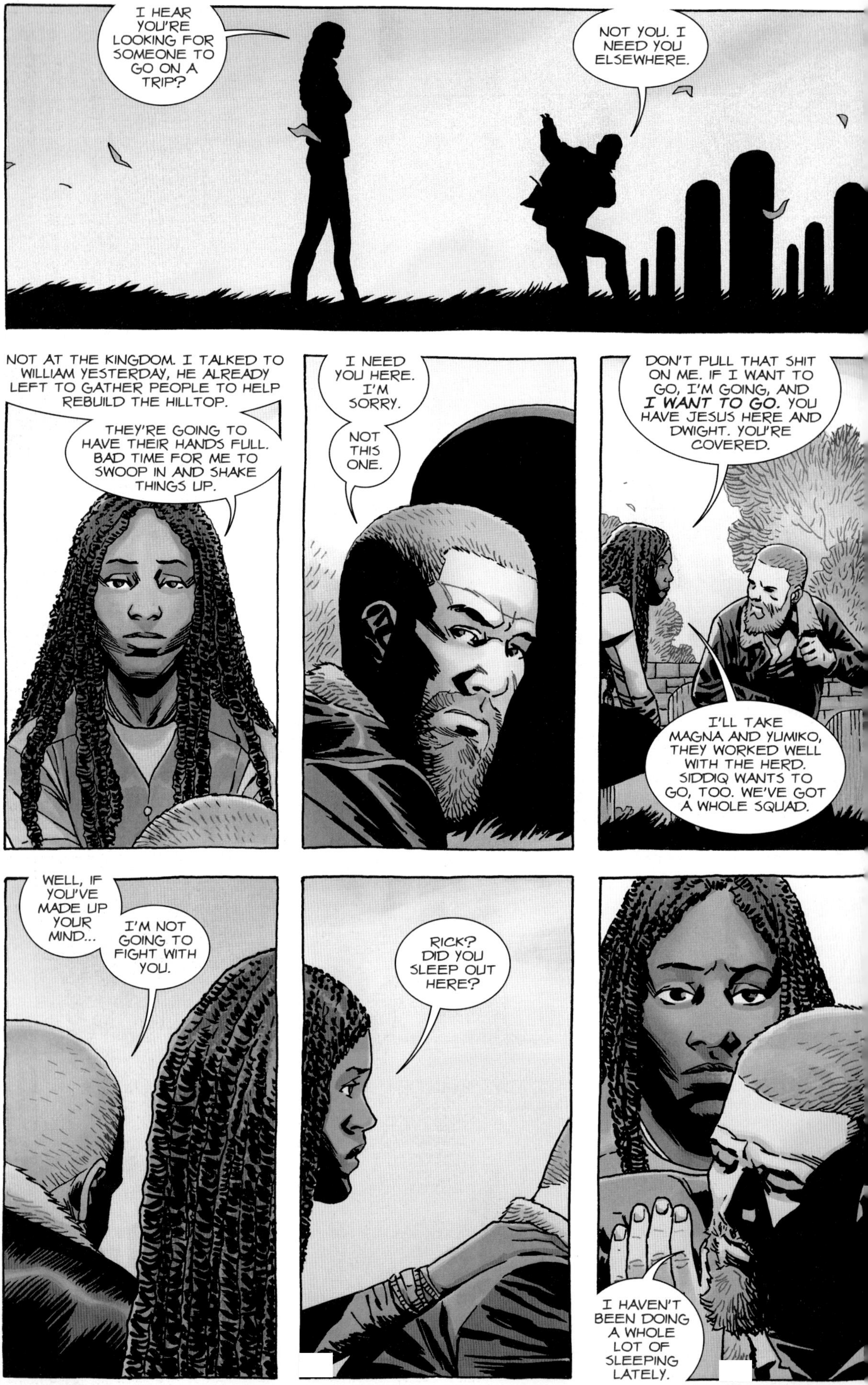
I HEAR YOU'RE LOOKING FOR SOMEONE TO GO ON A TRIP?
NOT YOU. I NEED YOU ELSEWHERE.
NOT AT THE KINGDOM. I TALKED TO WILLIAM YESTERDAY, HE ALREADY LEFT TO GATHER PEOPLE TO HELP REBUILD THE HILLTOP.
THEY'RE GOING TO HAVE THEIR HANDS FULL. BAD TIME FOR ME TO SWOOP IN AND SHAKE THINGS UP.
I NEED YOU HERE. I'M SORRY.
NOT THIS ONE.
DON'T PULL THAT SHIT ON ME. IF I WANT TO GO, I'M GOING, AND *I WANT TO GO.* YOU HAVE JESUS HERE AND DWIGHT. YOU'RE COVERED.
I'LL TAKE MAGNA AND YUMIKO, THEY WORKED WELL WITH THE HERD. SIDDIQ WANTS TO GO, TOO. WE'VE GOT A WHOLE SQUAD.
WELL, IF YOU'VE MADE UP YOUR MIND...
I'M NOT GOING TO FIGHT WITH YOU.
RICK? DID YOU SLEEP OUT HERE?
I HAVEN'T BEEN DOING A WHOLE LOT OF SLEEPING LATELY.

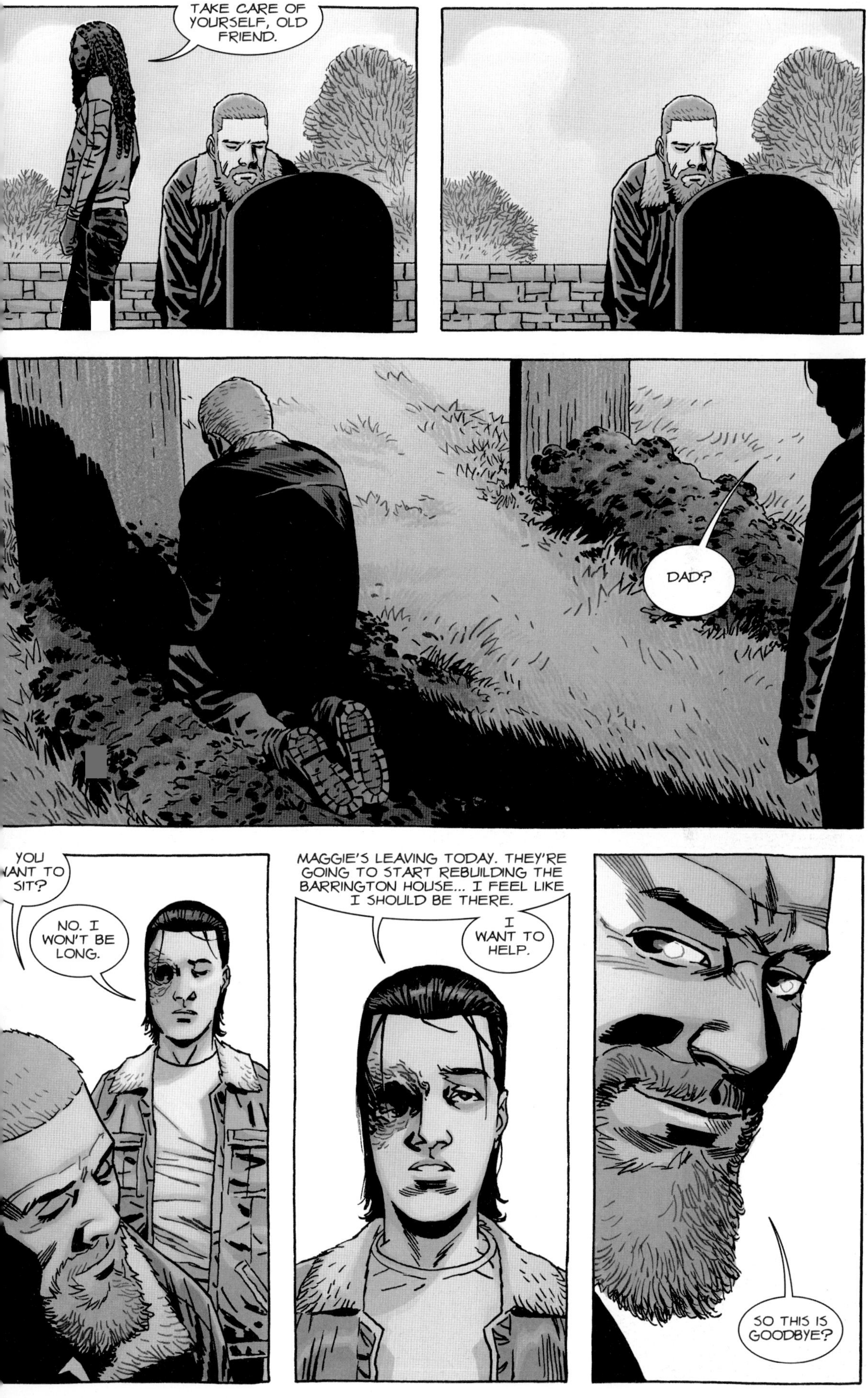
TAKE CARE OF YOURSELF, OLD FRIEND.
DAD?
YOU ANT TO SIT?
NO. I WON'T BE LONG.
MAGGIE'S LEAVING TODAY. THEY'RE GOING TO START REBUILDING THE BARRINGTON HOUSE... I FEEL LIKE I SHOULD BE THERE.
I WANT TO HELP.
SO THIS IS GOODBYE?

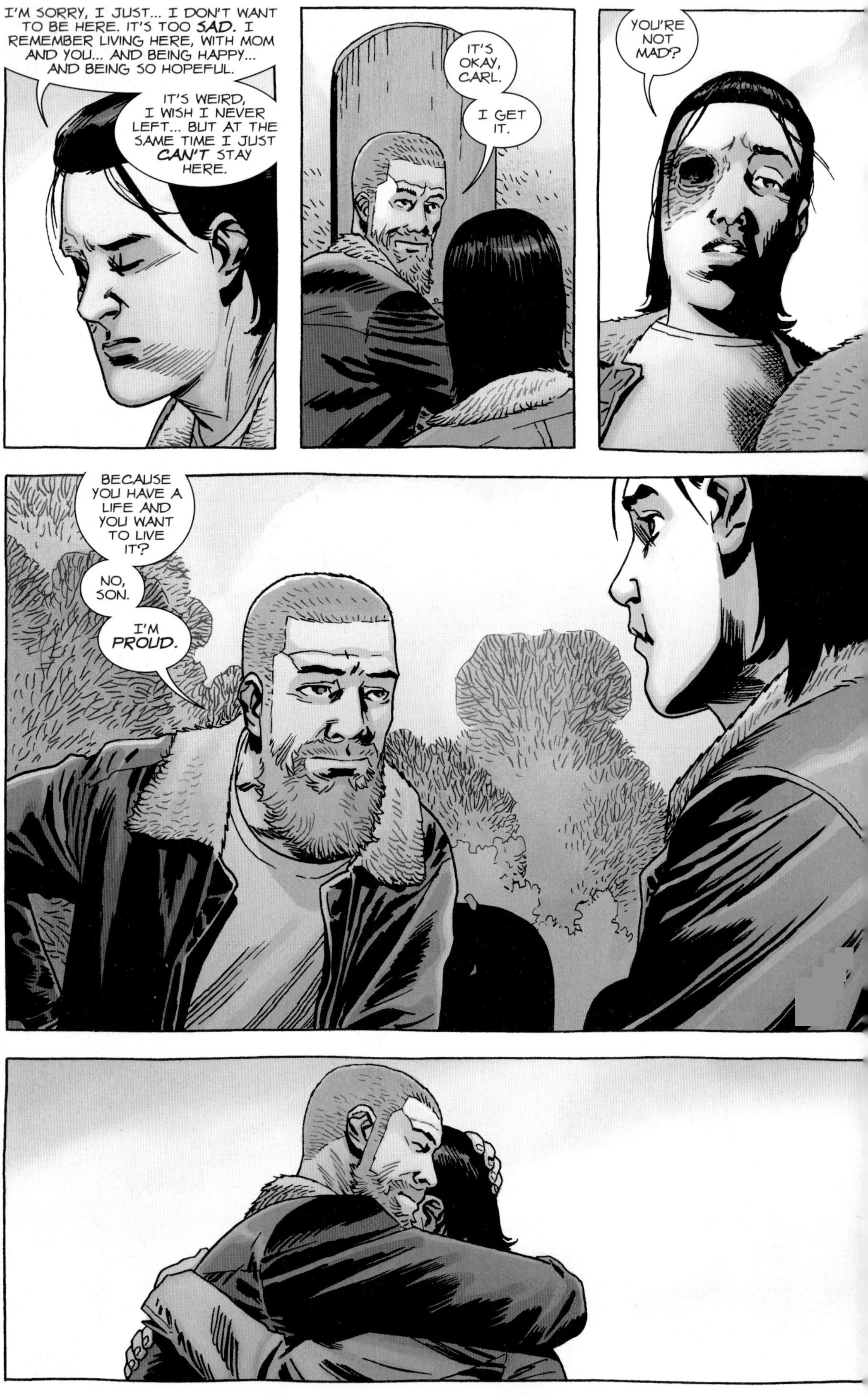
I'M SORRY, I JUST... I DON'T WANT TO BE HERE. IT'S TOO SAD. I REMEMBER LIVING HERE, WITH MOM AND YOU... AND BEING HAPPY... AND BEING SO HOPEFUL.
IT'S WEIRD, I WISH I NEVER LEFT... BUT AT THE SAME TIME I JUST CAN'T STAY HERE.
IT'S OKAY, CARL.
I GET IT.
YOU'RE NOT MAD?
BECAUSE YOU HAVE A LIFE AND YOU WANT TO LIVE IT?
NO, SON.
I'M PROUD.

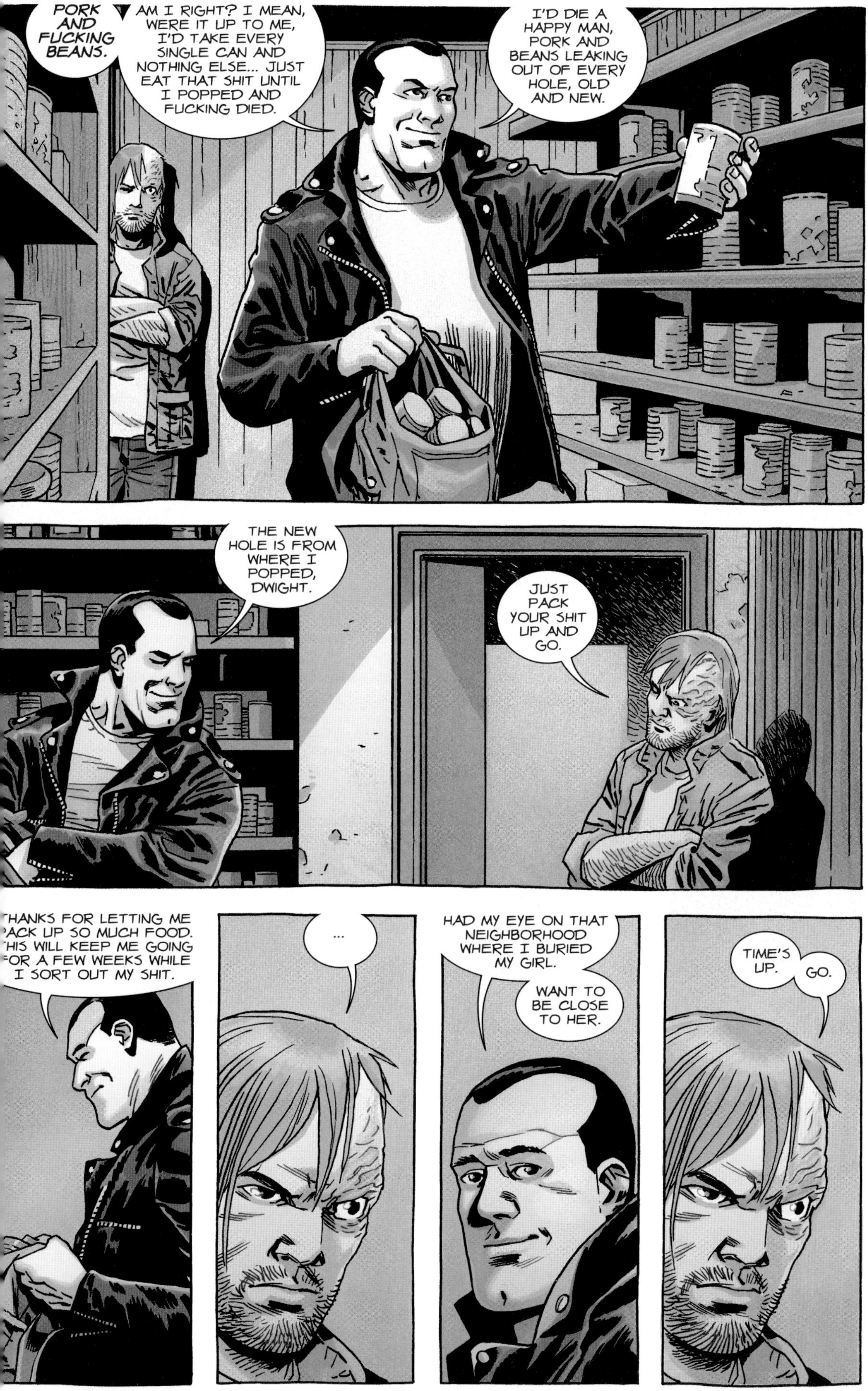
PORK AND FUCKING BEANS.
AM I RIGHT? I MEAN, WERE IT UP TO ME, I'D TAKE EVERY SINGLE CAN AND NOTHING ELSE... JUST EAT THAT SHIT UNTIL I POPPED AND FUCKING DIED.
I'D DIE A HAPPY MAN, PORK AND BEANS LEAKING OUT OF EVERY HOLE, OLD AND NEW.
THE NEW HOLE IS FROM WHERE I POPPED, DWIGHT.
JUST PACK YOUR SHIT UP AND GO.
THANKS FOR LETTING ME PACK UP SO MUCH FOOD. THIS WILL KEEP ME GOING FOR A FEW WEEKS WHILE I SORT OUT MY SHIT.
...
HAD MY EYE ON THAT NEIGHBORHOOD WHERE I BURIED MY GIRL.
WANT TO BE CLOSE TO HER.
TIME'S UP.
GO.

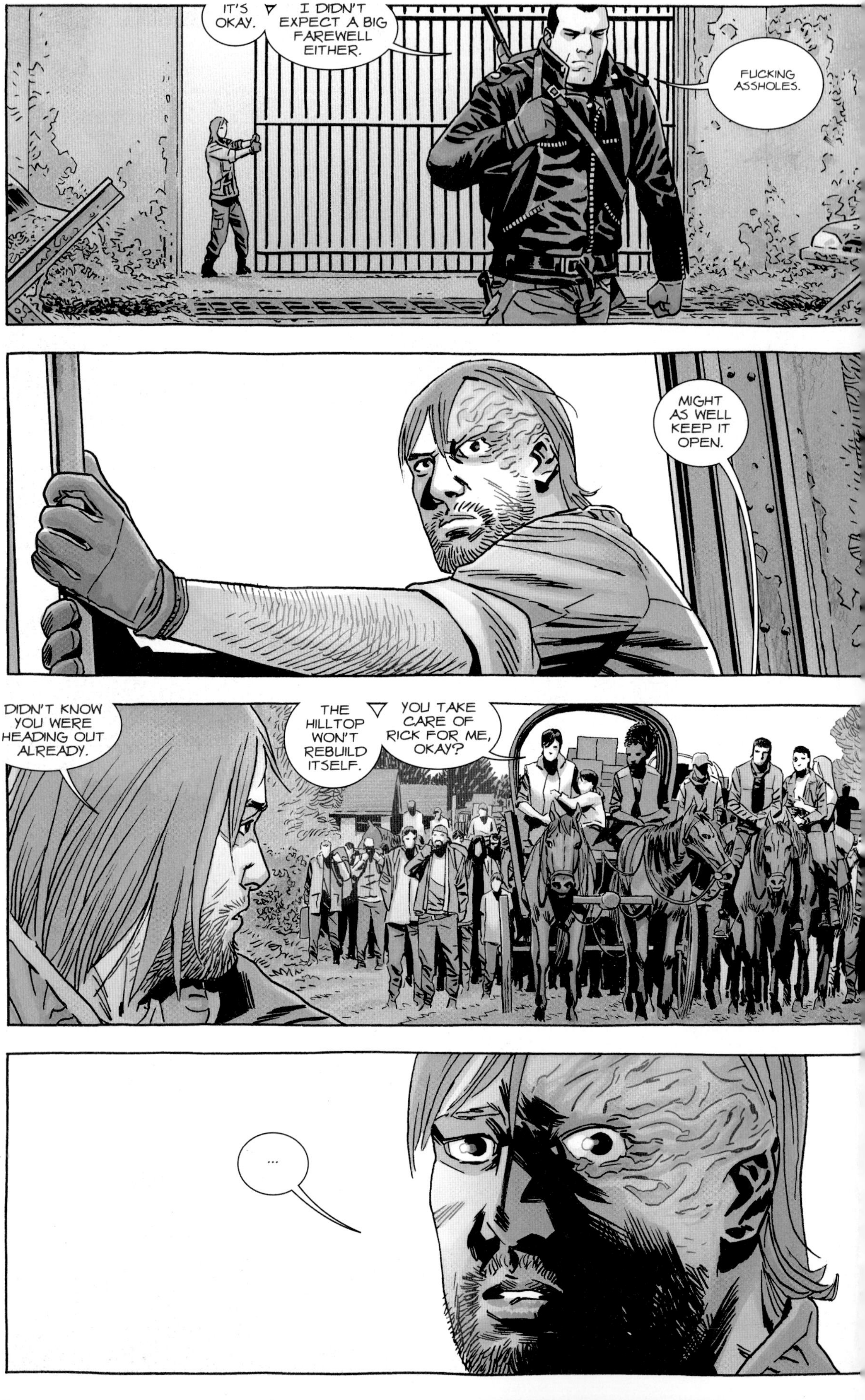
IT'S OKAY.
I DIDN'T EXPECT A BIG FAREWELL EITHER.
FUCKING ASSHOLES.
MIGHT AS WELL KEEP IT OPEN.
DIDN'T KNOW YOU WERE HEADING OUT ALREADY.
THE HILLTOP WON'T REBUILD ITSELF.
YOU TAKE CARE OF RICK FOR ME, OKAY?
...

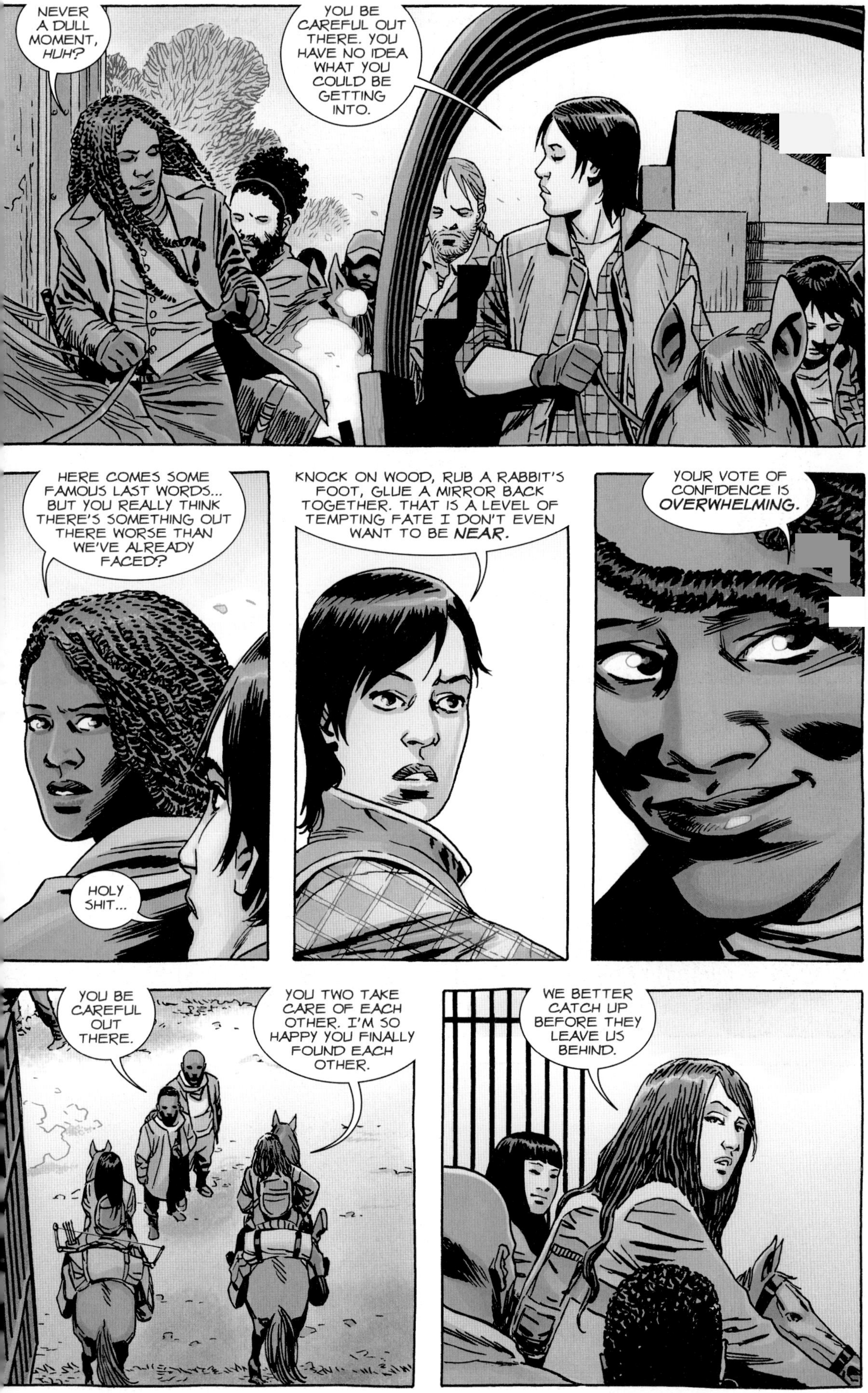
NEVER A DULL MOMENT, *HUH?*
YOU BE CAREFUL OUT THERE. YOU HAVE NO IDEA WHAT YOU COULD BE GETTING INTO.
HERE COMES SOME FAMOUS LAST WORDS... BUT YOU REALLY THINK THERE'S SOMETHING OUT THERE WORSE THAN WE'VE ALREADY FACED?
HOLY SHIT...
KNOCK ON WOOD, RUB A RABBIT'S FOOT, GLUE A MIRROR BACK TOGETHER. THAT IS A LEVEL OF TEMPTING FATE I DON'T EVEN WANT TO BE ***NEAR.***
YOUR VOTE OF CONFIDENCE IS ***OVERWHELMING.***
YOU BE CAREFUL OUT THERE.
YOU TWO TAKE CARE OF EACH OTHER. I'M SO HAPPY YOU FINALLY FOUND EACH OTHER.
WE BETTER CATCH UP BEFORE THEY LEAVE US BEHIND.

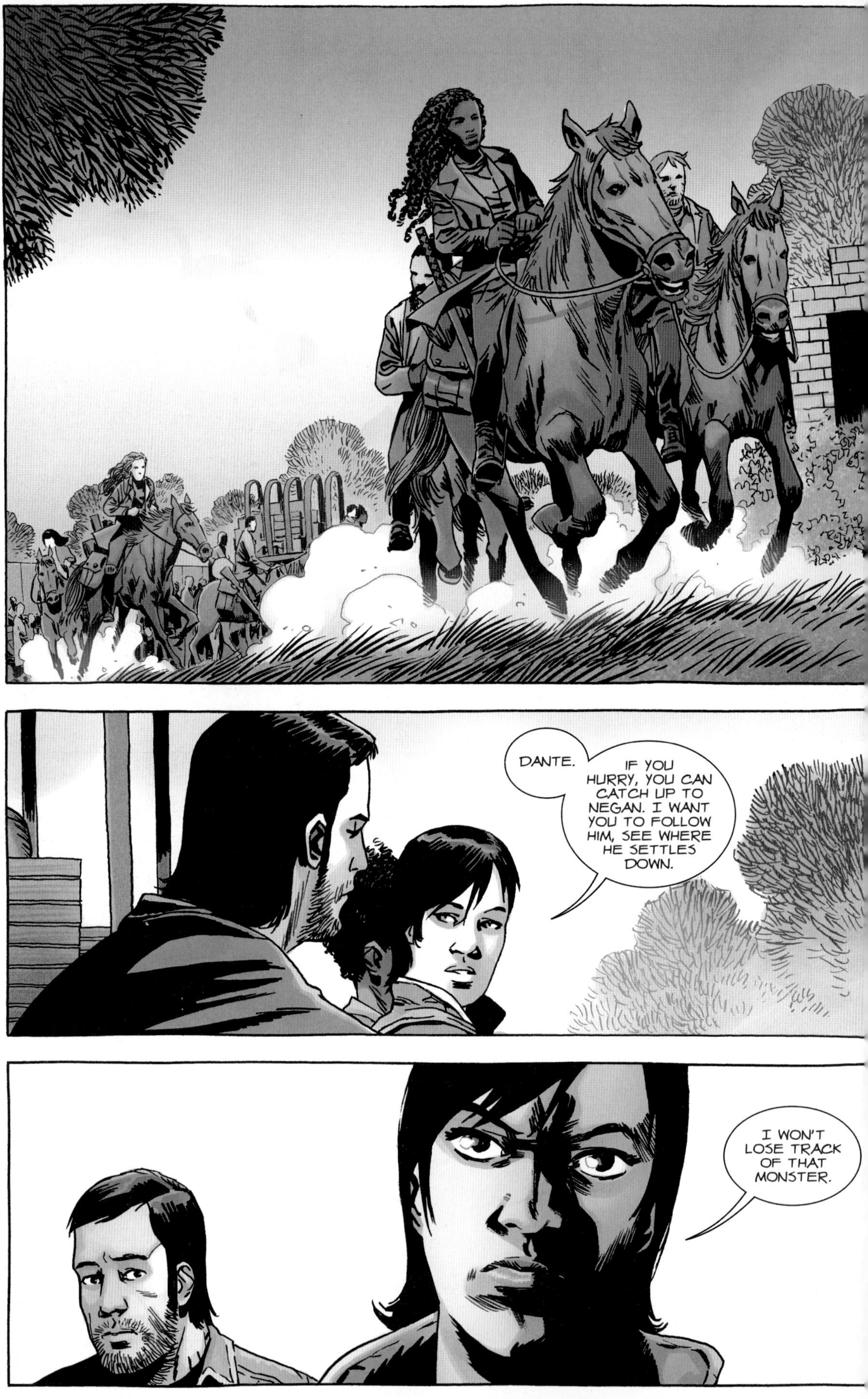
DANTE.
IF YOU HURRY, YOU CAN CATCH UP TO NEGAN. I WANT YOU TO FOLLOW HIM, SEE WHERE HE SETTLES DOWN.
I WON'T LOSE TRACK OF THAT MONSTER.

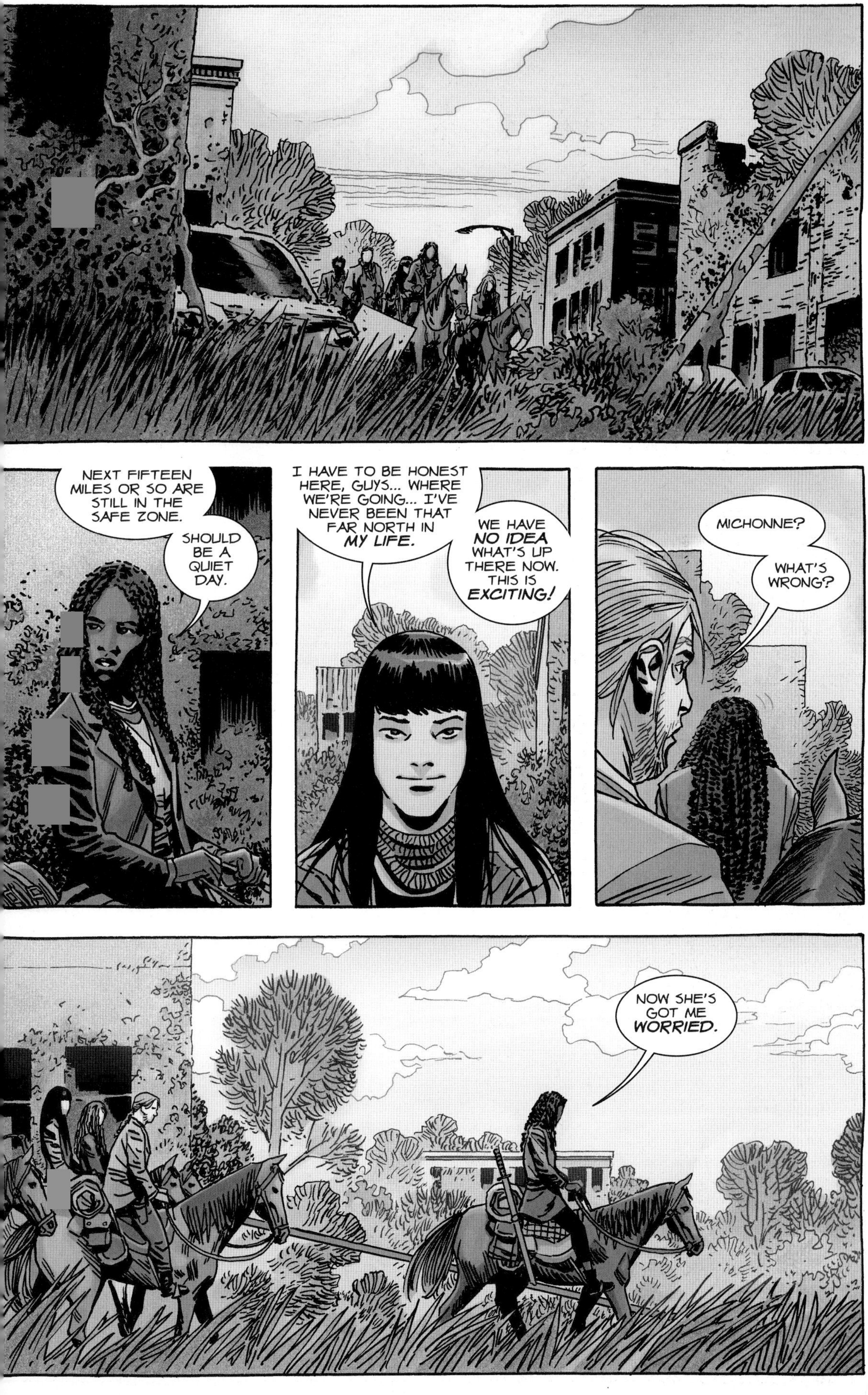
NEXT FIFTEEN MILES OR SO ARE STILL IN THE SAFE ZONE.
SHOULD BE A QUIET DAY.
I HAVE TO BE HONEST HERE, GUYS... WHERE WE'RE GOING... I'VE NEVER BEEN THAT FAR NORTH IN MY LIFE.
WE HAVE NO IDEA WHAT'S UP THERE NOW. THIS IS EXCITING!
MICHONNE?
WHAT'S WRONG?
NOW SHE'S GOT ME WORRIED.

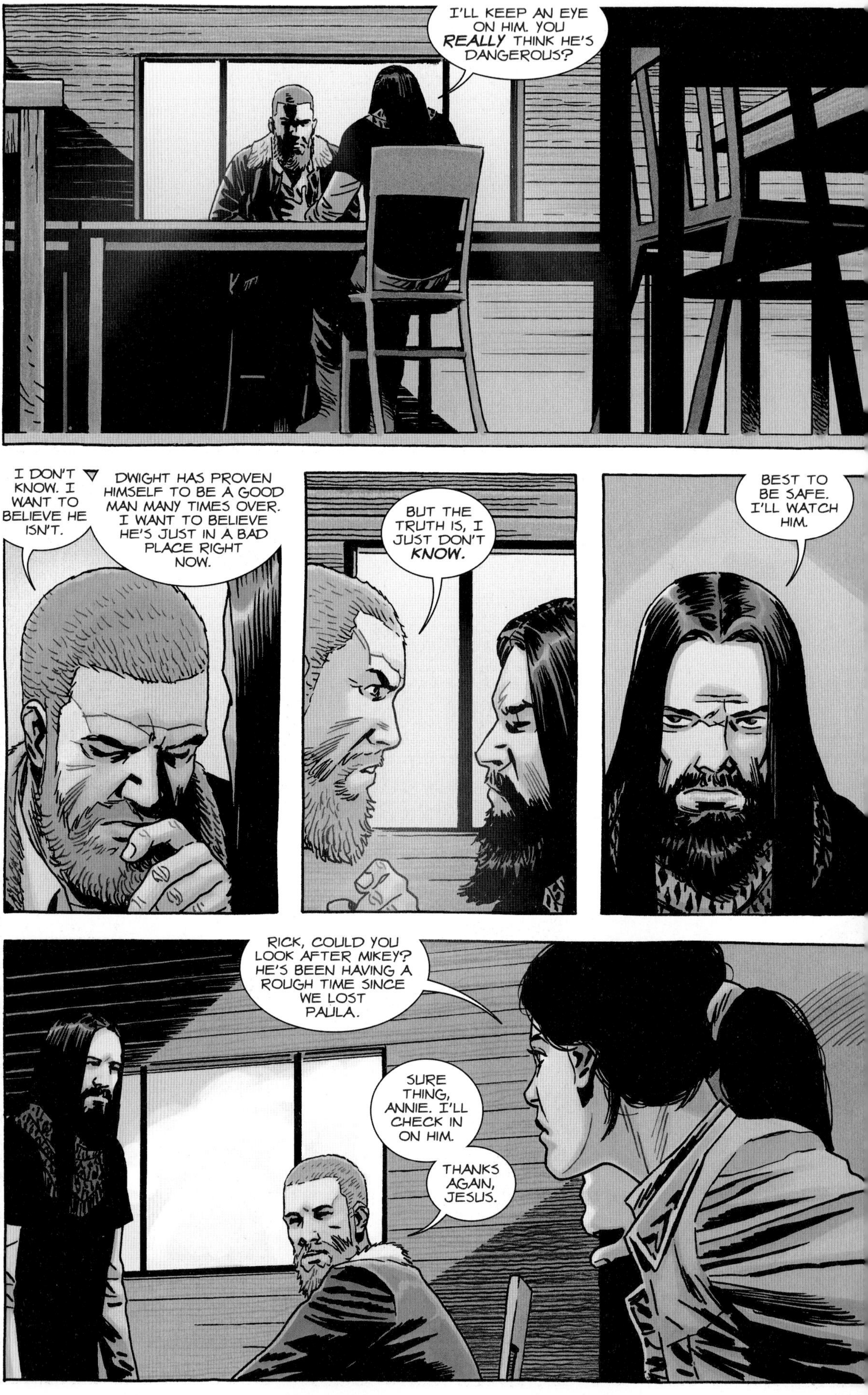
I'LL KEEP AN EYE ON HIM. YOU REALLY THINK HE'S DANGEROUS?
I DON'T KNOW. I WANT TO BELIEVE HE ISN'T.
DWIGHT HAS PROVEN HIMSELF TO BE A GOOD MAN MANY TIMES OVER. I WANT TO BELIEVE HE'S JUST IN A BAD PLACE RIGHT NOW.
BUT THE TRUTH IS, I JUST DON'T KNOW.
BEST TO BE SAFE. I'LL WATCH HIM.
RICK, COULD YOU LOOK AFTER MIKEY? HE'S BEEN HAVING A ROUGH TIME SINCE WE LOST PAULA.
SURE THING, ANNIE. I'LL CHECK IN ON HIM.
THANKS AGAIN, JESUS.

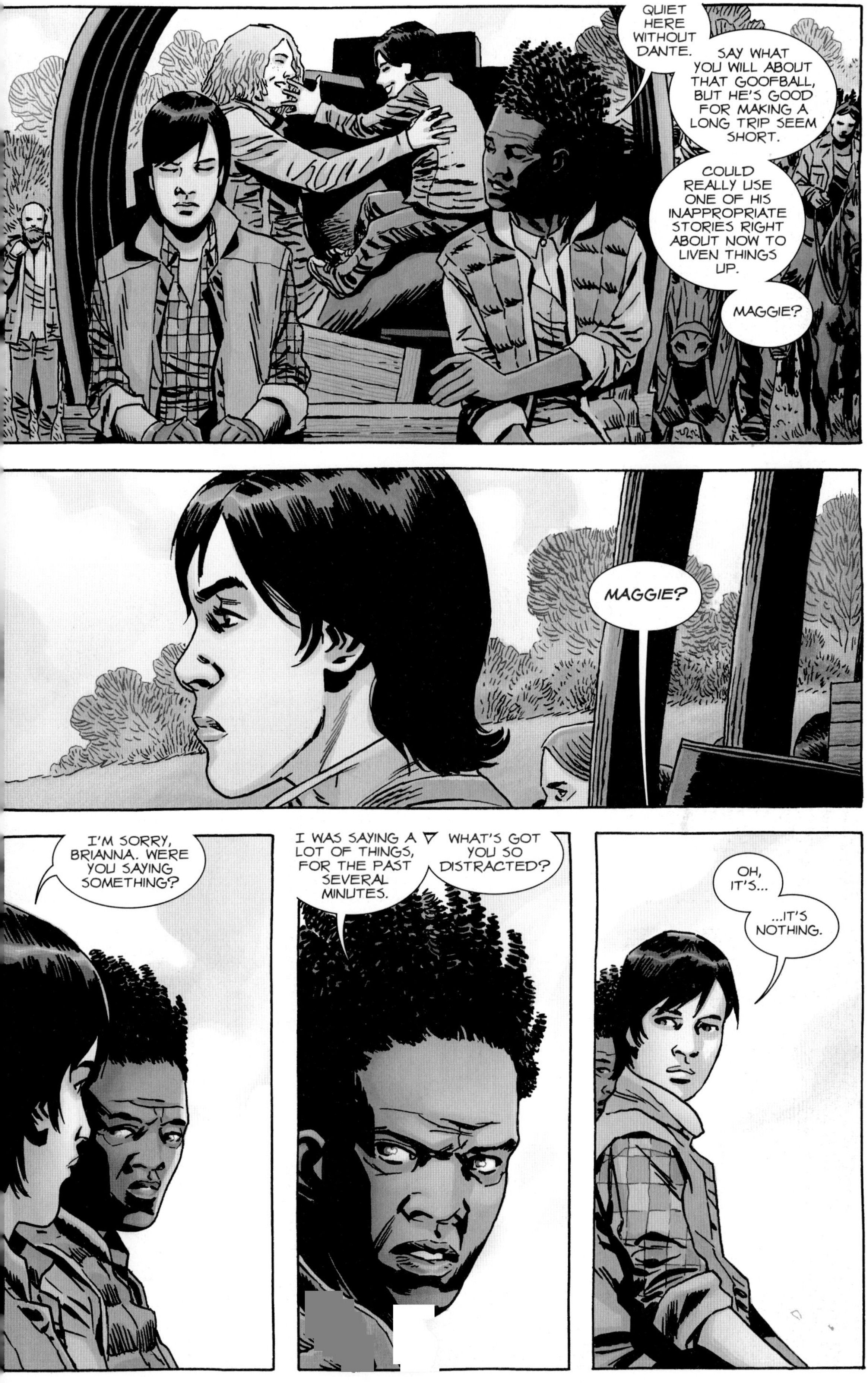
QUIET HERE WITHOUT DANTE.
SAY WHAT YOU WILL ABOUT THAT GOOFBALL, BUT HE'S GOOD FOR MAKING A LONG TRIP SEEM SHORT.
COULD REALLY USE ONE OF HIS INAPPROPRIATE STORIES RIGHT ABOUT NOW TO LIVEN THINGS UP.
MAGGIE?
MAGGIE?
I'M SORRY, BRIANNA. WERE YOU SAYING SOMETHING?
I WAS SAYING A LOT OF THINGS, FOR THE PAST SEVERAL MINUTES.
WHAT'S GOT YOU SO DISTRACTED?
OH, IT'S...
...IT'S NOTHING.

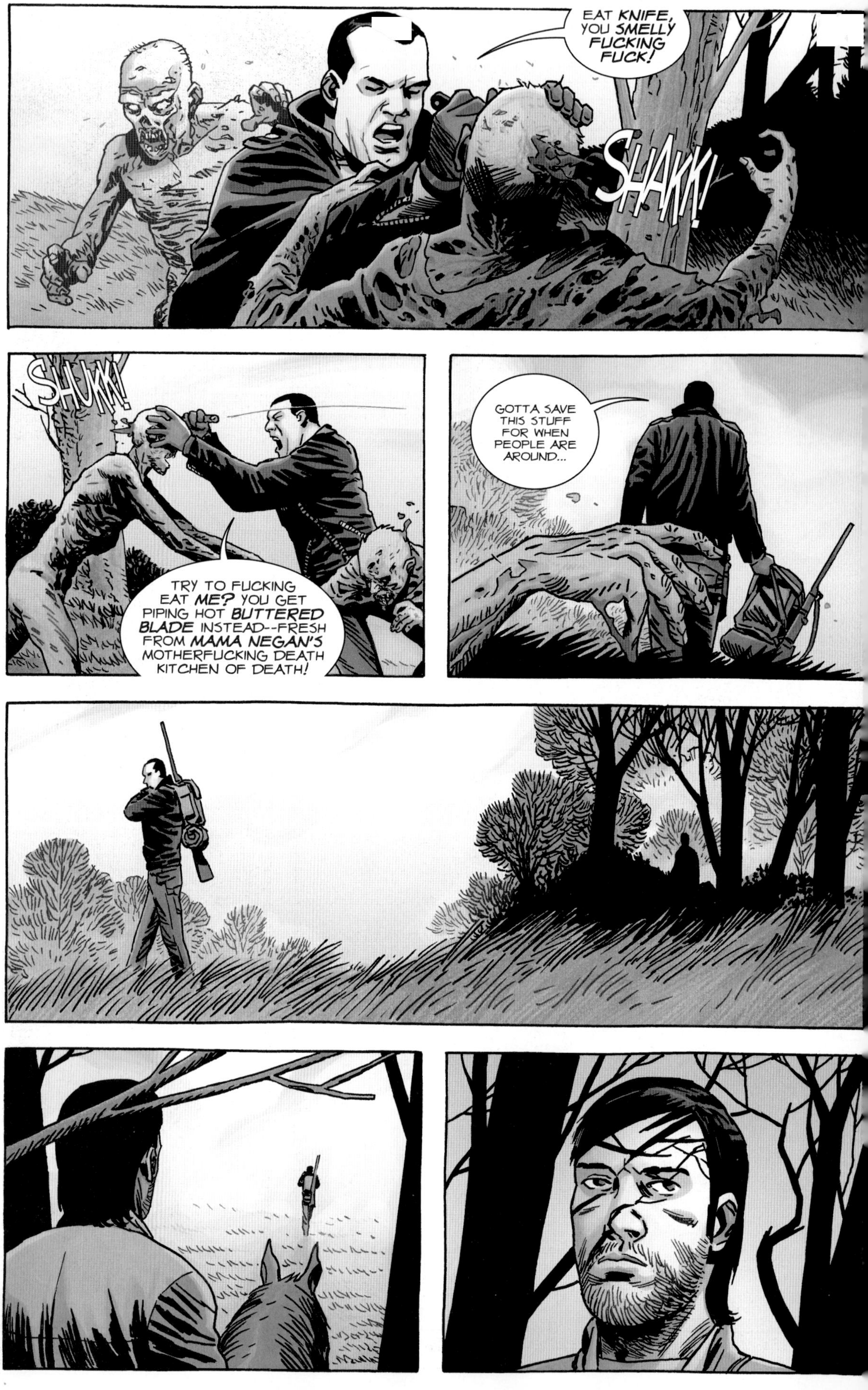
EAT KNIFE, YOU SMELLY FUCKING FUCK!
SHAKK!
SHUKK!
TRY TO FUCKING EAT ME? YOU GET PIPING HOT BUTTERED BLADE INSTEAD--FRESH FROM MAMA NEGAN'S MOTHERFUCKING DEATH KITCHEN OF DEATH!
GOTTA SAVE THIS STUFF FOR WHEN PEOPLE ARE AROUND...

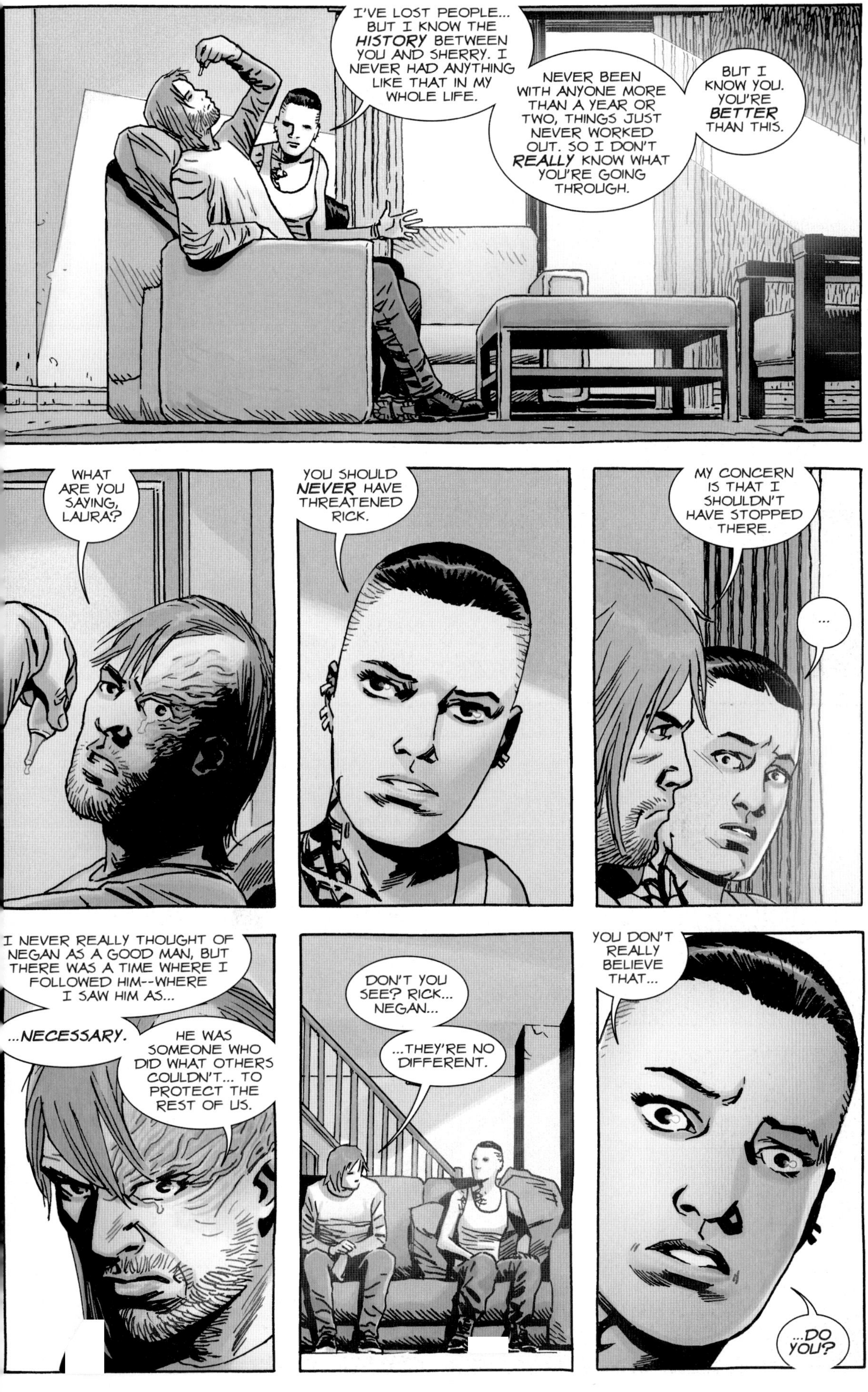
I'VE LOST PEOPLE... BUT I KNOW THE HISTORY BETWEEN YOU AND SHERRY. I NEVER HAD ANYTHING LIKE THAT IN MY WHOLE LIFE.
NEVER BEEN WITH ANYONE MORE THAN A YEAR OR TWO, THINGS JUST NEVER WORKED OUT. SO I DON'T REALLY KNOW WHAT YOU'RE GOING THROUGH.
BUT I KNOW YOU. YOU'RE BETTER THAN THIS.
WHAT ARE YOU SAYING, LAURA?
YOU SHOULD NEVER HAVE THREATENED RICK.
MY CONCERN IS THAT I SHOULDN'T HAVE STOPPED THERE.
...
I NEVER REALLY THOUGHT OF NEGAN AS A GOOD MAN, BUT THERE WAS A TIME WHERE I FOLLOWED HIM--WHERE I SAW HIM AS...
...NECESSARY.
HE WAS SOMEONE WHO DID WHAT OTHERS COULDN'T... TO PROTECT THE REST OF US.
DON'T YOU SEE? RICK... NEGAN...
...THEY'RE NO DIFFERENT.
YOU DON'T REALLY BELIEVE THAT...
...DO YOU?

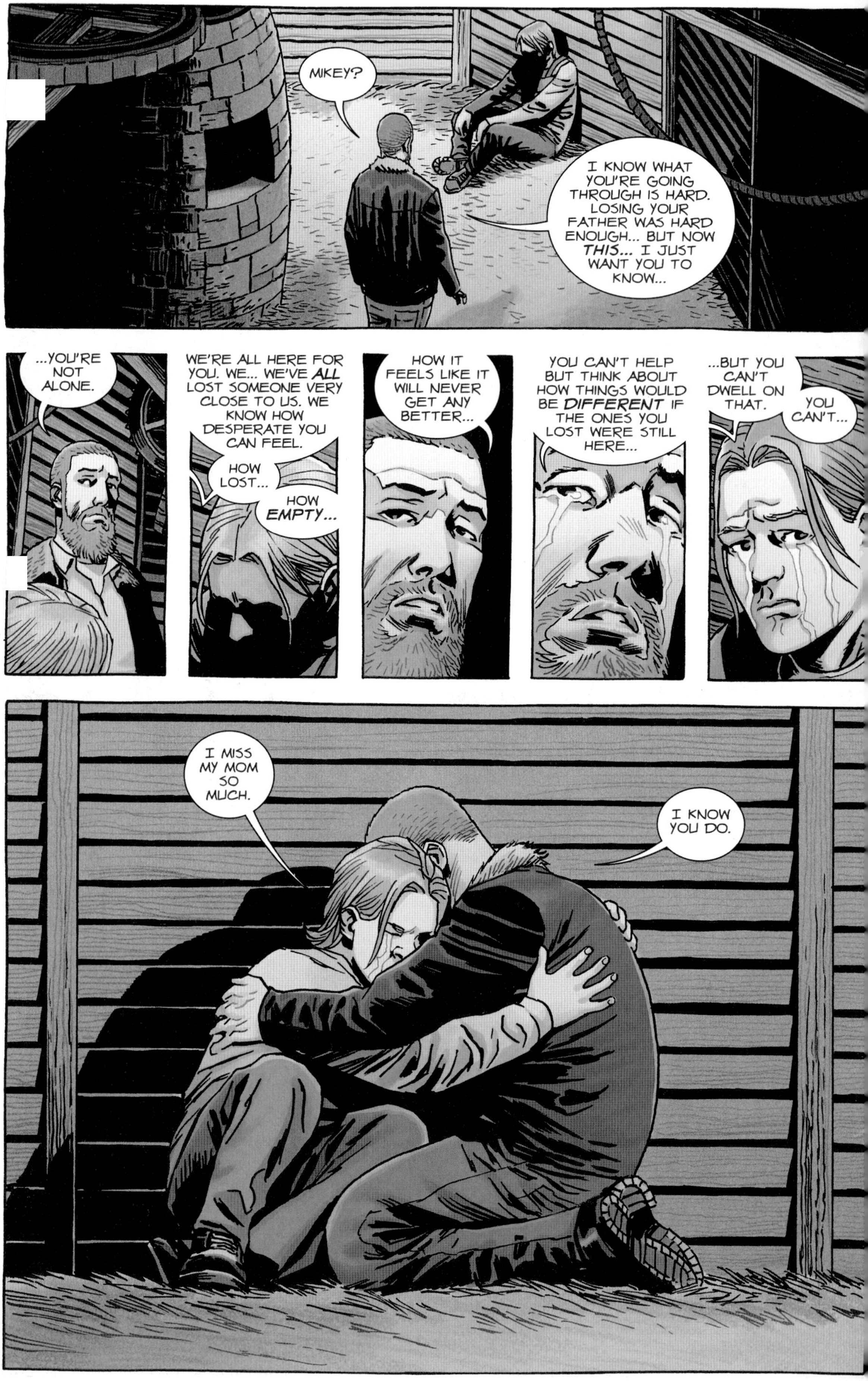
MIKEY?
I KNOW WHAT YOU'RE GOING THROUGH IS HARD. LOSING YOUR FATHER WAS HARD ENOUGH... BUT NOW THIS... I JUST WANT YOU TO KNOW...
...YOU'RE NOT ALONE.
WE'RE ALL HERE FOR YOU. WE... WE'VE ALL LOST SOMEONE VERY CLOSE TO US. WE KNOW HOW DESPERATE YOU CAN FEEL.
HOW LOST...
HOW EMPTY...
HOW IT FEELS LIKE IT WILL NEVER GET ANY BETTER...
YOU CAN'T HELP BUT THINK ABOUT HOW THINGS WOULD BE DIFFERENT IF THE ONES YOU LOST WERE STILL HERE...
...BUT YOU CAN'T DWELL ON THAT.
YOU CAN'T...
I MISS MY MOM SO MUCH.
I KNOW YOU DO.

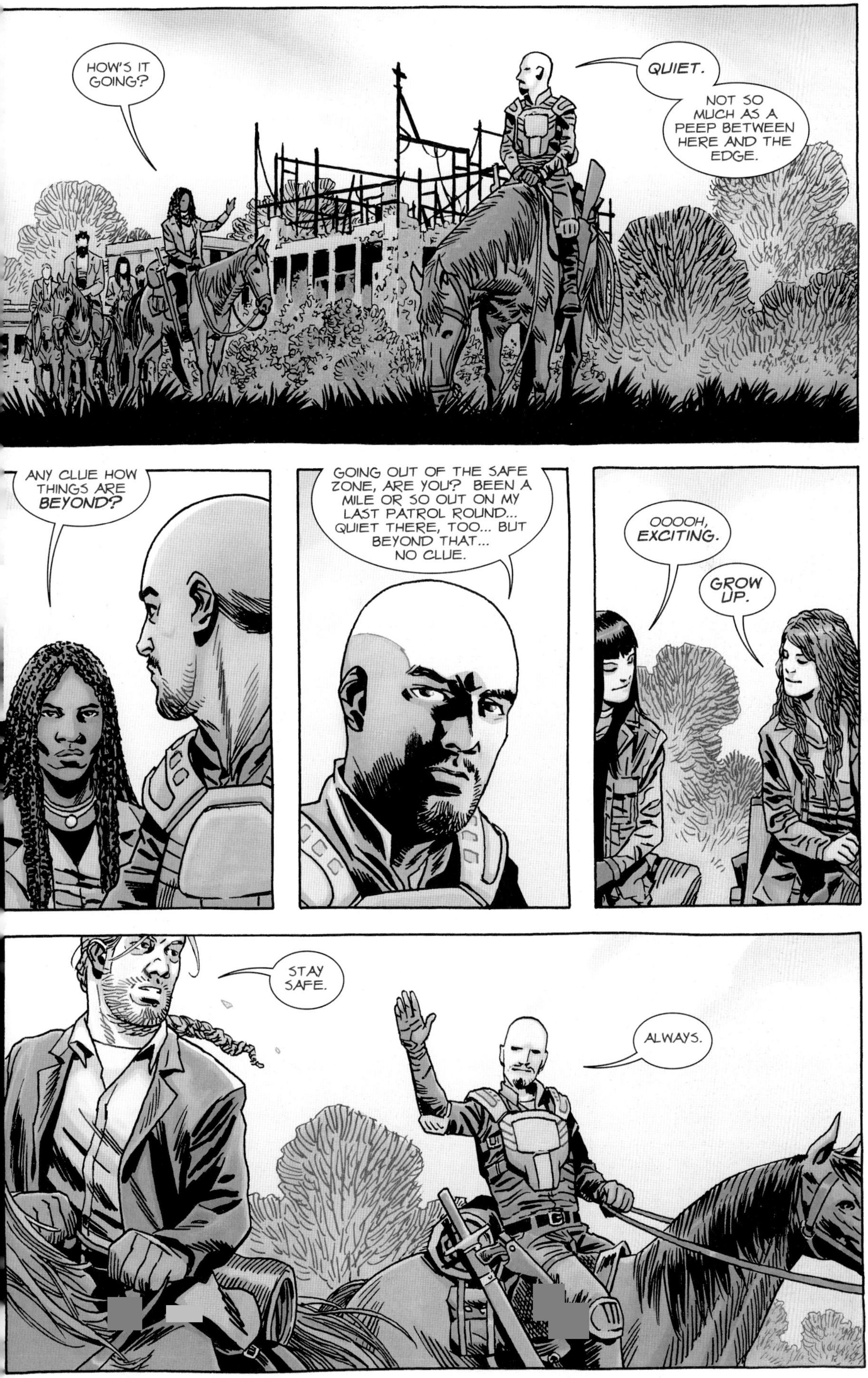
HOW'S IT GOING?
QUIET.
NOT SO MUCH AS A PEEP BETWEEN HERE AND THE EDGE.
ANY CLUE HOW THINGS ARE BEYOND?
GOING OUT OF THE SAFE ZONE, ARE YOU? BEEN A MILE OR SO OUT ON MY LAST PATROL ROUND... QUIET THERE, TOO... BUT BEYOND THAT... NO CLUE.
OOOOH, EXCITING.
GROW UP.
STAY SAFE.
ALWAYS.

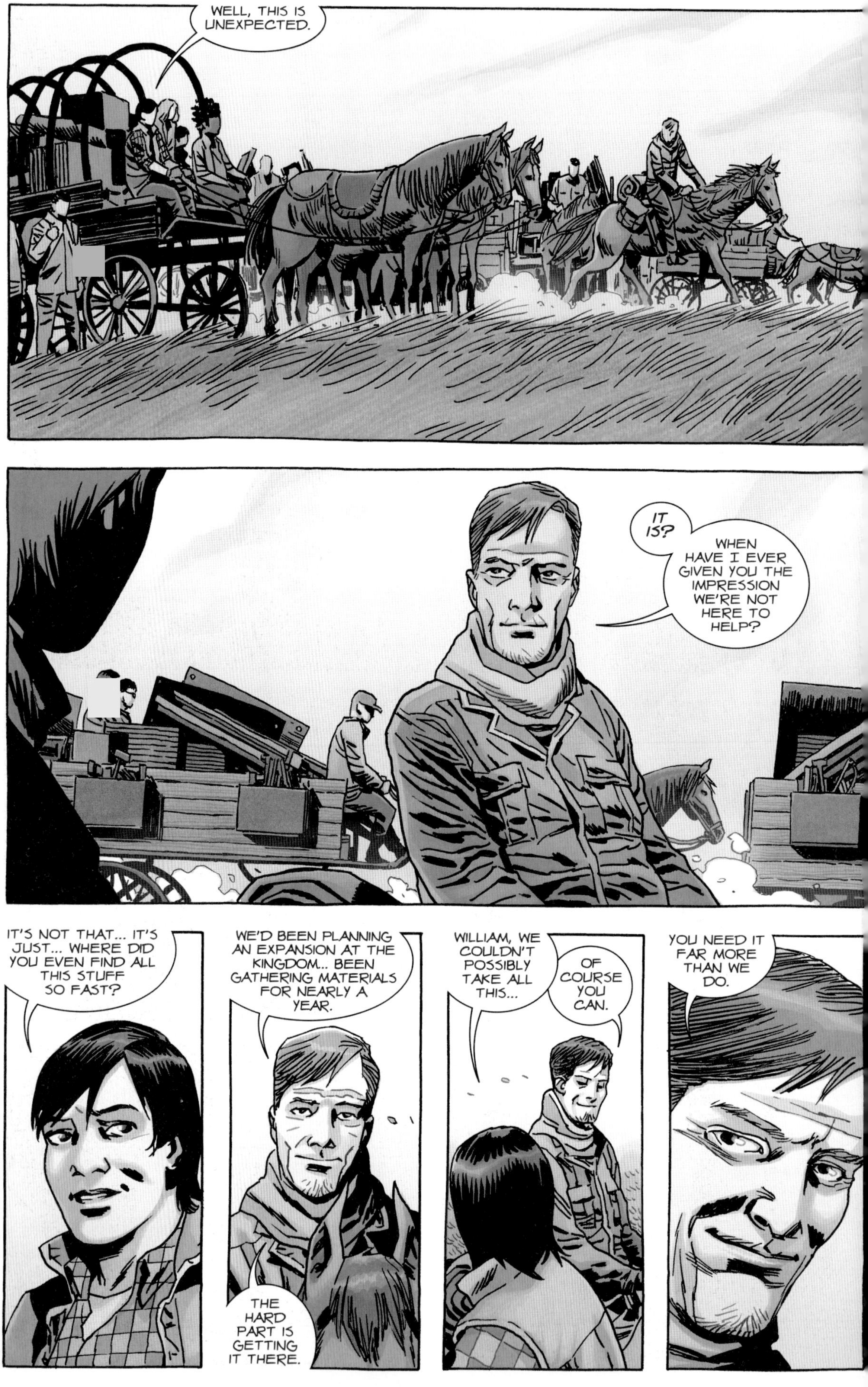
WELL, THIS IS UNEXPECTED.
IT IS?
WHEN HAVE I EVER GIVEN YOU THE IMPRESSION WE'RE NOT HERE TO HELP?
IT'S NOT THAT... IT'S JUST... WHERE DID YOU EVEN FIND ALL THIS STUFF SO FAST?
WE'D BEEN PLANNING AN EXPANSION AT THE KINGDOM... BEEN GATHERING MATERIALS FOR NEARLY A YEAR.
THE HARD PART IS GETTING IT THERE.
WILLIAM, WE COULDN'T POSSIBLY TAKE ALL THIS...
OF COURSE YOU CAN.
YOU NEED IT FAR MORE THAN WE DO.

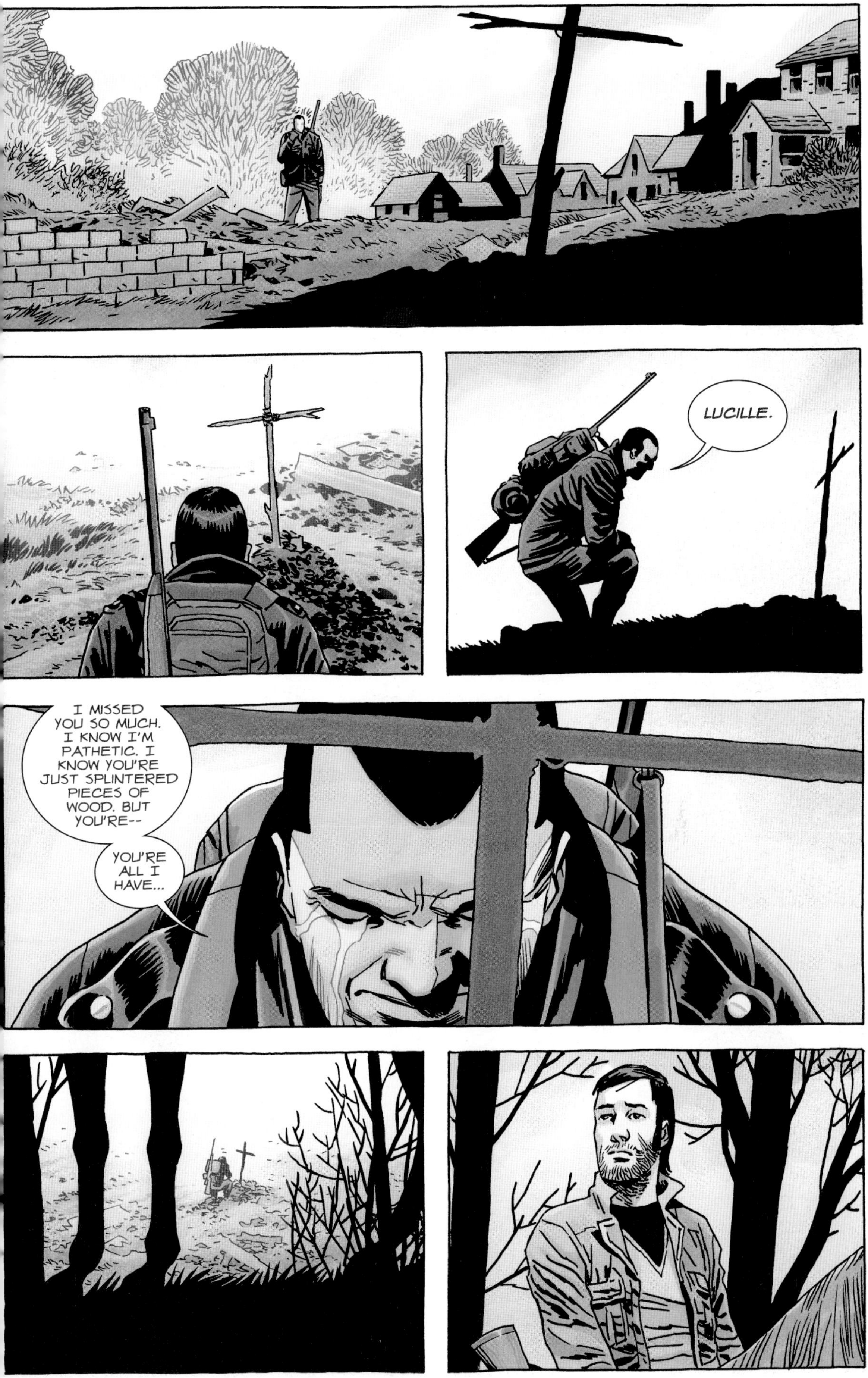
LUCILLE.
I MISSED YOU SO MUCH. I KNOW I'M PATHETIC. I KNOW YOU'RE JUST SPLINTERED PIECES OF WOOD. BUT YOU'RE--
YOU'RE ALL I HAVE...

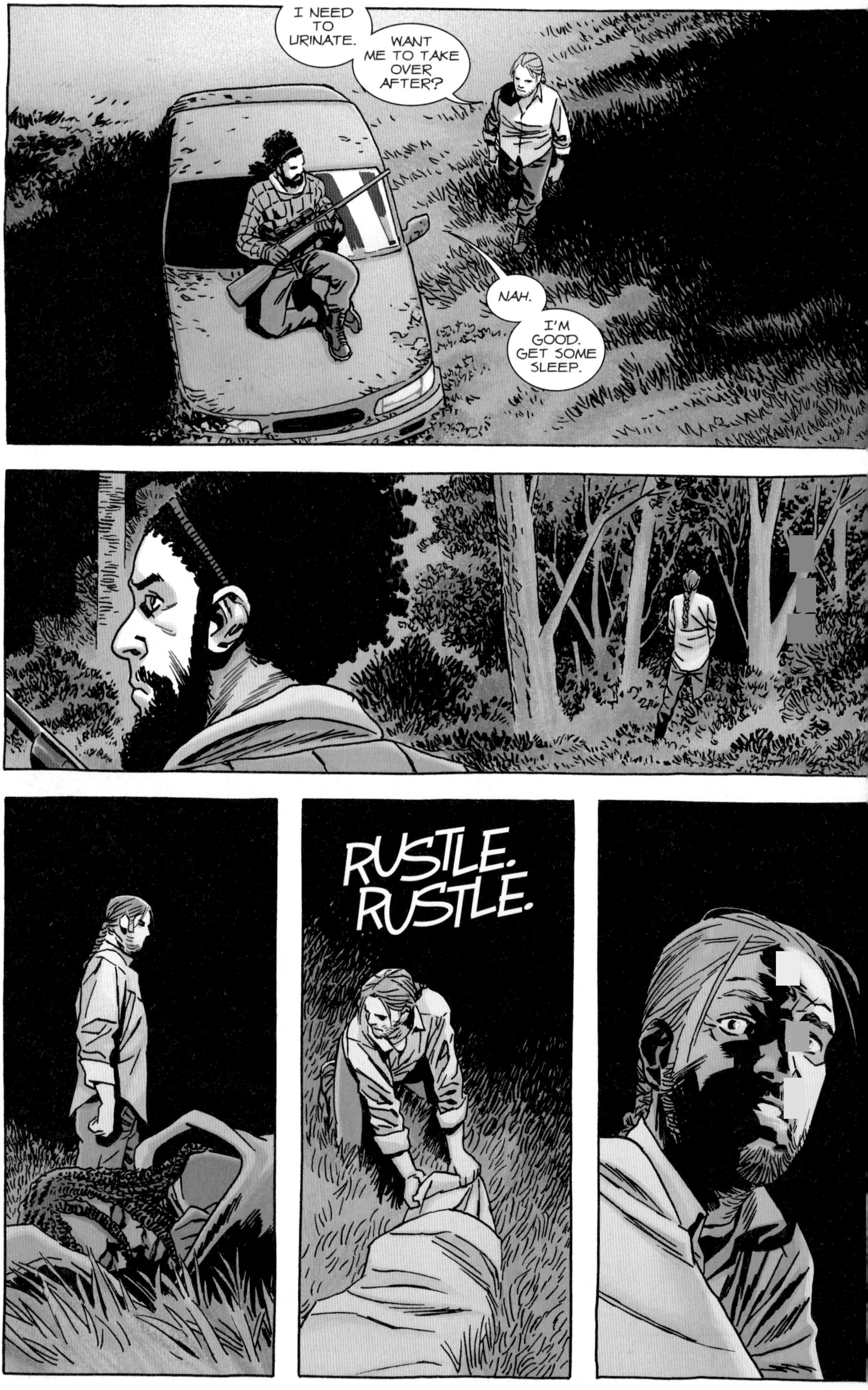

I NEED TO URINATE.
WANT ME TO TAKE OVER AFTER?
NAH.
I'M GOOD. GET SOME SLEEP.
RUSTLE. RUSTLE.

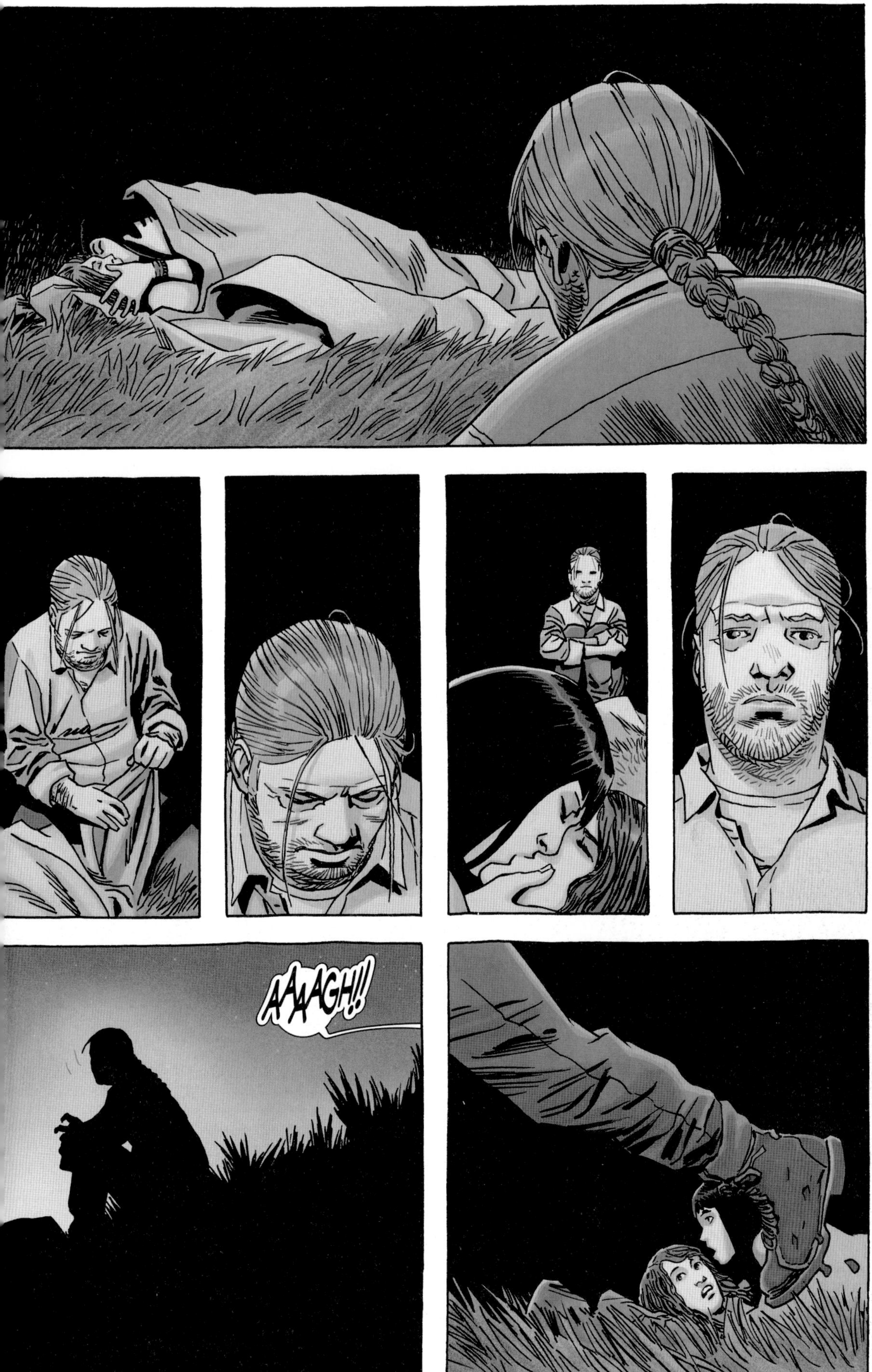
AAAAGH!!

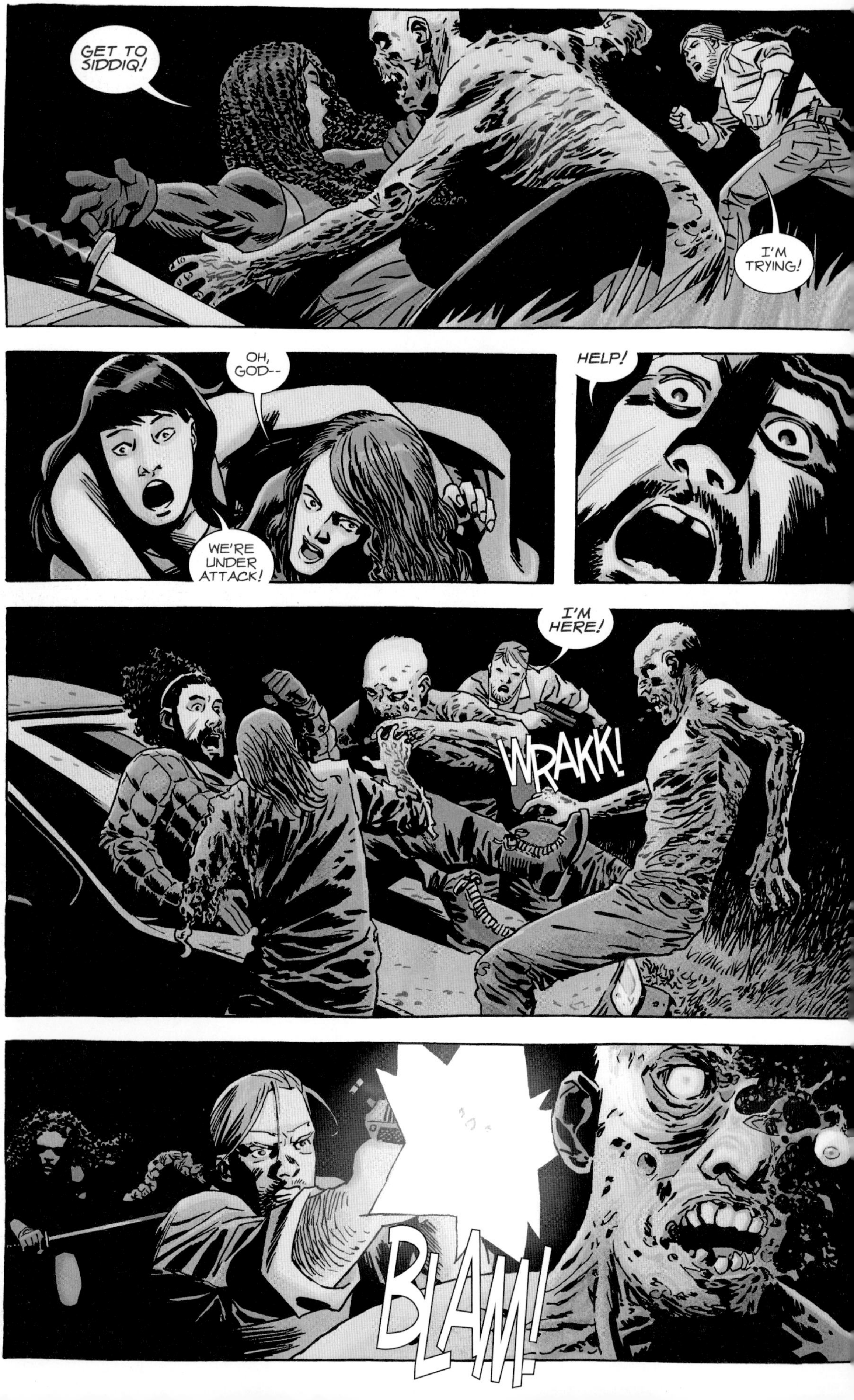
GET TO SIDDIQ!
I'M TRYING!
OH, GOD--
WE'RE UNDER ATTACK!
HELP!
I'M HERE!
WRAKK!
BLAM!

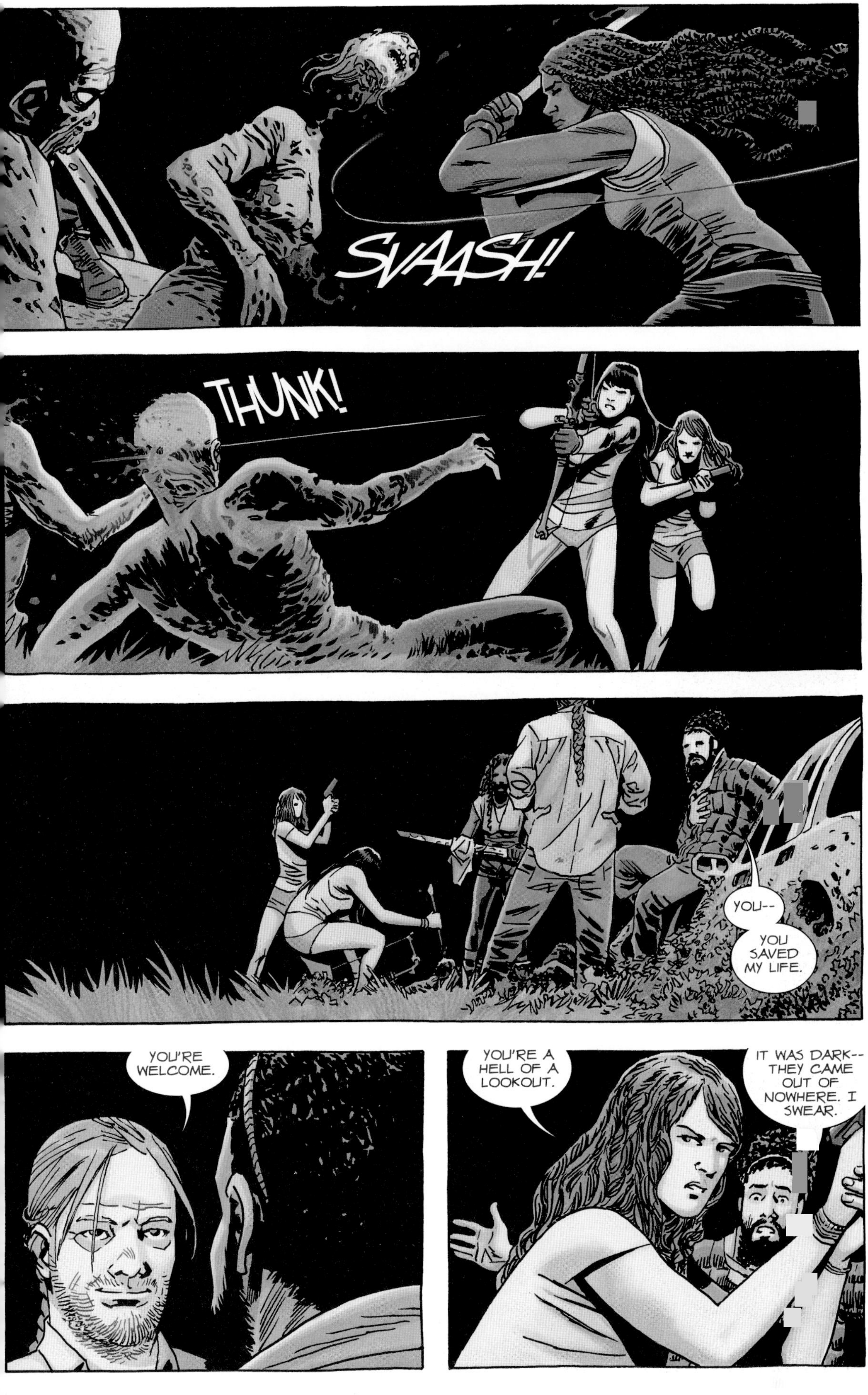
SVAASH!
THUNK!
YOU--
YOU SAVED MY LIFE.
YOU'RE WELCOME.
YOU'RE A HELL OF A LOOKOUT.
IT WAS DARK-- THEY CAME OUT OF NOWHERE. I SWEAR.

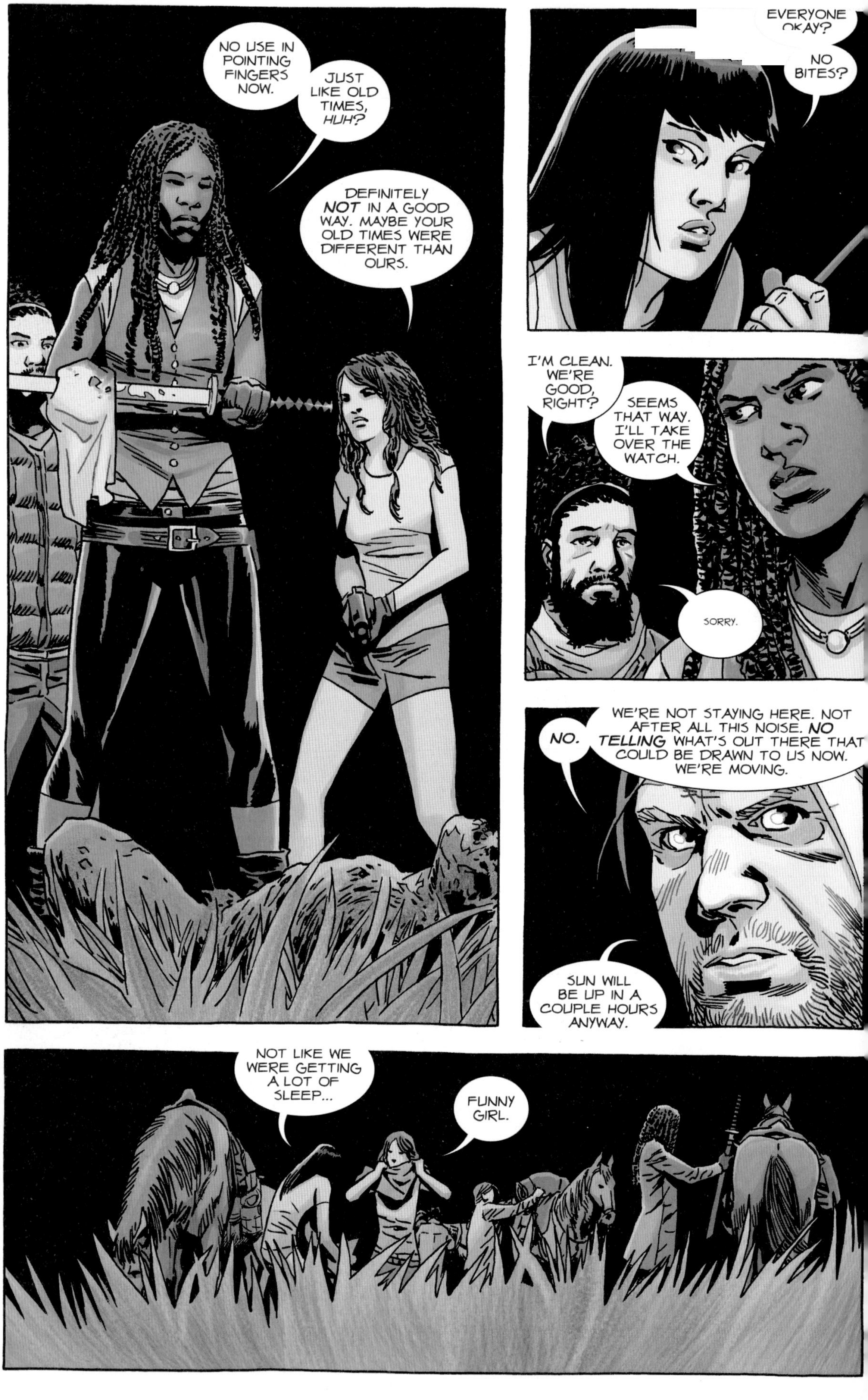
NO USE IN POINTING FINGERS NOW.
JUST LIKE OLD TIMES, HUH?
DEFINITELY NOT IN A GOOD WAY. MAYBE YOUR OLD TIMES WERE DIFFERENT THAN OURS.
EVERYONE OKAY?
NO BITES?
I'M CLEAN. WE'RE GOOD, RIGHT?
SEEMS THAT WAY. I'LL TAKE OVER THE WATCH.
SORRY.
NO.
WE'RE NOT STAYING HERE. NOT AFTER ALL THIS NOISE. NO TELLING WHAT'S OUT THERE THAT COULD BE DRAWN TO US NOW. WE'RE MOVING.
SUN WILL BE UP IN A COUPLE HOURS ANYWAY.
NOT LIKE WE WERE GETTING A LOT OF SLEEP...
FUNNY GIRL.

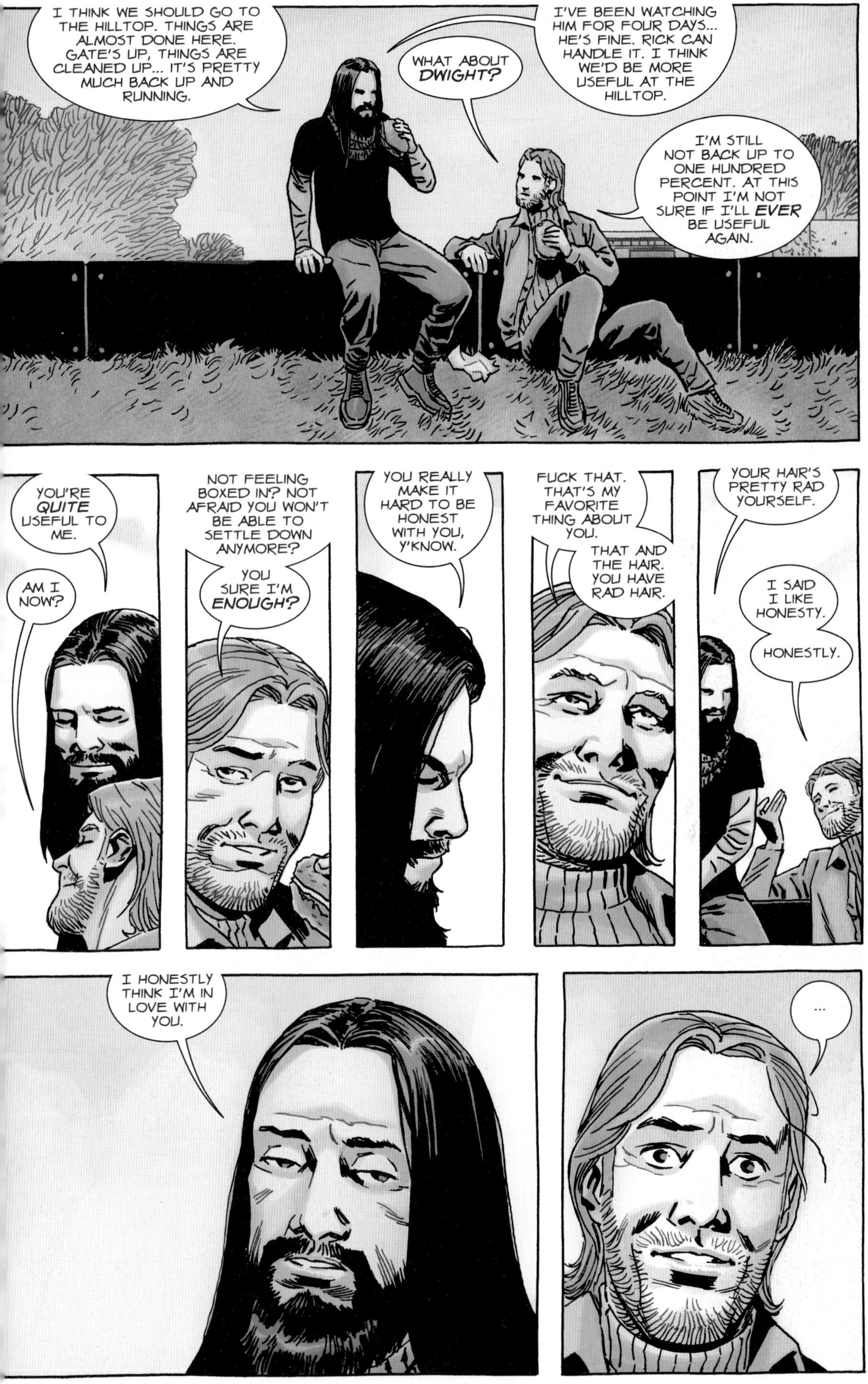

I THINK WE SHOULD GO TO THE HILLTOP. THINGS ARE ALMOST DONE HERE. GATE'S UP, THINGS ARE CLEANED UP... IT'S PRETTY MUCH BACK UP AND RUNNING.
WHAT ABOUT *DWIGHT?*
I'VE BEEN WATCHING HIM FOR FOUR DAYS... HE'S FINE. RICK CAN HANDLE IT. I THINK WE'D BE MORE USEFUL AT THE HILLTOP.
I'M STILL NOT BACK UP TO ONE HUNDRED PERCENT. AT THIS POINT I'M NOT SURE IF I'LL *EVER* BE USEFUL AGAIN.
YOU'RE *QUITE* USEFUL TO ME.
AM I NOW?
NOT FEELING BOXED IN? NOT AFRAID YOU WON'T BE ABLE TO SETTLE DOWN ANYMORE?
YOU SURE I'M *ENOUGH?*
YOU REALLY MAKE IT HARD TO BE HONEST WITH YOU, Y'KNOW.
FUCK THAT. THAT'S MY FAVORITE THING ABOUT YOU.
THAT AND THE HAIR. YOU HAVE RAD HAIR.
YOUR HAIR'S PRETTY RAD YOURSELF.
I SAID I LIKE HONESTY.
HONESTLY.
I HONESTLY THINK I'M IN LOVE WITH YOU.
...

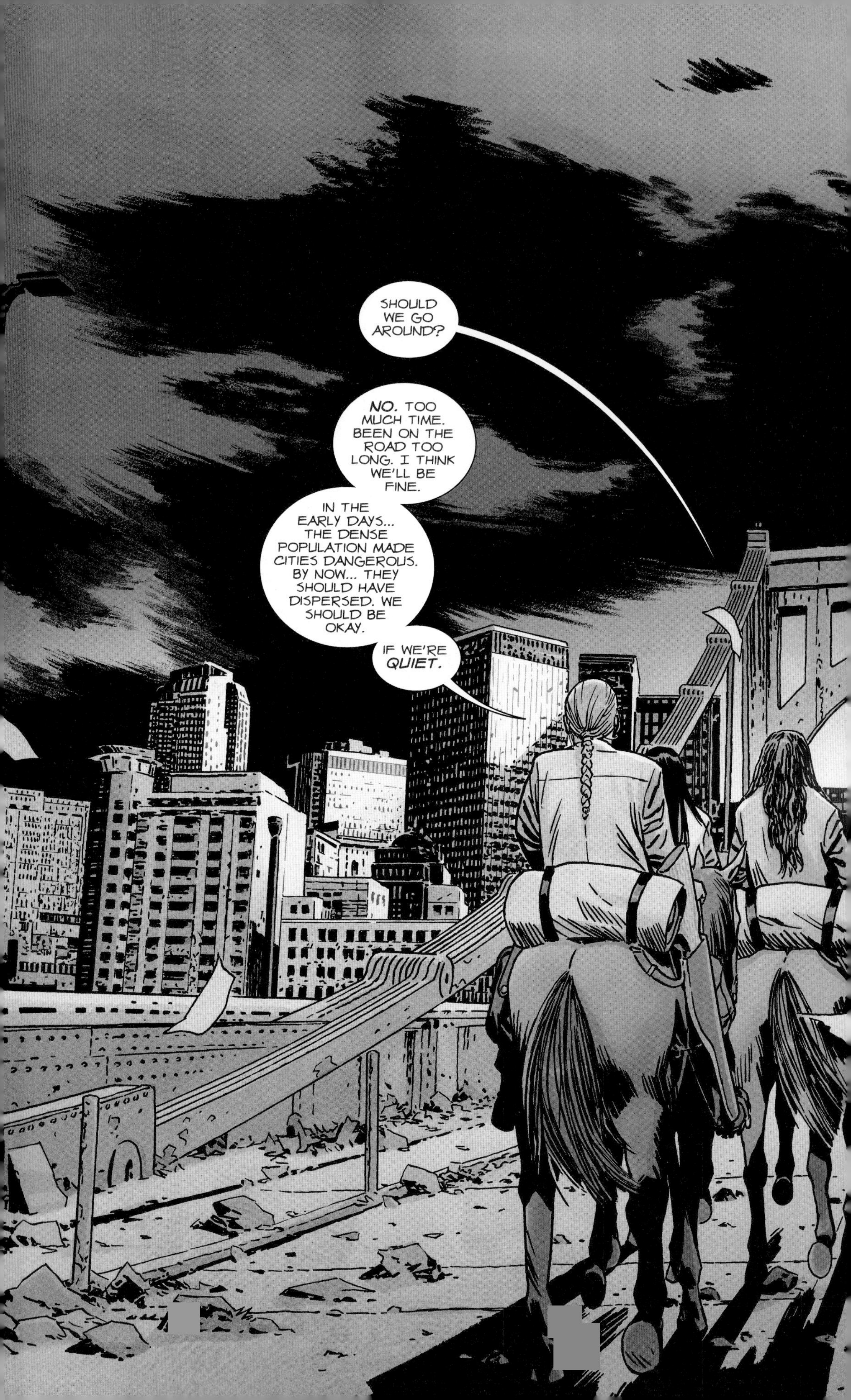

SHOULD WE GO AROUND?
NO. TOO MUCH TIME. BEEN ON THE ROAD TOO LONG. I THINK WE'LL BE FINE.
IN THE EARLY DAYS... THE DENSE POPULATION MADE CITIES DANGEROUS. BY NOW... THEY SHOULD HAVE DISPERSED. WE SHOULD BE OKAY.
IF WE'RE QUIET.

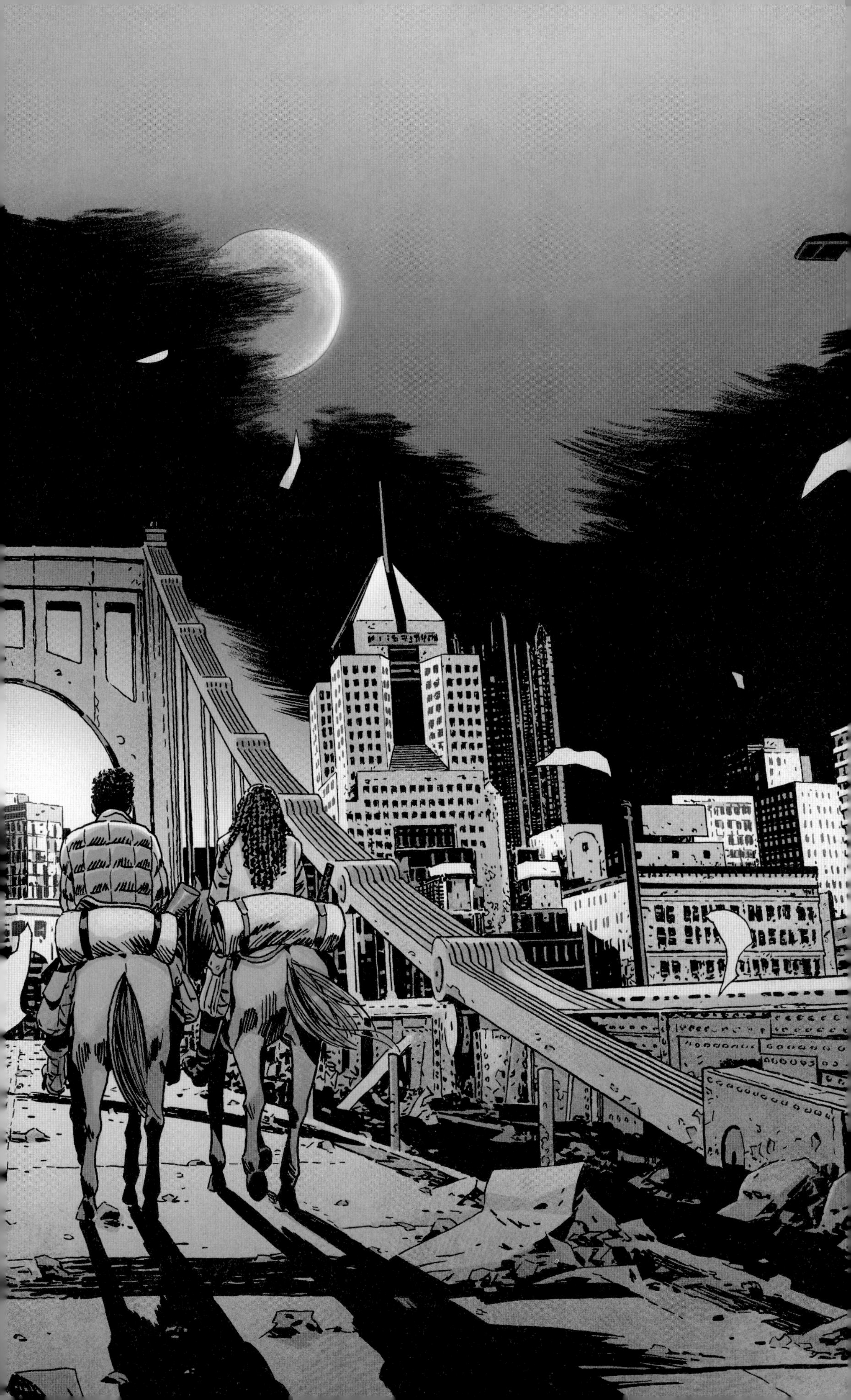

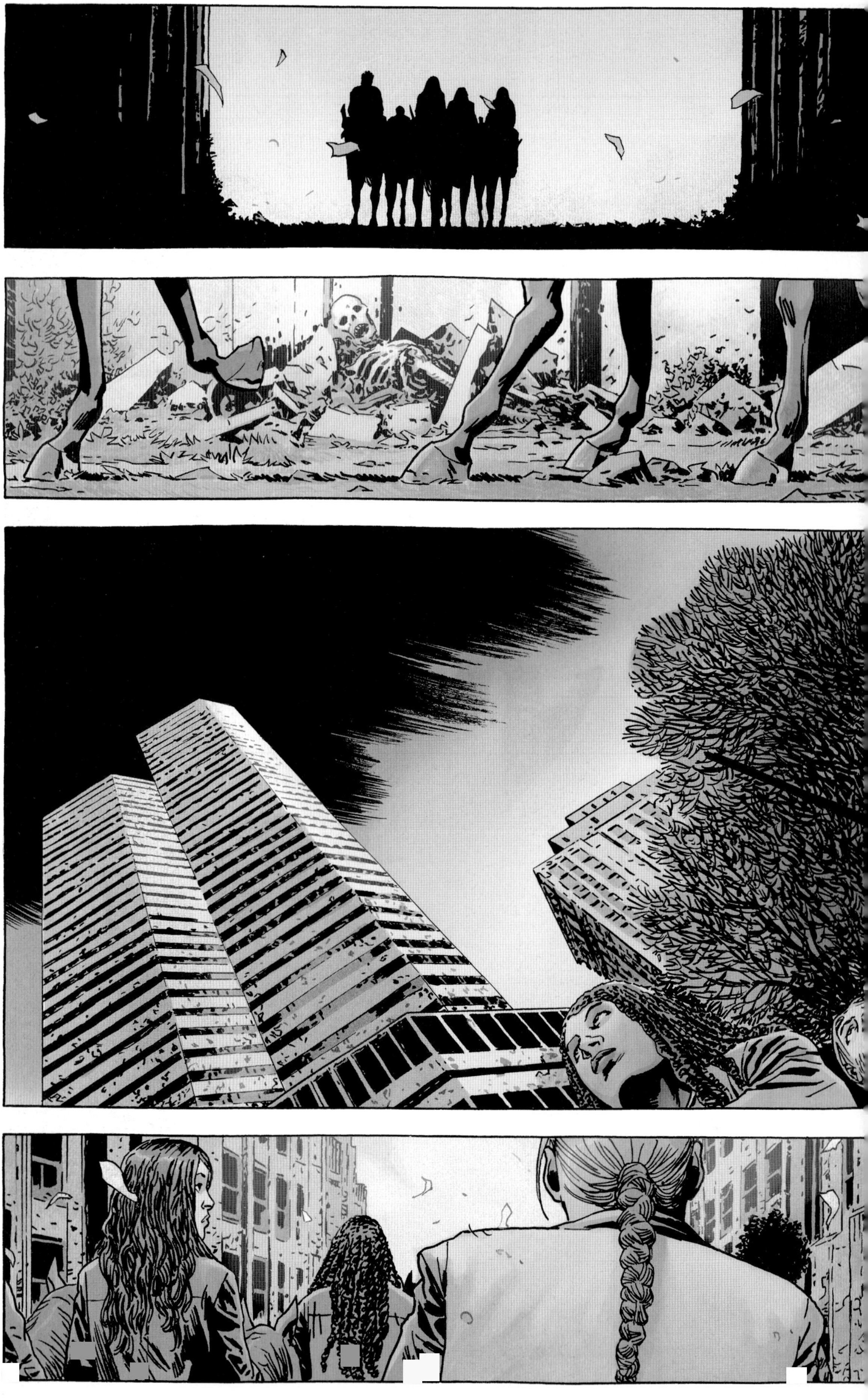

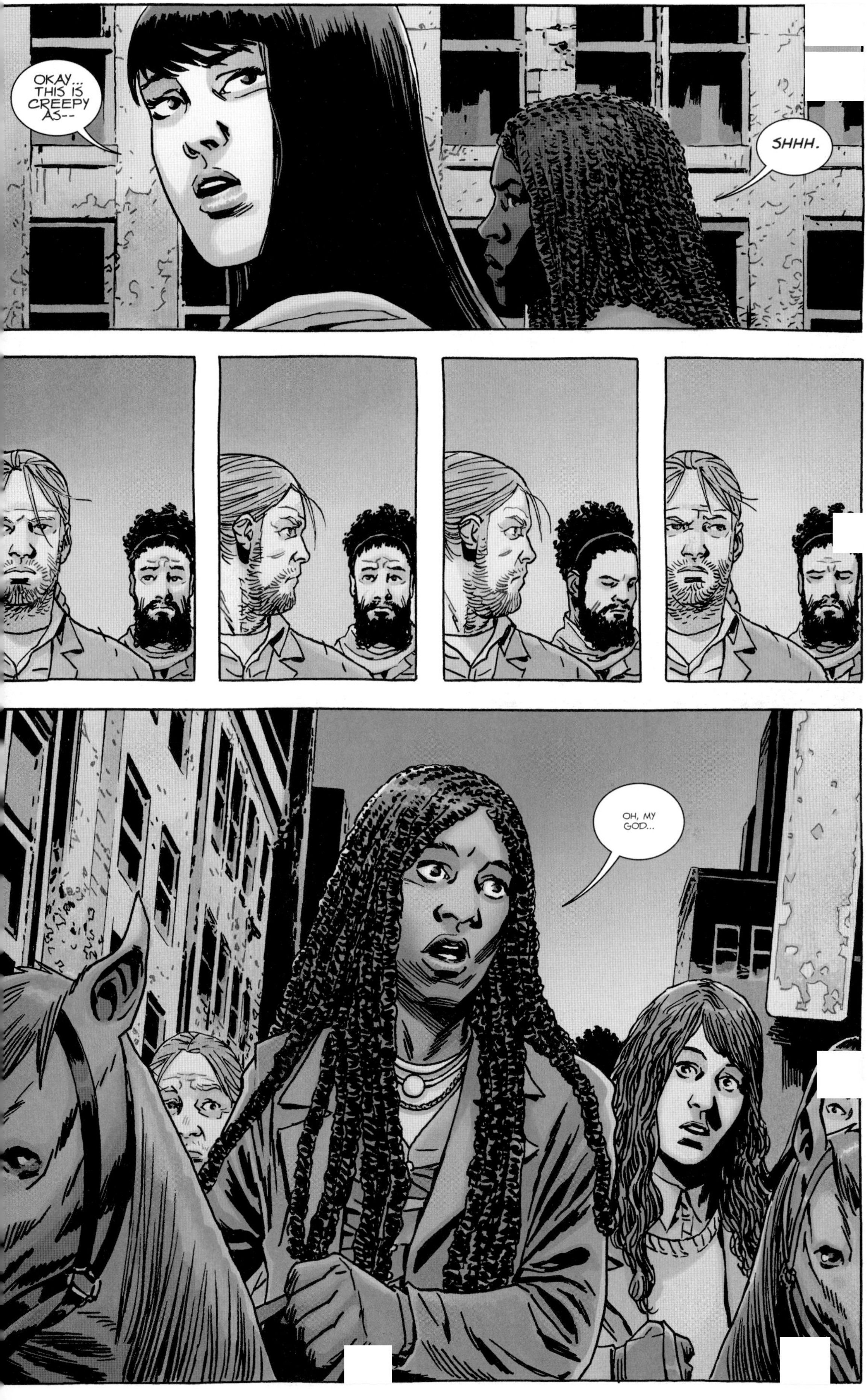
OKAY... THIS IS CREEPY AS--
SHHH.
OH, MY GOD...

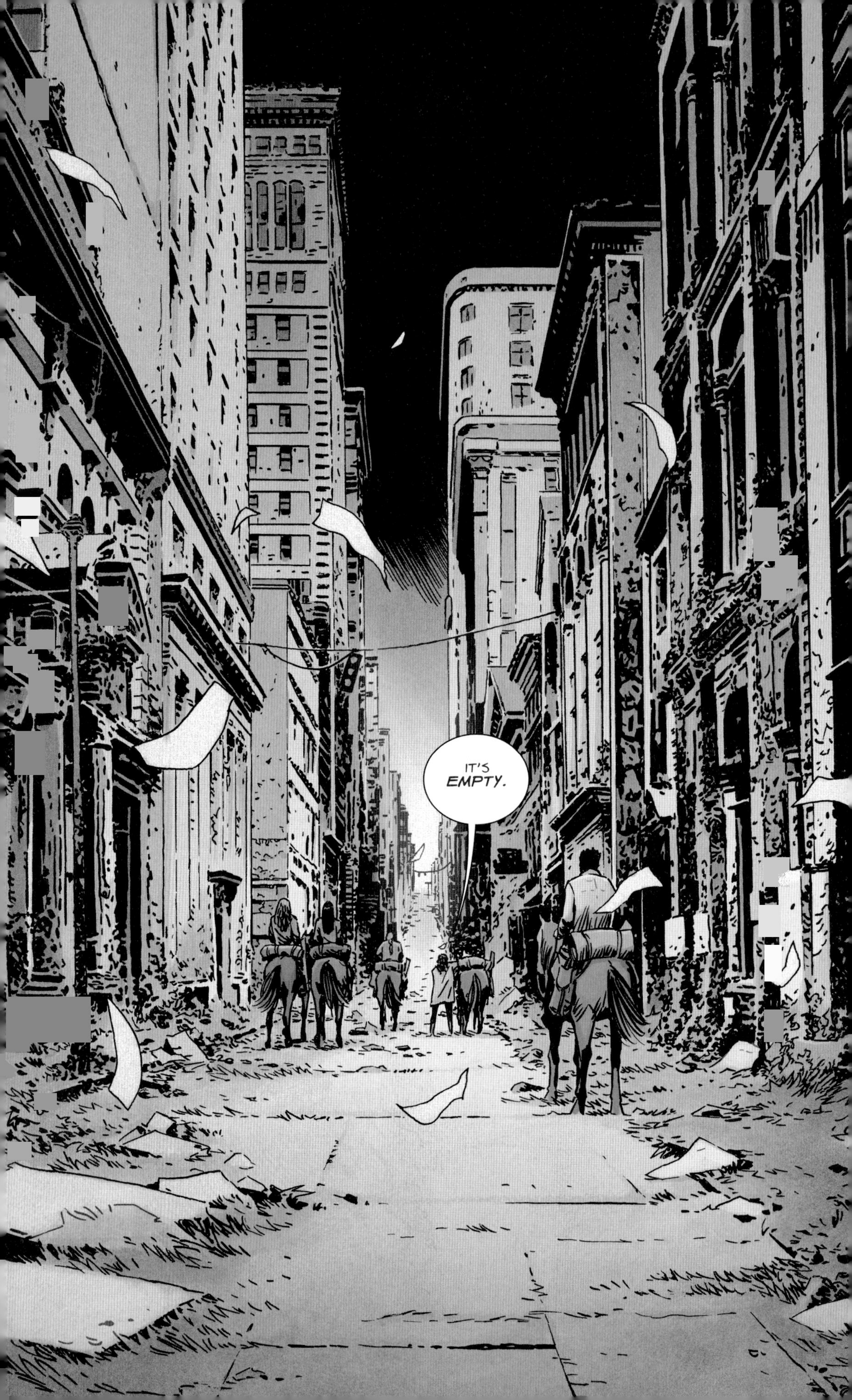
IT'S EMPTY.

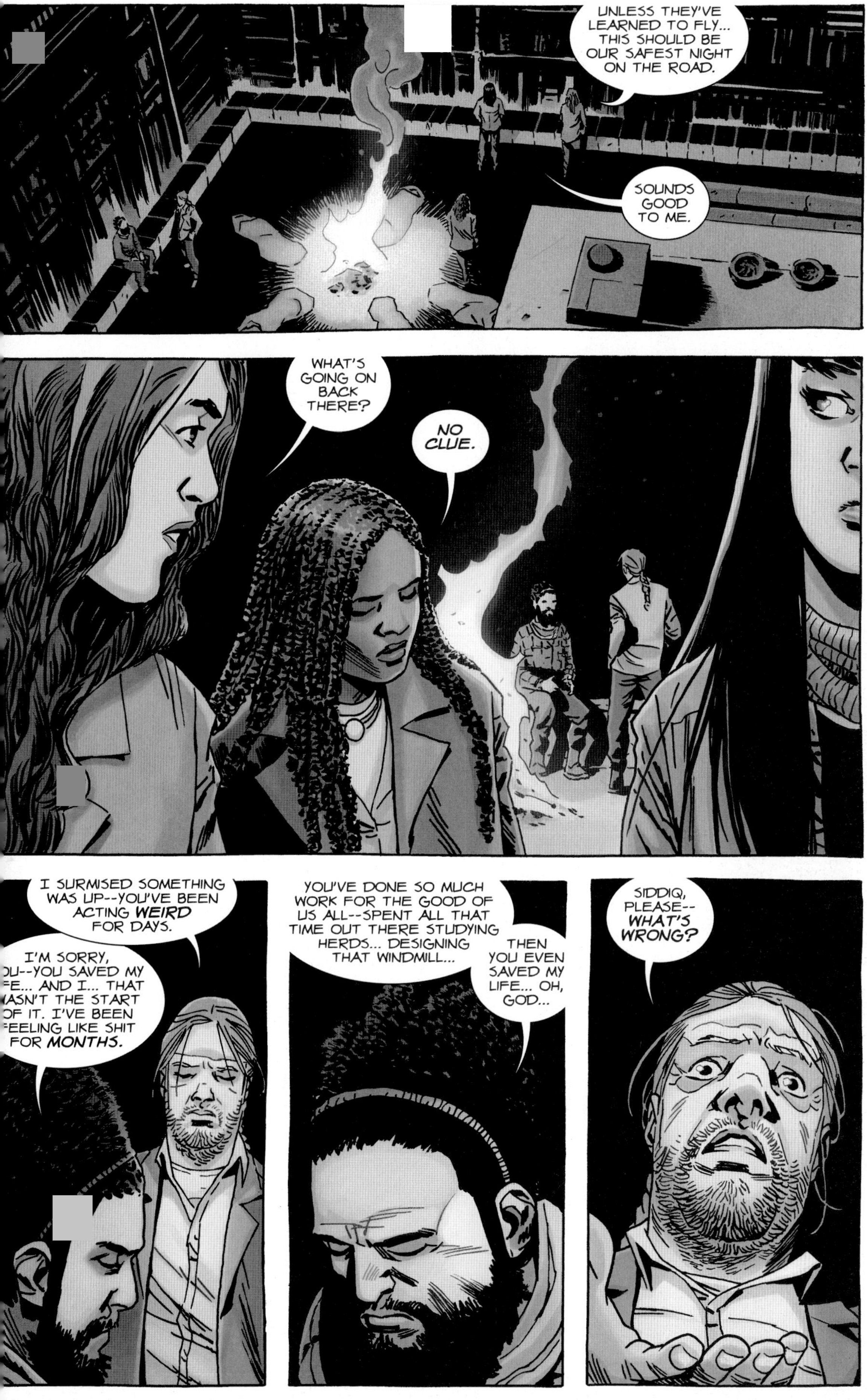
UNLESS THEY'VE LEARNED TO FLY... THIS SHOULD BE OUR SAFEST NIGHT ON THE ROAD.
SOUNDS GOOD TO ME.
WHAT'S GOING ON BACK THERE?
NO CLUE.
I SURMISED SOMETHING WAS UP--YOU'VE BEEN ACTING WEIRD FOR DAYS.
I'M SORRY, OU--YOU SAVED MY FE... AND I... THAT ASN'T THE START OF IT. I'VE BEEN FEELING LIKE SHIT FOR MONTHS.
YOU'VE DONE SO MUCH WORK FOR THE GOOD OF US ALL--SPENT ALL THAT TIME OUT THERE STUDYING HERDS... DESIGNING THAT WINDMILL...
THEN YOU EVEN SAVED MY LIFE... OH, GOD...
SIDDIQ, PLEASE-- WHAT'S WRONG?

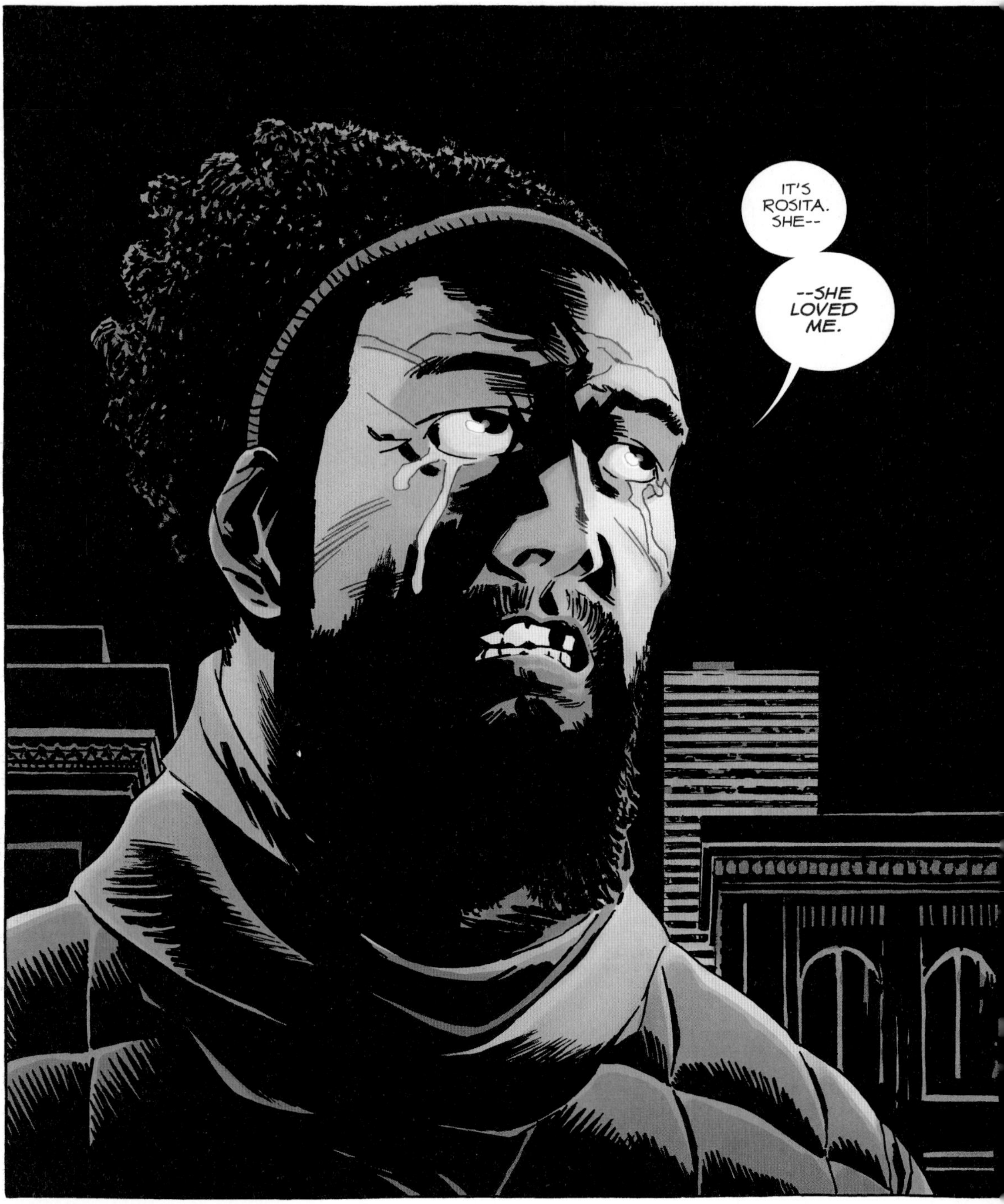
IT'S ROSITA. SHE--
--SHE LOVED ME.

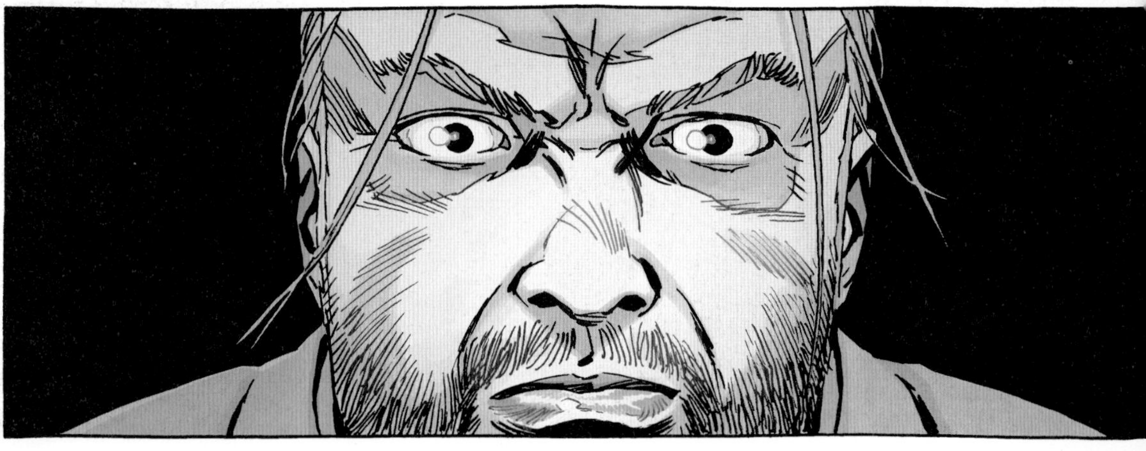

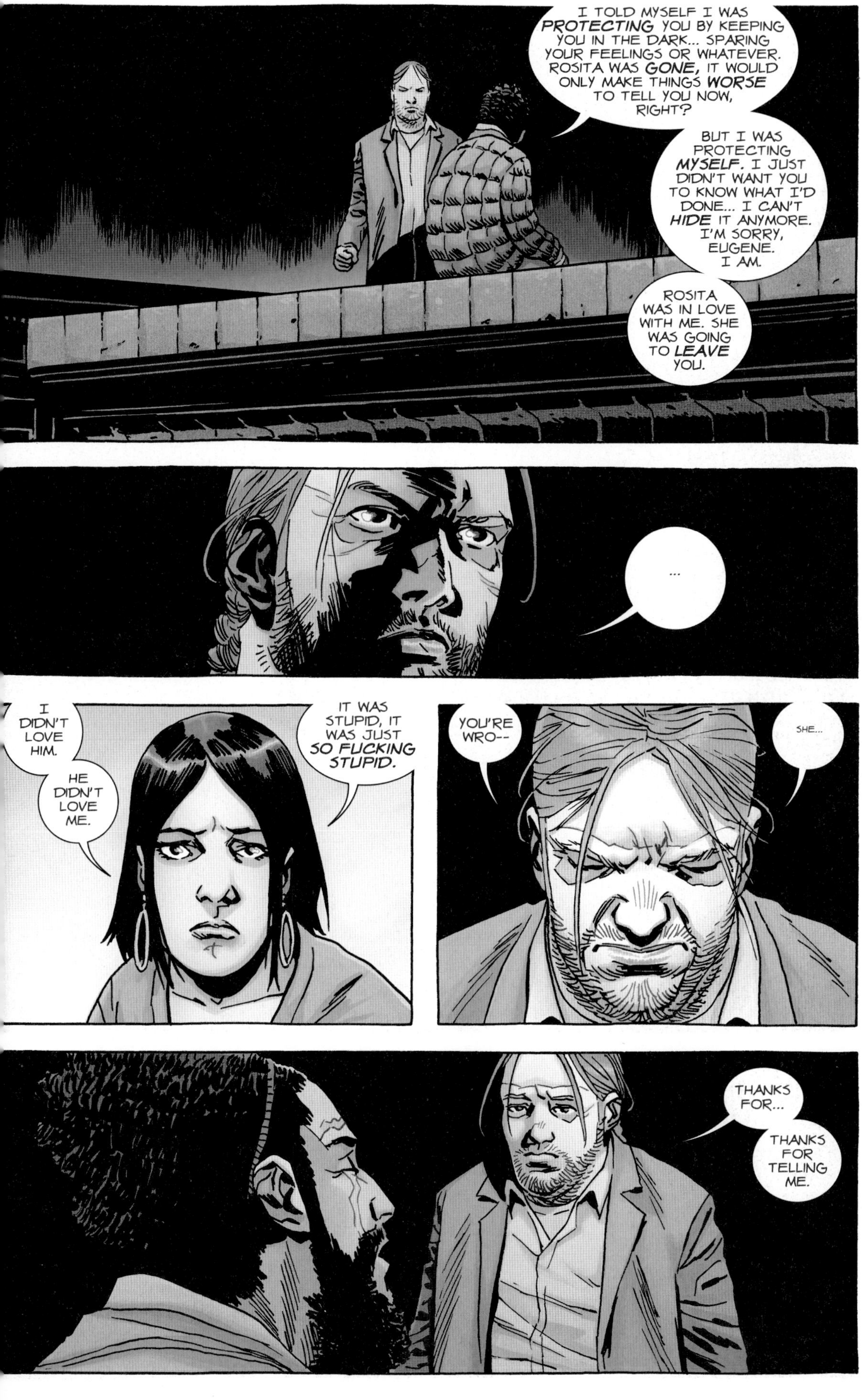
I TOLD MYSELF I WAS PROTECTING YOU BY KEEPING YOU IN THE DARK... SPARING YOUR FEELINGS OR WHATEVER. ROSITA WAS GONE, IT WOULD ONLY MAKE THINGS WORSE TO TELL YOU NOW, RIGHT?
BUT I WAS PROTECTING MYSELF. I JUST DIDN'T WANT YOU TO KNOW WHAT I'D DONE... I CAN'T HIDE IT ANYMORE. I'M SORRY, EUGENE. I AM.
ROSITA WAS IN LOVE WITH ME. SHE WAS GOING TO LEAVE YOU.
...
I DIDN'T LOVE HIM.
HE DIDN'T LOVE ME.
IT WAS STUPID, IT WAS JUST SO FUCKING STUPID.
YOU'RE WRO--
SHE...
THANKS FOR...
THANKS FOR TELLING ME.

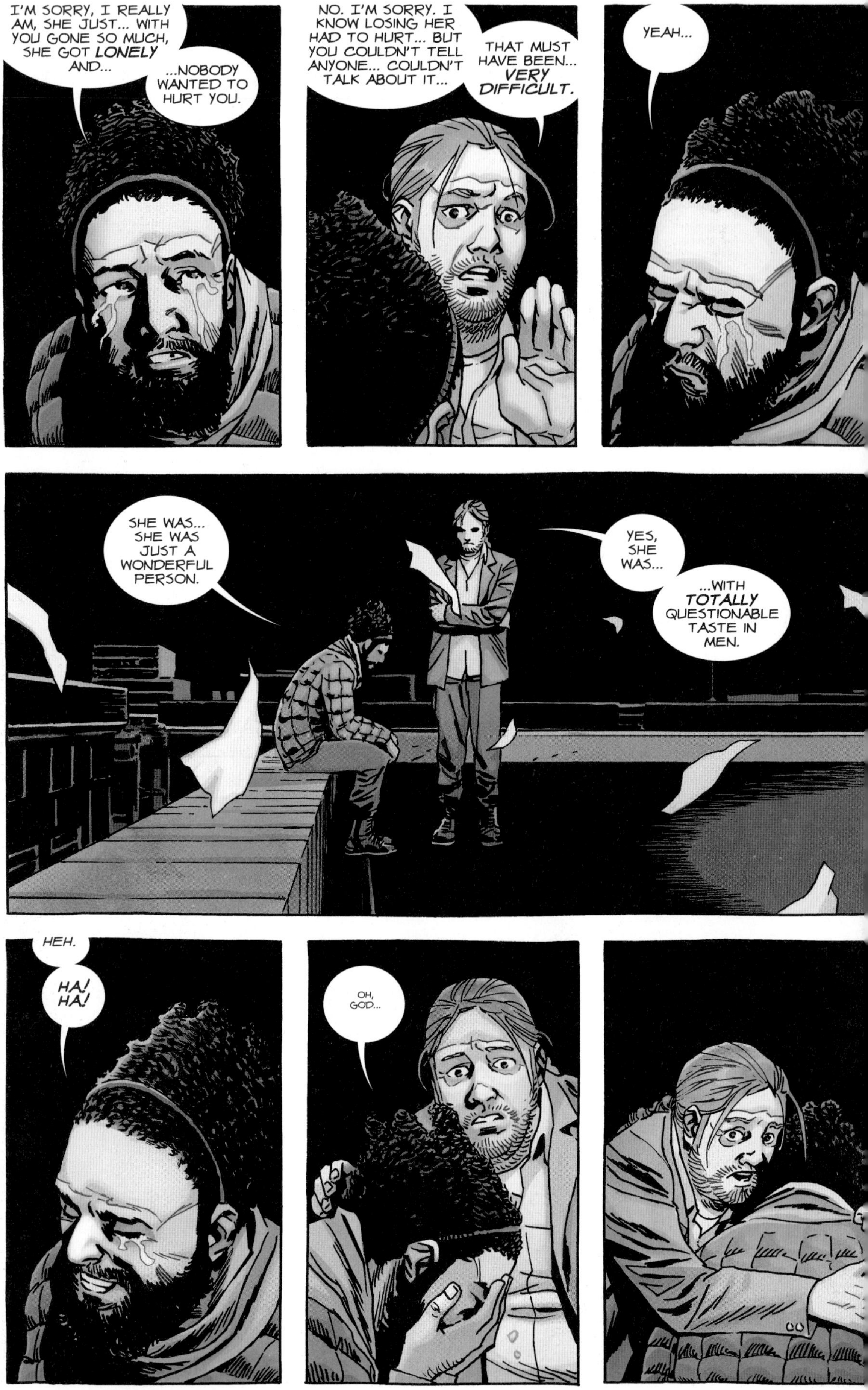
I'M SORRY, I REALLY AM, SHE JUST... WITH YOU GONE SO MUCH, SHE GOT LONELY AND...
...NOBODY WANTED TO HURT YOU.
NO. I'M SORRY. I KNOW LOSING HER HAD TO HURT... BUT YOU COULDN'T TELL ANYONE... COULDN'T TALK ABOUT IT...
THAT MUST HAVE BEEN... VERY DIFFICULT.
YEAH...
SHE WAS... SHE WAS JUST A WONDERFUL PERSON.
YES, SHE WAS...
...WITH TOTALLY QUESTIONABLE TASTE IN MEN.
HEH.
HA! HA!
OH, GOD...

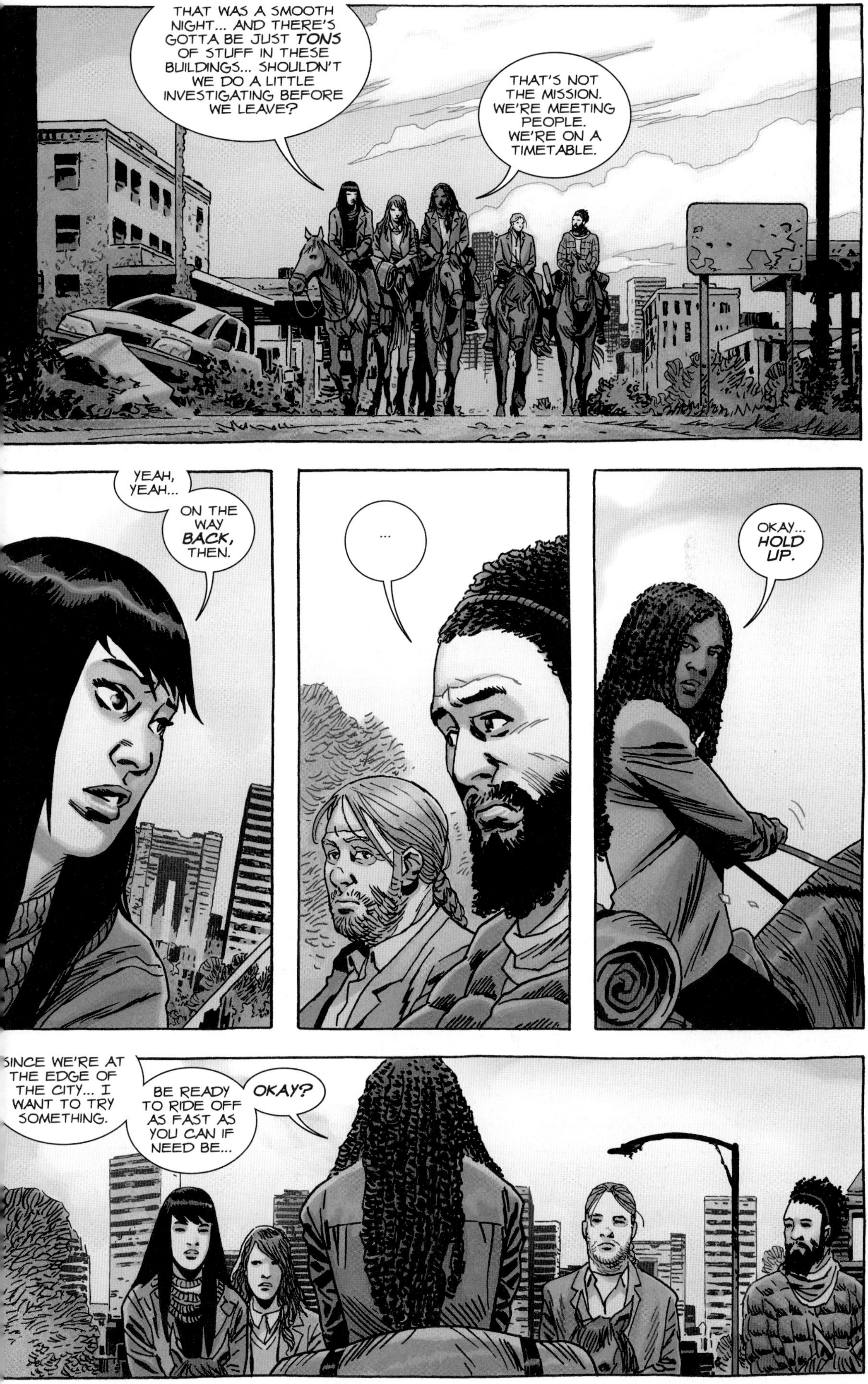
THAT WAS A SMOOTH NIGHT... AND THERE'S GOTTA BE JUST TONS OF STUFF IN THESE BUILDINGS... SHOULDN'T WE DO A LITTLE INVESTIGATING BEFORE WE LEAVE?
THAT'S NOT THE MISSION. WE'RE MEETING PEOPLE. WE'RE ON A TIMETABLE.
YEAH, YEAH...
ON THE WAY BACK, THEN.
...
OKAY... HOLD UP.
SINCE WE'RE AT THE EDGE OF THE CITY... I WANT TO TRY SOMETHING.
BE READY TO RIDE OFF AS FAST AS YOU CAN IF NEED BE...
OKAY?

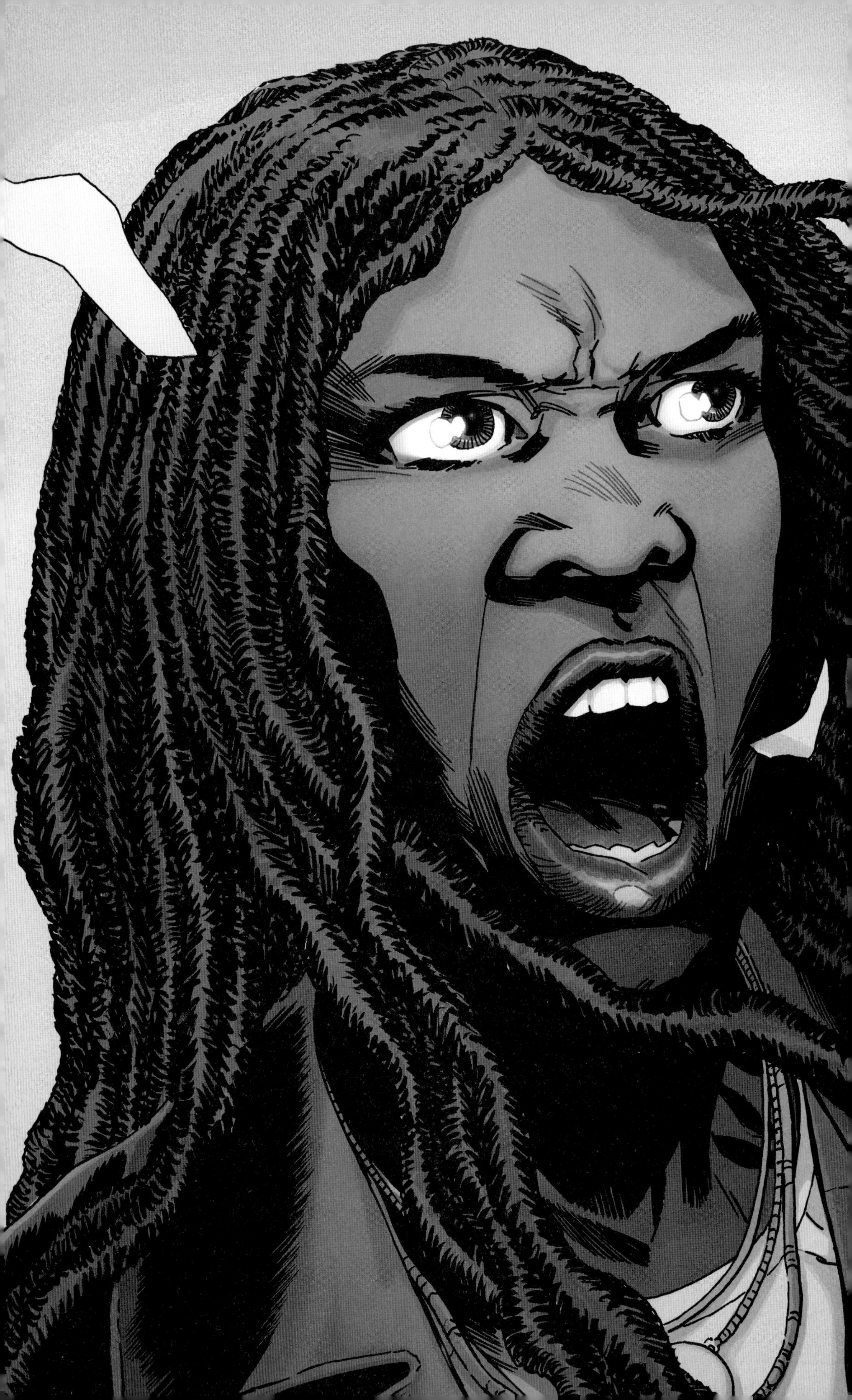

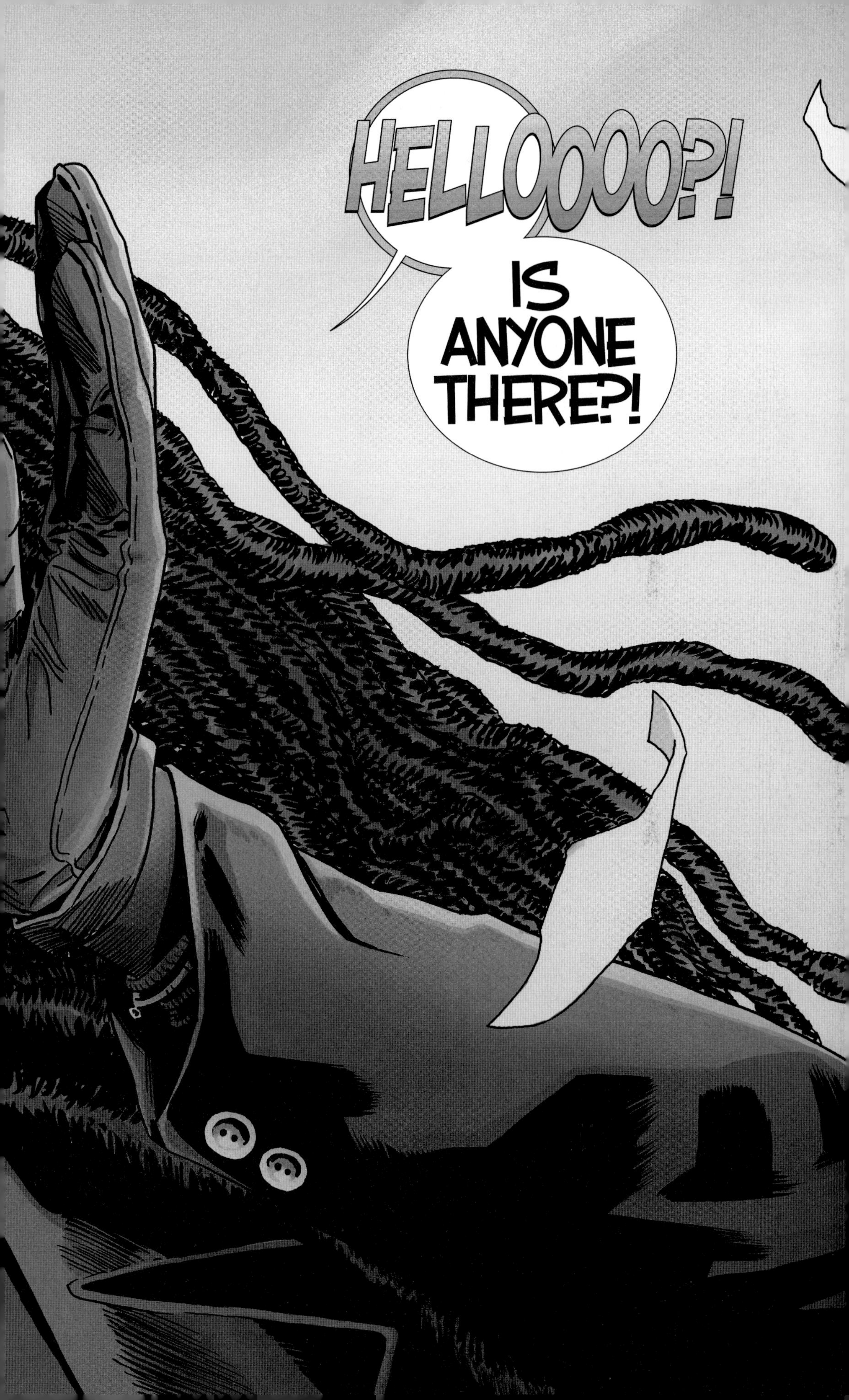
HELLOOOO?!
IS ANYONE THERE?!

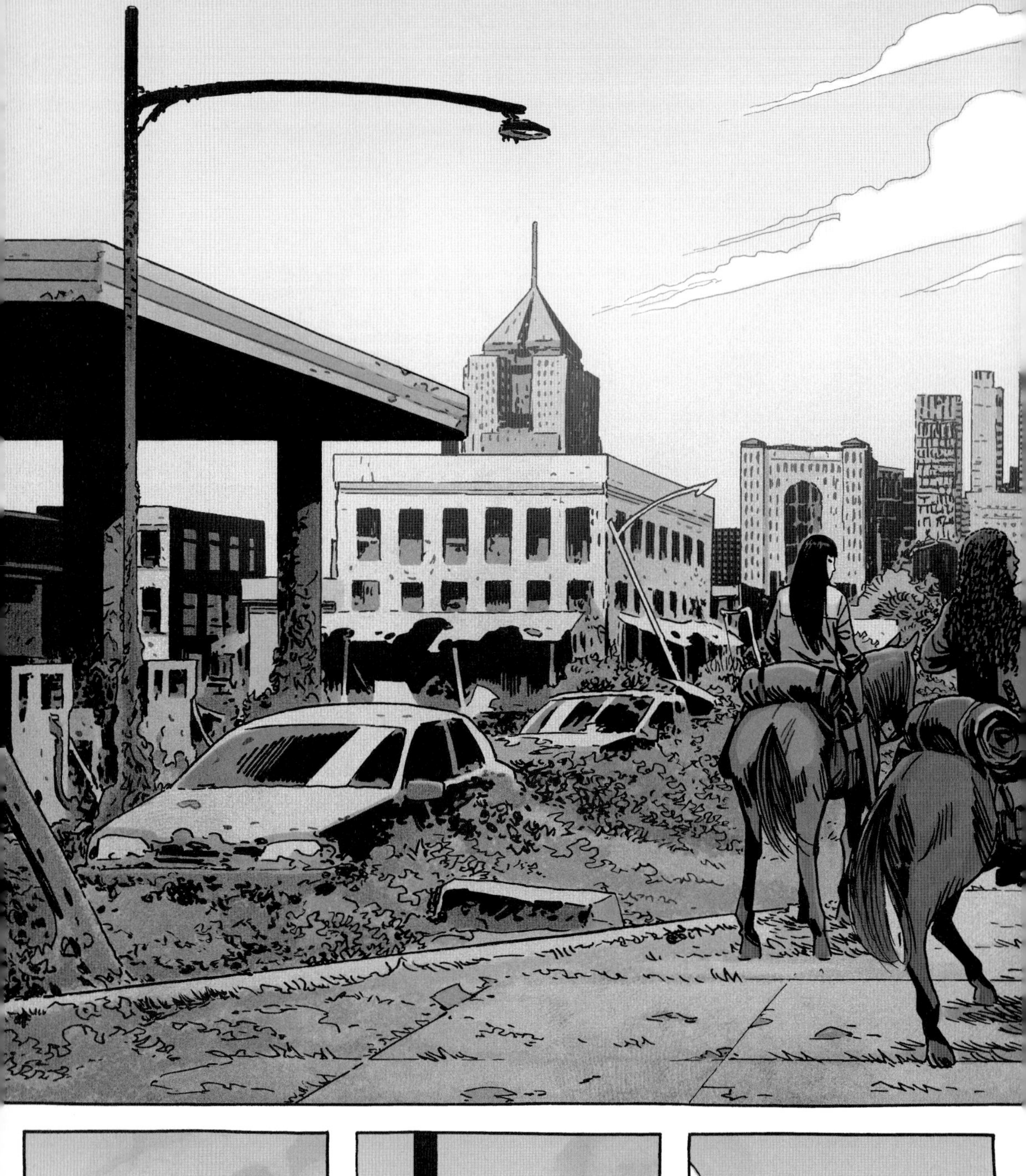
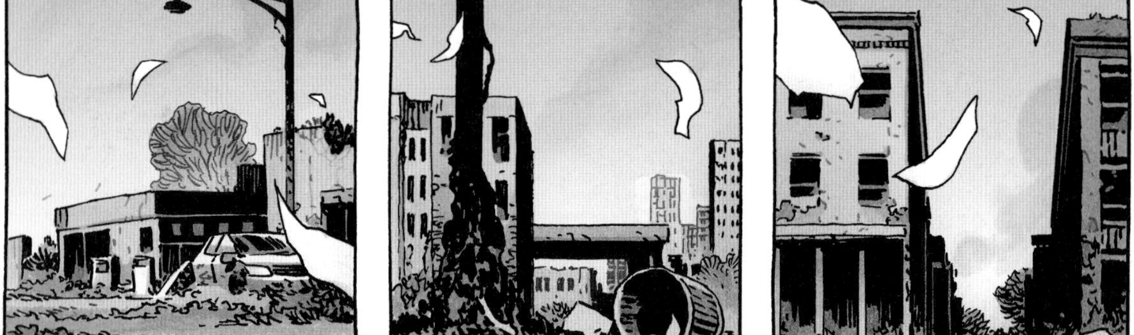

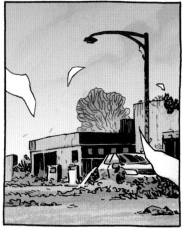

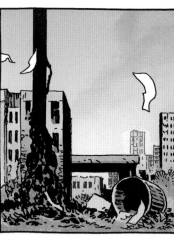

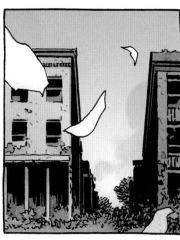

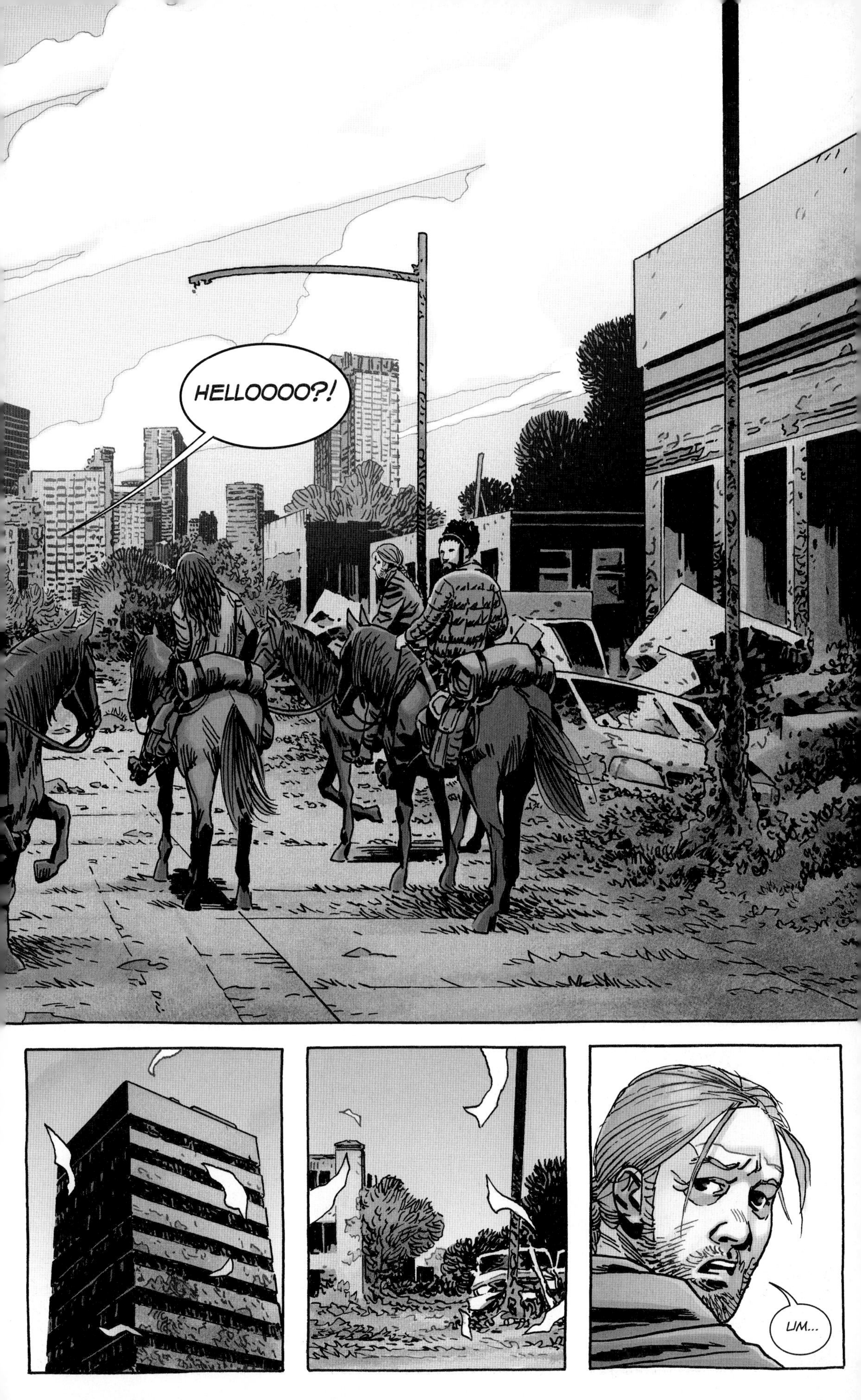
HELLOOOO?!
UM...

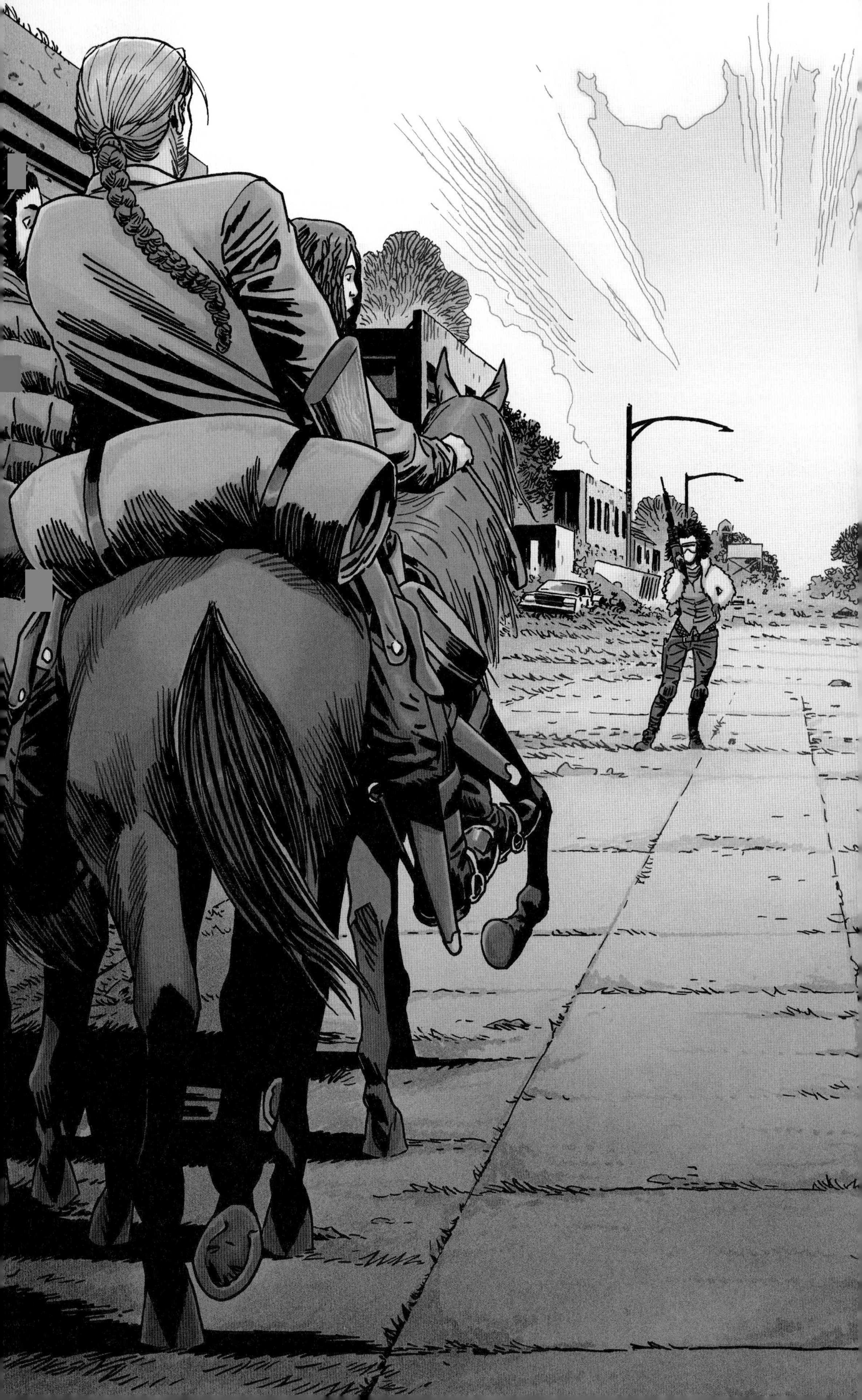

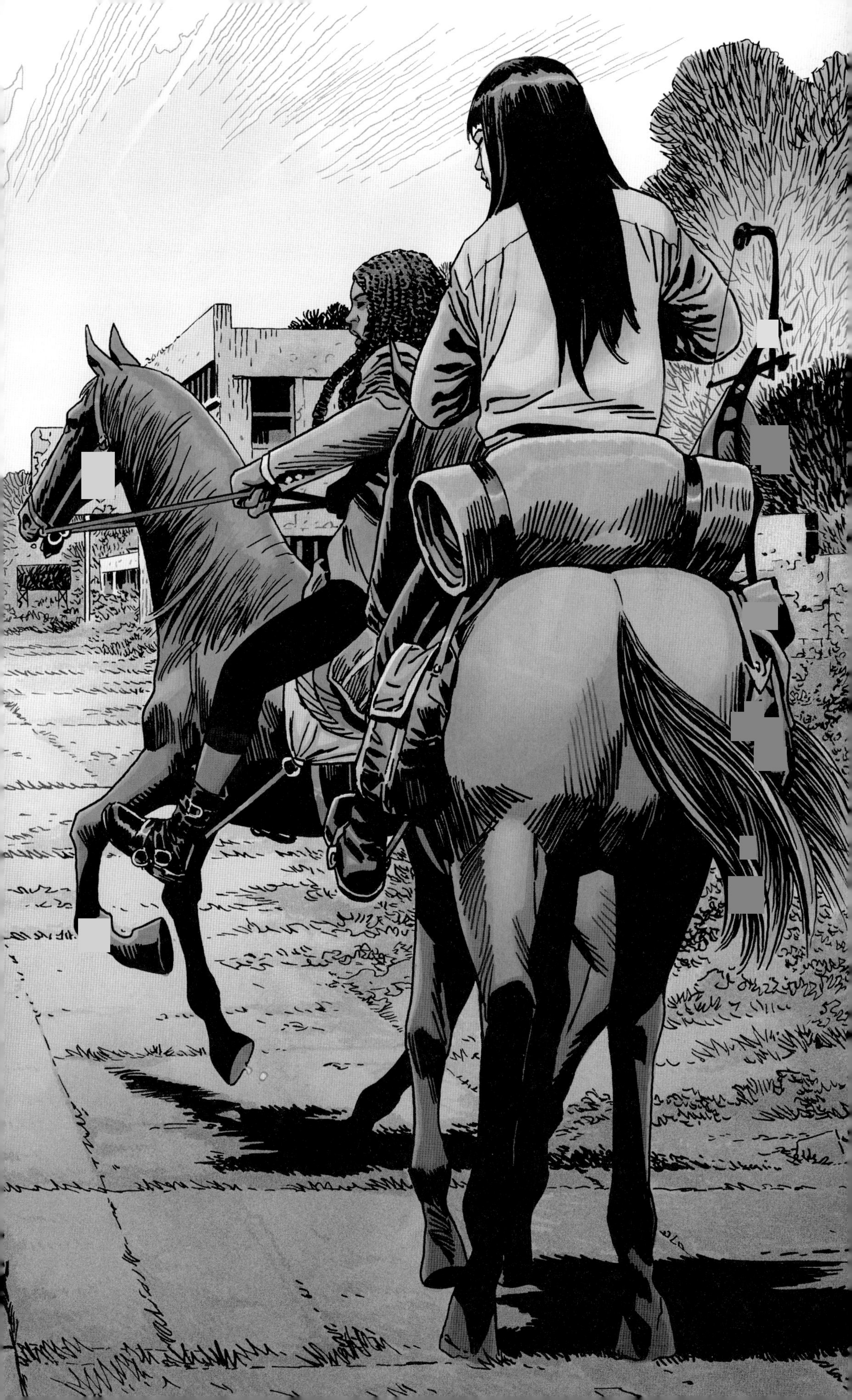

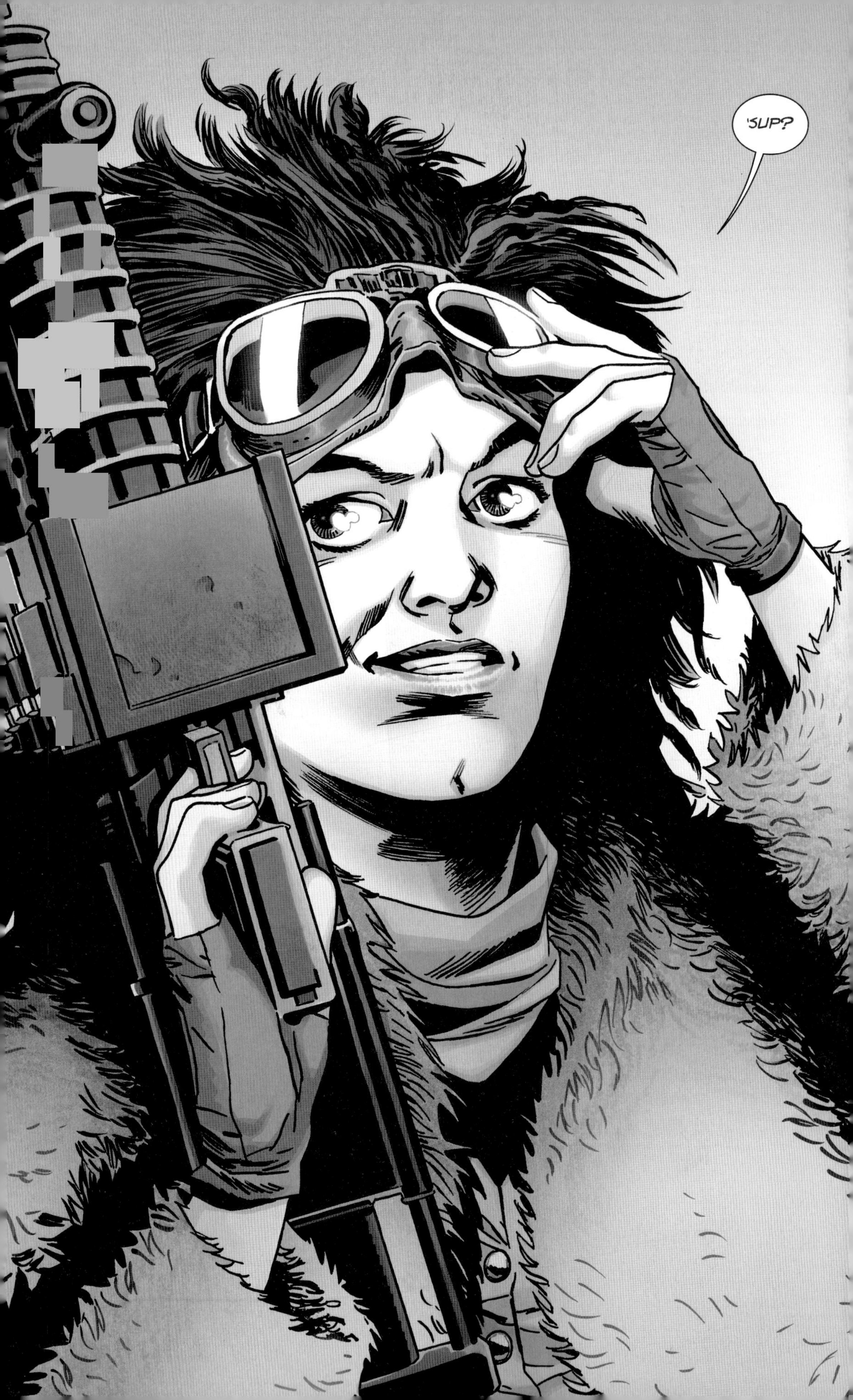
'SUP?

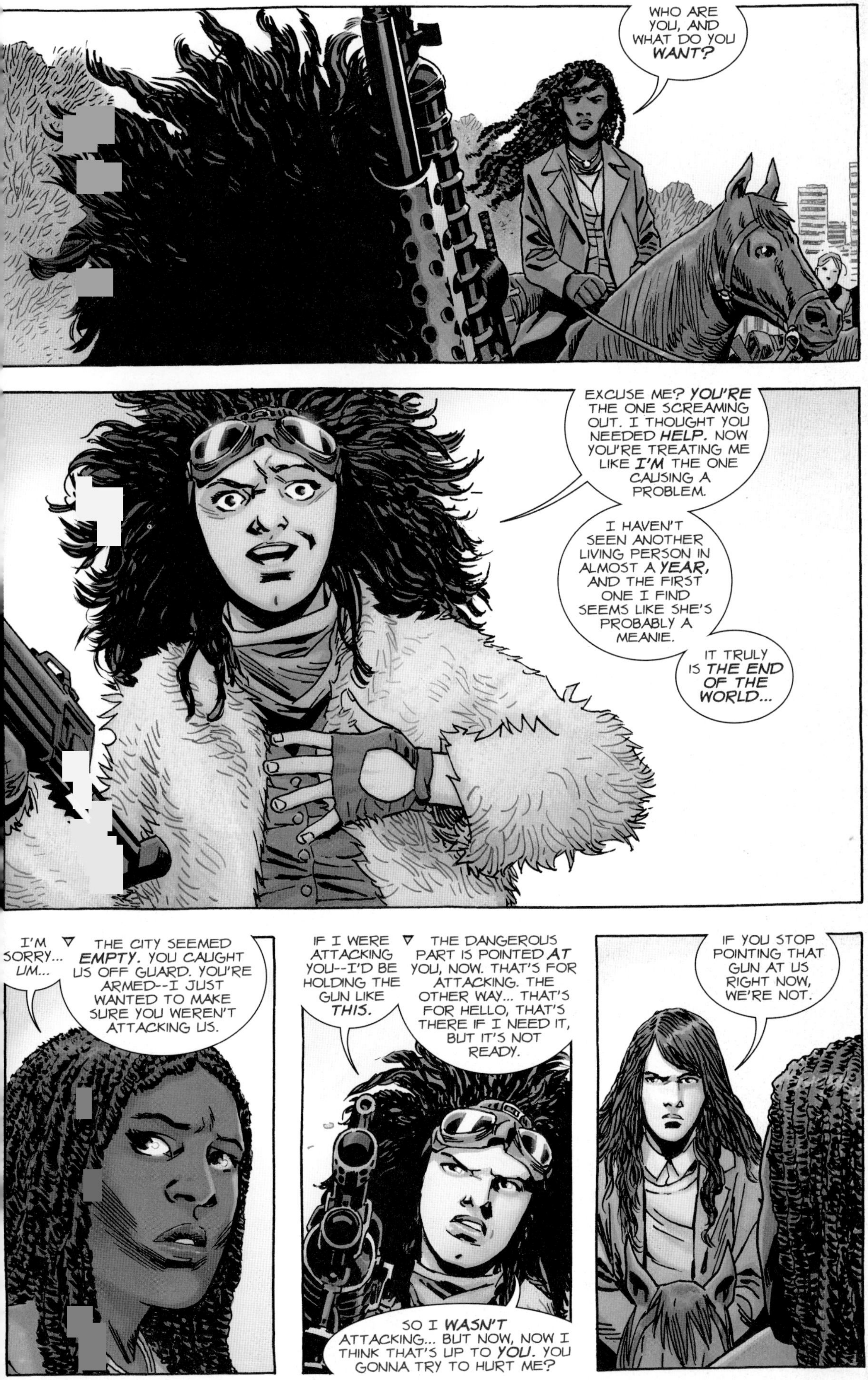
WHO ARE YOU, AND WHAT DO YOU WANT?
EXCUSE ME? YOU'RE THE ONE SCREAMING OUT. I THOUGHT YOU NEEDED HELP. NOW YOU'RE TREATING ME LIKE I'M THE ONE CAUSING A PROBLEM.
I HAVEN'T SEEN ANOTHER LIVING PERSON IN ALMOST A YEAR, AND THE FIRST ONE I FIND SEEMS LIKE SHE'S PROBABLY A MEANIE.
IT TRULY IS THE END OF THE WORLD...
I'M SORRY... UM...
THE CITY SEEMED EMPTY. YOU CAUGHT US OFF GUARD. YOU'RE ARMED--I JUST WANTED TO MAKE SURE YOU WEREN'T ATTACKING US.
IF I WERE ATTACKING YOU--I'D BE HOLDING THE GUN LIKE THIS.
THE DANGEROUS PART IS POINTED AT YOU, NOW. THAT'S FOR ATTACKING. THE OTHER WAY... THAT'S FOR HELLO, THAT'S THERE IF I NEED IT, BUT IT'S NOT READY.
SO I WASN'T ATTACKING... BUT NOW, NOW I THINK THAT'S UP TO YOU. YOU GONNA TRY TO HURT ME?
IF YOU STOP POINTING THAT GUN AT US RIGHT NOW, WE'RE NOT.

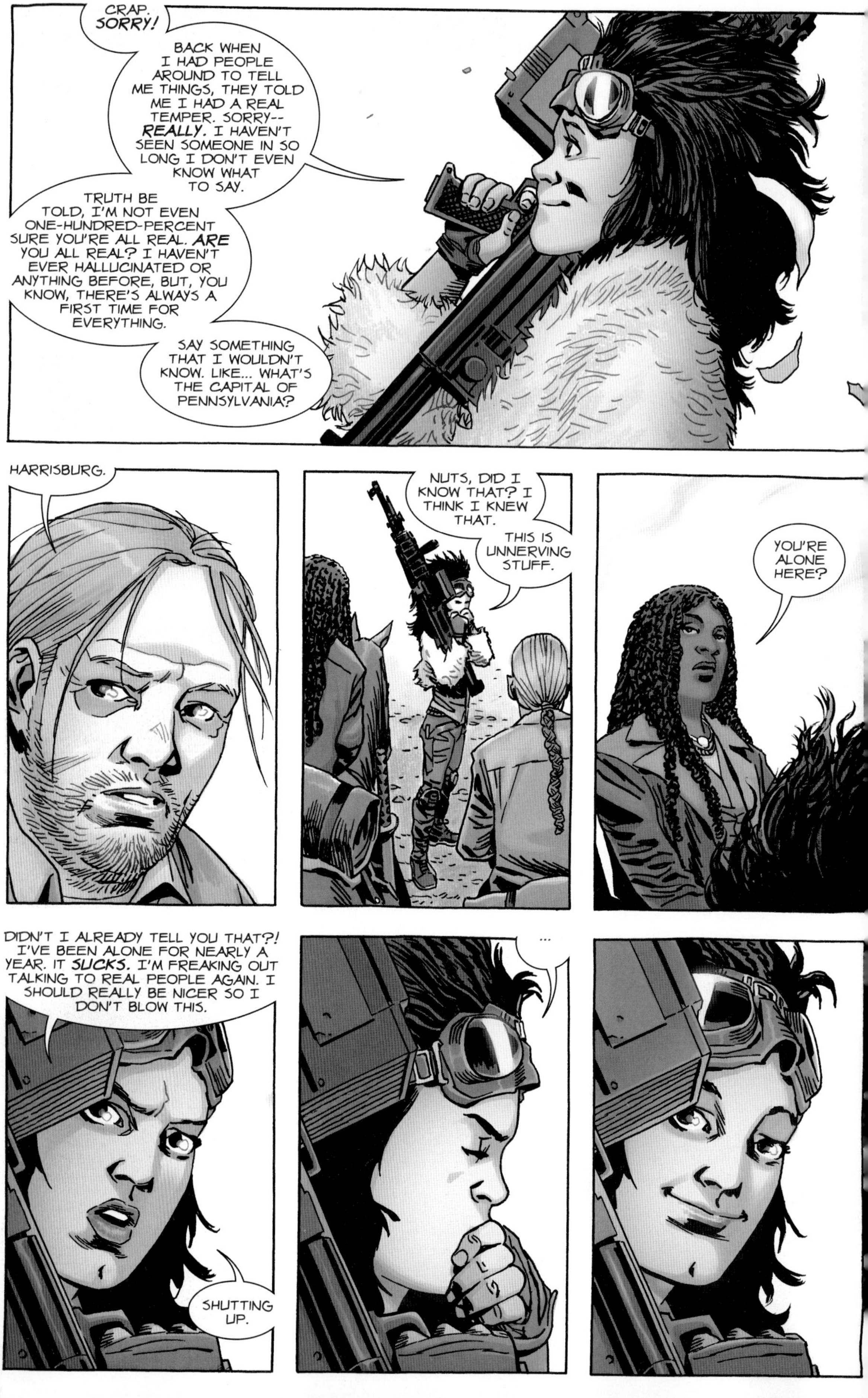
CRAP. SORRY!
BACK WHEN I HAD PEOPLE AROUND TO TELL ME THINGS, THEY TOLD ME I HAD A REAL TEMPER. SORRY-- REALLY. I HAVEN'T SEEN SOMEONE IN SO LONG I DON'T EVEN KNOW WHAT TO SAY.
TRUTH BE TOLD, I'M NOT EVEN ONE-HUNDRED-PERCENT SURE YOU'RE ALL REAL. ARE YOU ALL REAL? I HAVEN'T EVER HALLUCINATED OR ANYTHING BEFORE, BUT, YOU KNOW, THERE'S ALWAYS A FIRST TIME FOR EVERYTHING.
SAY SOMETHING THAT I WOULDN'T KNOW. LIKE... WHAT'S THE CAPITAL OF PENNSYLVANIA?
HARRISBURG.
NUTS, DID I KNOW THAT? I THINK I KNEW THAT.
THIS IS UNNERVING STUFF.
YOU'RE ALONE HERE?
DIDN'T I ALREADY TELL YOU THAT?! I'VE BEEN ALONE FOR NEARLY A YEAR. IT SUCKS. I'M FREAKING OUT TALKING TO REAL PEOPLE AGAIN. I SHOULD REALLY BE NICER SO I DON'T BLOW THIS.
SHUTTING UP.
...

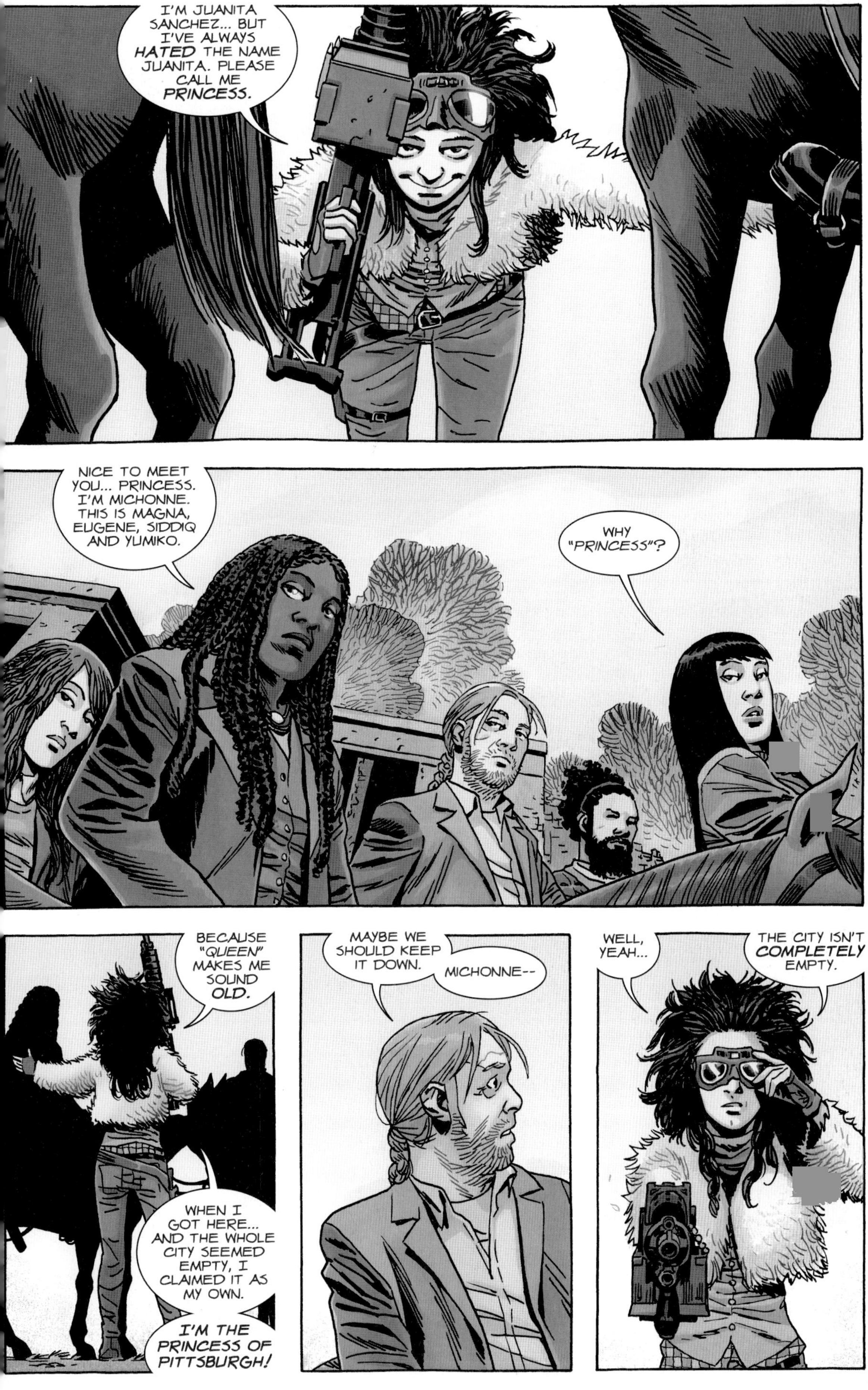
I'M JUANITA SANCHEZ... BUT I'VE ALWAYS HATED THE NAME JUANITA. PLEASE CALL ME PRINCESS.
NICE TO MEET YOU... PRINCESS. I'M MICHONNE. THIS IS MAGNA, EUGENE, SIDDIQ AND YUMIKO.
WHY "PRINCESS"?
BECAUSE "QUEEN" MAKES ME SOUND OLD.
WHEN I GOT HERE... AND THE WHOLE CITY SEEMED EMPTY, I CLAIMED IT AS MY OWN.
I'M THE PRINCESS OF PITTSBURGH!
MAYBE WE SHOULD KEEP IT DOWN.
MICHONNE--
WELL, YEAH...
THE CITY ISN'T COMPLETELY EMPTY.

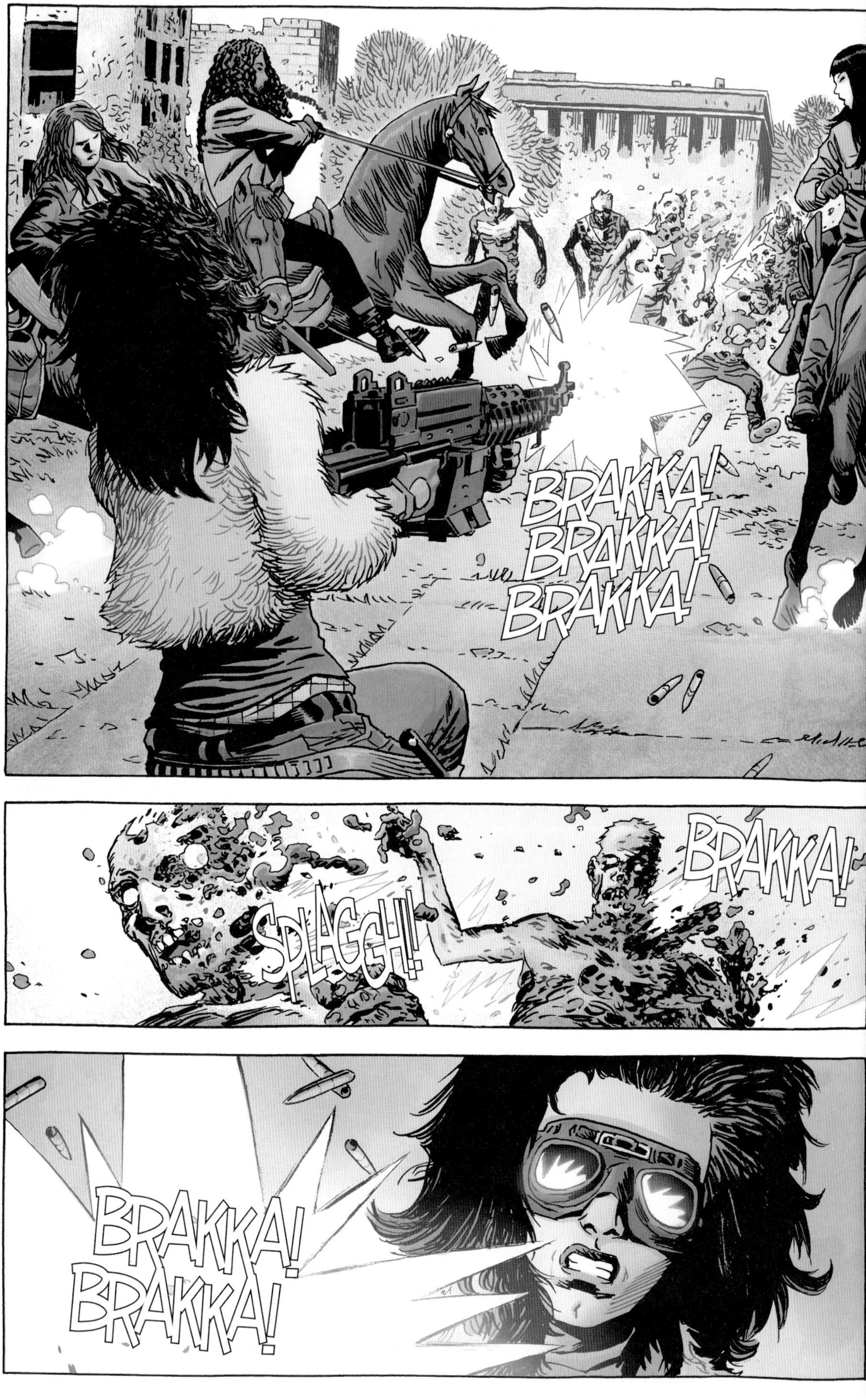
BRAKKA! BRAKKA! BRAKKA!
SPLAGGH!!
BRAKKA!
BRAKKA! BRAKKA!

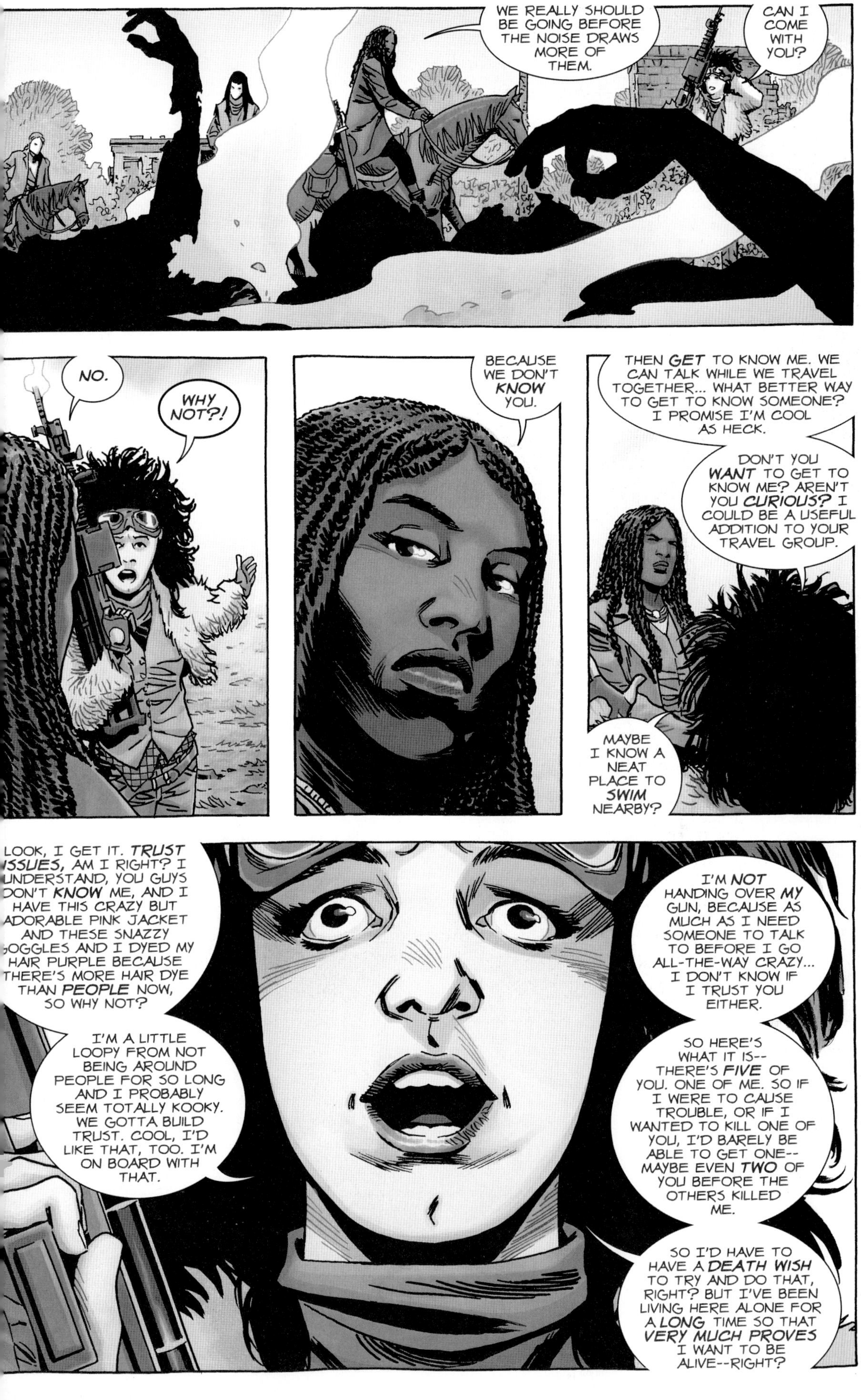
WE REALLY SHOULD BE GOING BEFORE THE NOISE DRAWS MORE OF THEM.
CAN I COME WITH YOU?
NO.
WHY NOT?!
BECAUSE WE DON'T KNOW YOU.
THEN GET TO KNOW ME. WE CAN TALK WHILE WE TRAVEL TOGETHER... WHAT BETTER WAY TO GET TO KNOW SOMEONE? I PROMISE I'M COOL AS HECK.
DON'T YOU WANT TO GET TO KNOW ME? AREN'T YOU CURIOUS? I COULD BE A USEFUL ADDITION TO YOUR TRAVEL GROUP.
MAYBE I KNOW A NEAT PLACE TO SWIM NEARBY?
LOOK, I GET IT. TRUST ISSUES, AM I RIGHT? I UNDERSTAND, YOU GUYS DON'T KNOW ME, AND I HAVE THIS CRAZY BUT ADORABLE PINK JACKET AND THESE SNAZZY GOGGLES AND I DYED MY HAIR PURPLE BECAUSE THERE'S MORE HAIR DYE THAN PEOPLE NOW, SO WHY NOT?
I'M A LITTLE LOOPY FROM NOT BEING AROUND PEOPLE FOR SO LONG AND I PROBABLY SEEM TOTALLY KOOKY. WE GOTTA BUILD TRUST. COOL, I'D LIKE THAT, TOO. I'M ON BOARD WITH THAT.
I'M NOT HANDING OVER MY GUN, BECAUSE AS MUCH AS I NEED SOMEONE TO TALK TO BEFORE I GO ALL-THE-WAY CRAZY... I DON'T KNOW IF I TRUST YOU EITHER.
SO HERE'S WHAT IT IS-- THERE'S FIVE OF YOU. ONE OF ME. SO IF I WERE TO CAUSE TROUBLE, OR IF I WANTED TO KILL ONE OF YOU, I'D BARELY BE ABLE TO GET ONE-- MAYBE EVEN TWO OF YOU BEFORE THE OTHERS KILLED ME.
SO I'D HAVE TO HAVE A DEATH WISH TO TRY AND DO THAT, RIGHT? BUT I'VE BEEN LIVING HERE ALONE FOR A LONG TIME SO THAT VERY MUCH PROVES I WANT TO BE ALIVE--RIGHT?

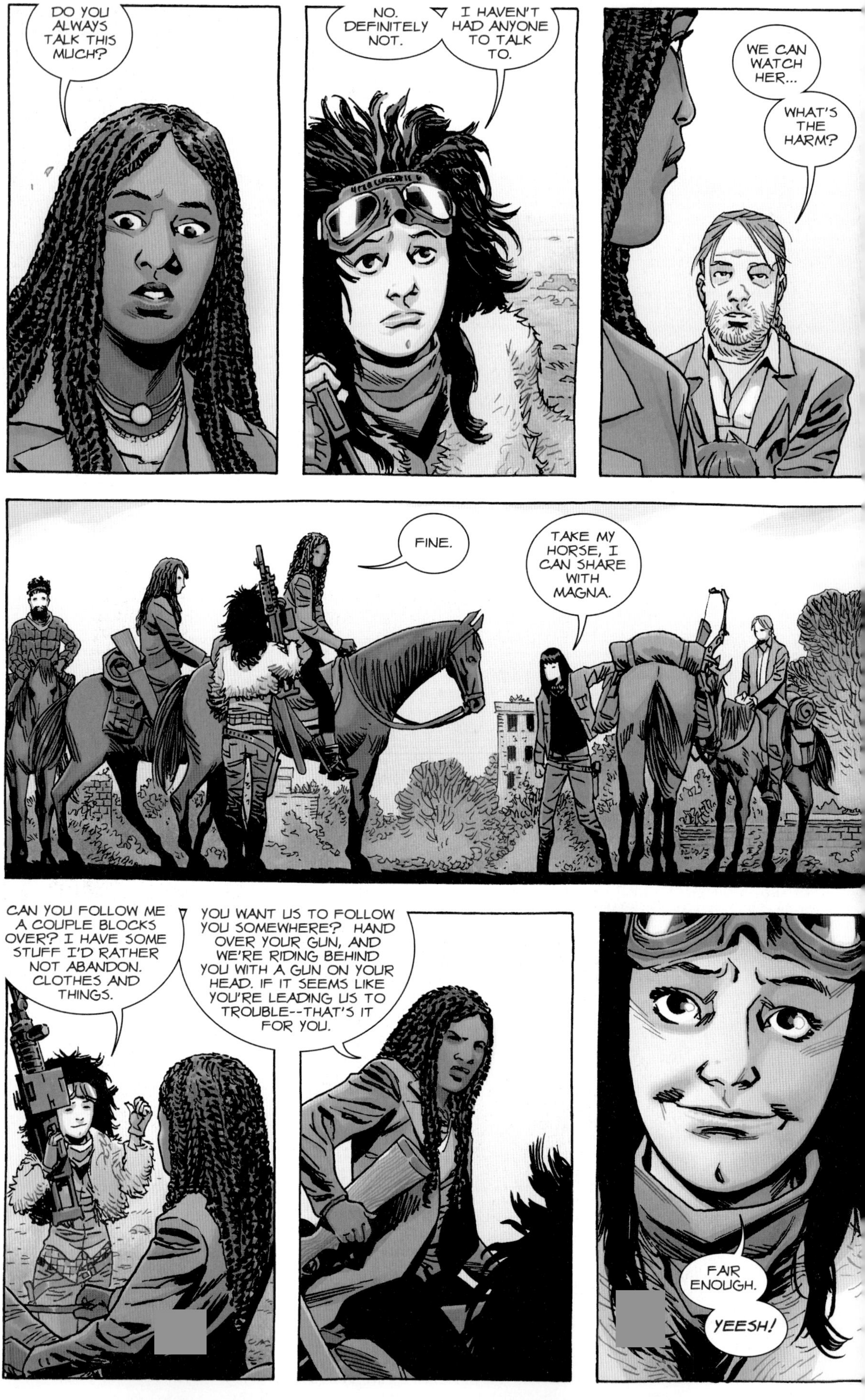
DO YOU ALWAYS TALK THIS MUCH?
NO. DEFINITELY NOT.
I HAVEN'T HAD ANYONE TO TALK TO.
WE CAN WATCH HER...
WHAT'S THE HARM?
FINE.
TAKE MY HORSE, I CAN SHARE WITH MAGNA.
CAN YOU FOLLOW ME A COUPLE BLOCKS OVER? I HAVE SOME STUFF I'D RATHER NOT ABANDON. CLOTHES AND THINGS.
YOU WANT US TO FOLLOW YOU SOMEWHERE? HAND OVER YOUR GUN, AND WE'RE RIDING BEHIND YOU WITH A GUN ON YOUR HEAD. IF IT SEEMS LIKE YOU'RE LEADING US TO TROUBLE--THAT'S IT FOR YOU.
FAIR ENOUGH.
YEESH!

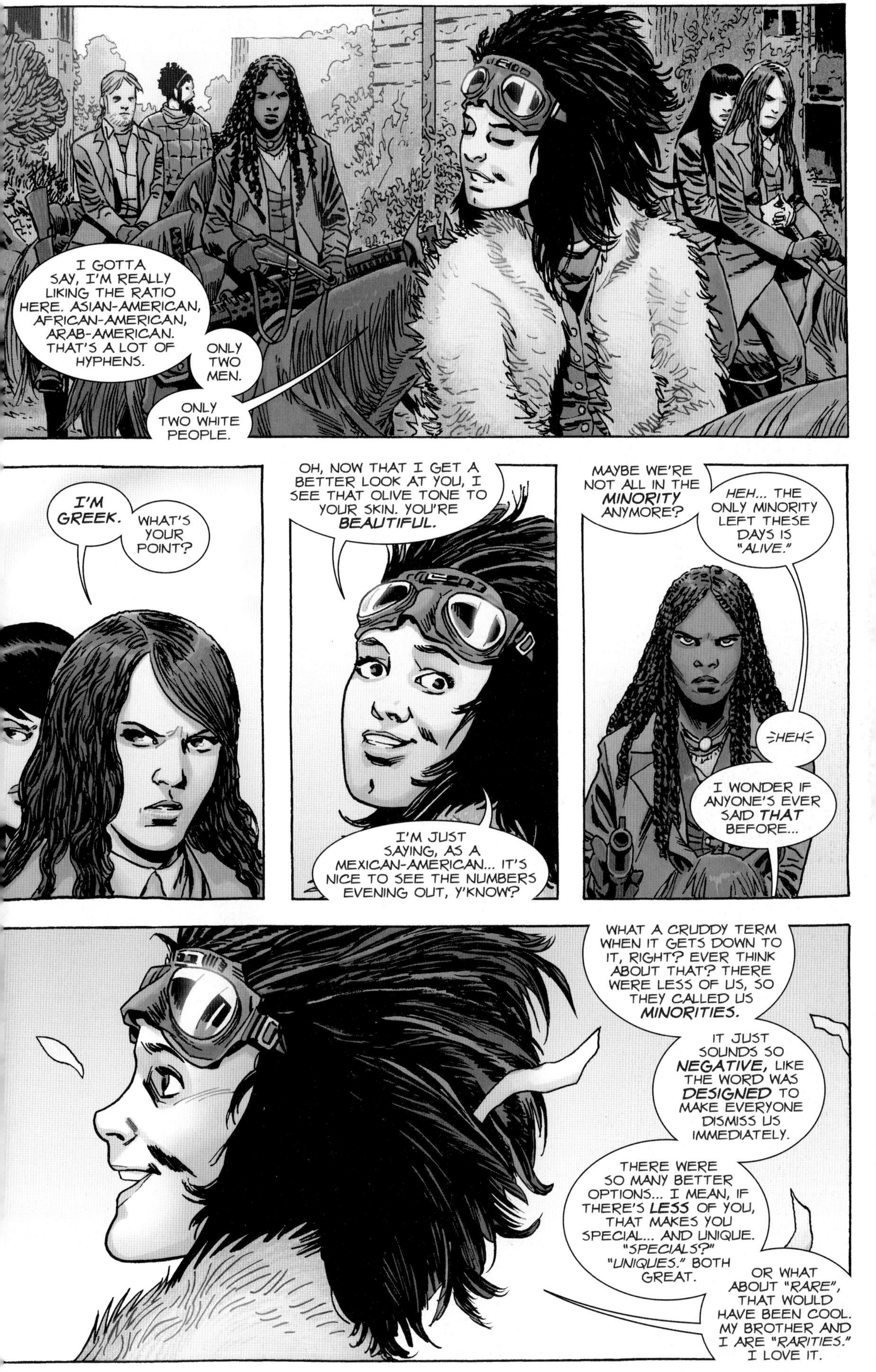
I GOTTA SAY, I'M REALLY LIKING THE RATIO HERE. ASIAN-AMERICAN, AFRICAN-AMERICAN, ARAB-AMERICAN. THAT'S A LOT OF HYPHENS.
ONLY TWO MEN.
ONLY TWO WHITE PEOPLE.
I'M GREEK.
WHAT'S YOUR POINT?
OH, NOW THAT I GET A BETTER LOOK AT YOU, I SEE THAT OLIVE TONE TO YOUR SKIN. YOU'RE ***BEAUTIFUL.***
I'M JUST SAYING, AS A MEXICAN-AMERICAN... IT'S NICE TO SEE THE NUMBERS EVENING OUT, Y'KNOW?
MAYBE WE'RE NOT ALL IN THE ***MINORITY*** ANYMORE?
HEH... THE ONLY MINORITY LEFT THESE DAYS IS "*ALIVE.*"
HEH
I WONDER IF ANYONE'S EVER SAID ***THAT*** BEFORE...
WHAT A CRUDDY TERM WHEN IT GETS DOWN TO IT, RIGHT? EVER THINK ABOUT THAT? THERE WERE LESS OF US, SO THEY CALLED US ***MINORITIES.***
IT JUST SOUNDS SO ***NEGATIVE,*** LIKE THE WORD WAS ***DESIGNED*** TO MAKE EVERYONE DISMISS US IMMEDIATELY.
THERE WERE SO MANY BETTER OPTIONS... I MEAN, IF THERE'S ***LESS*** OF YOU, THAT MAKES YOU SPECIAL... AND UNIQUE. "*SPECIALS?*" "*UNIQUES.*" BOTH GREAT.
OR WHAT ABOUT "*RARE*", THAT WOULD HAVE BEEN COOL. MY BROTHER AND I ARE "*RARITIES.*" I LOVE IT.

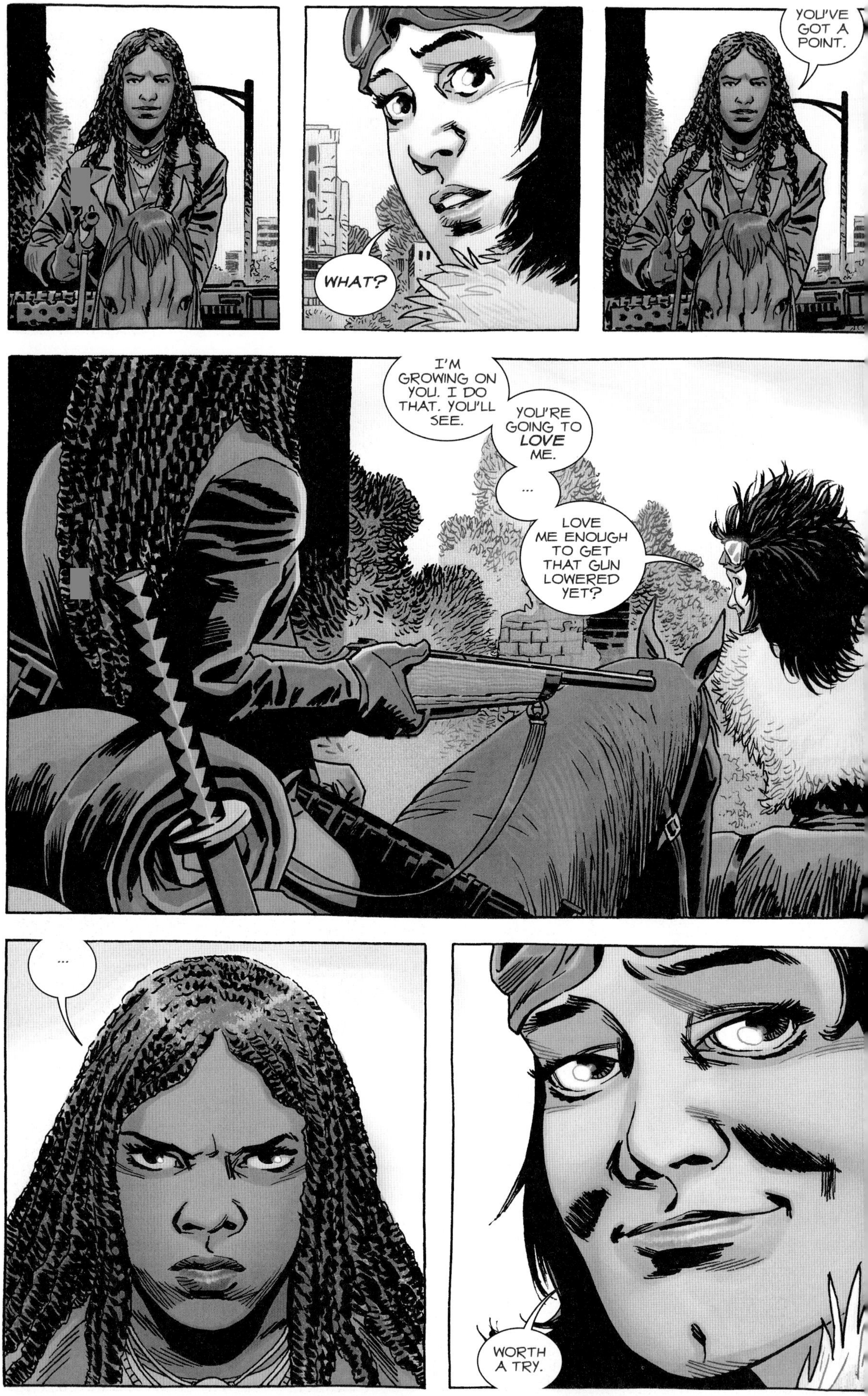
WHAT?
YOU'VE GOT A POINT.
I'M GROWING ON YOU. I DO THAT. YOU'LL SEE.
YOU'RE GOING TO *LOVE* ME.
...
LOVE ME ENOUGH TO GET THAT GUN LOWERED YET?
...
WORTH A TRY.

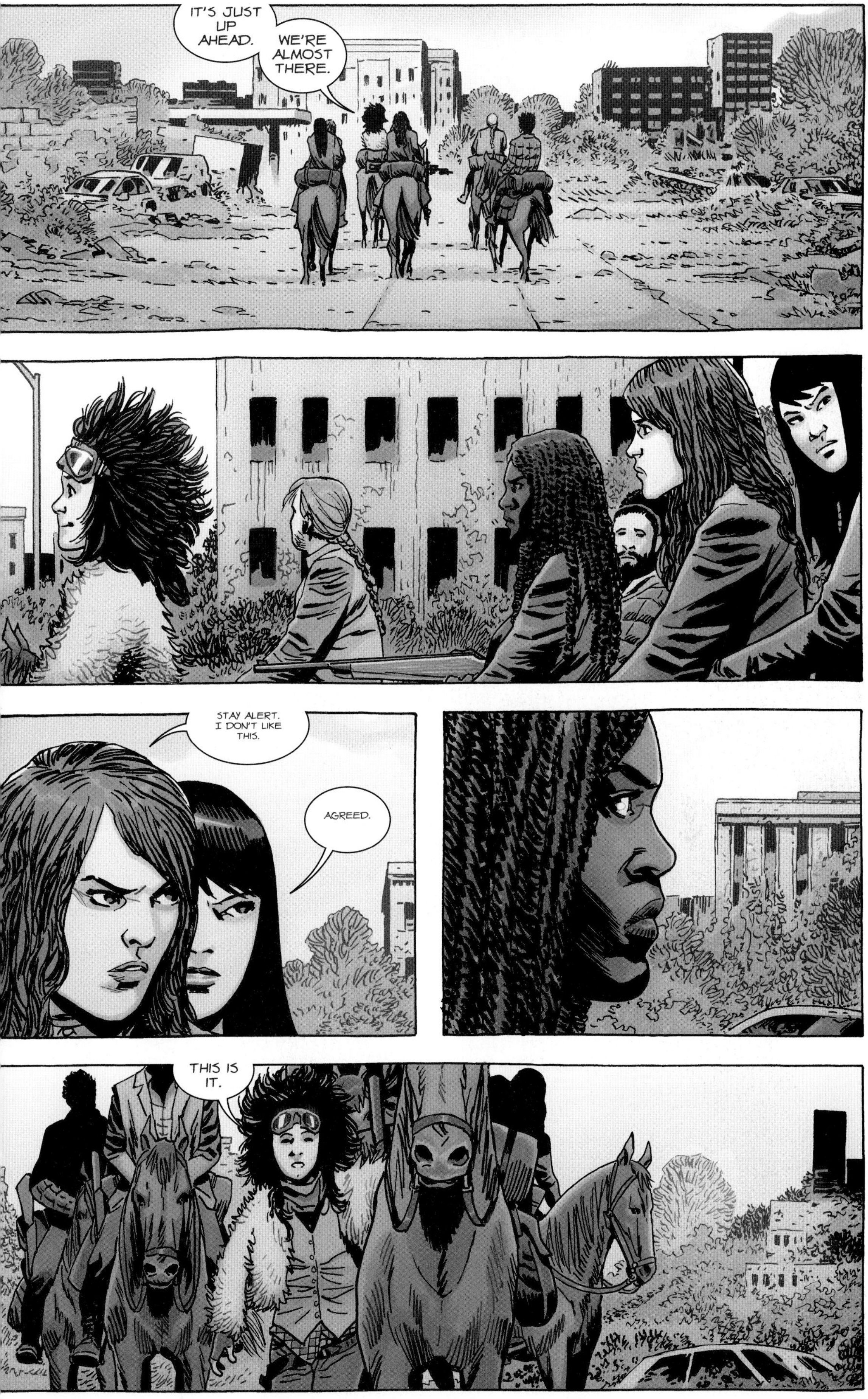
IT'S JUST UP AHEAD.
WE'RE ALMOST THERE.
STAY ALERT. I DON'T LIKE THIS.
AGREED.
THIS IS IT.

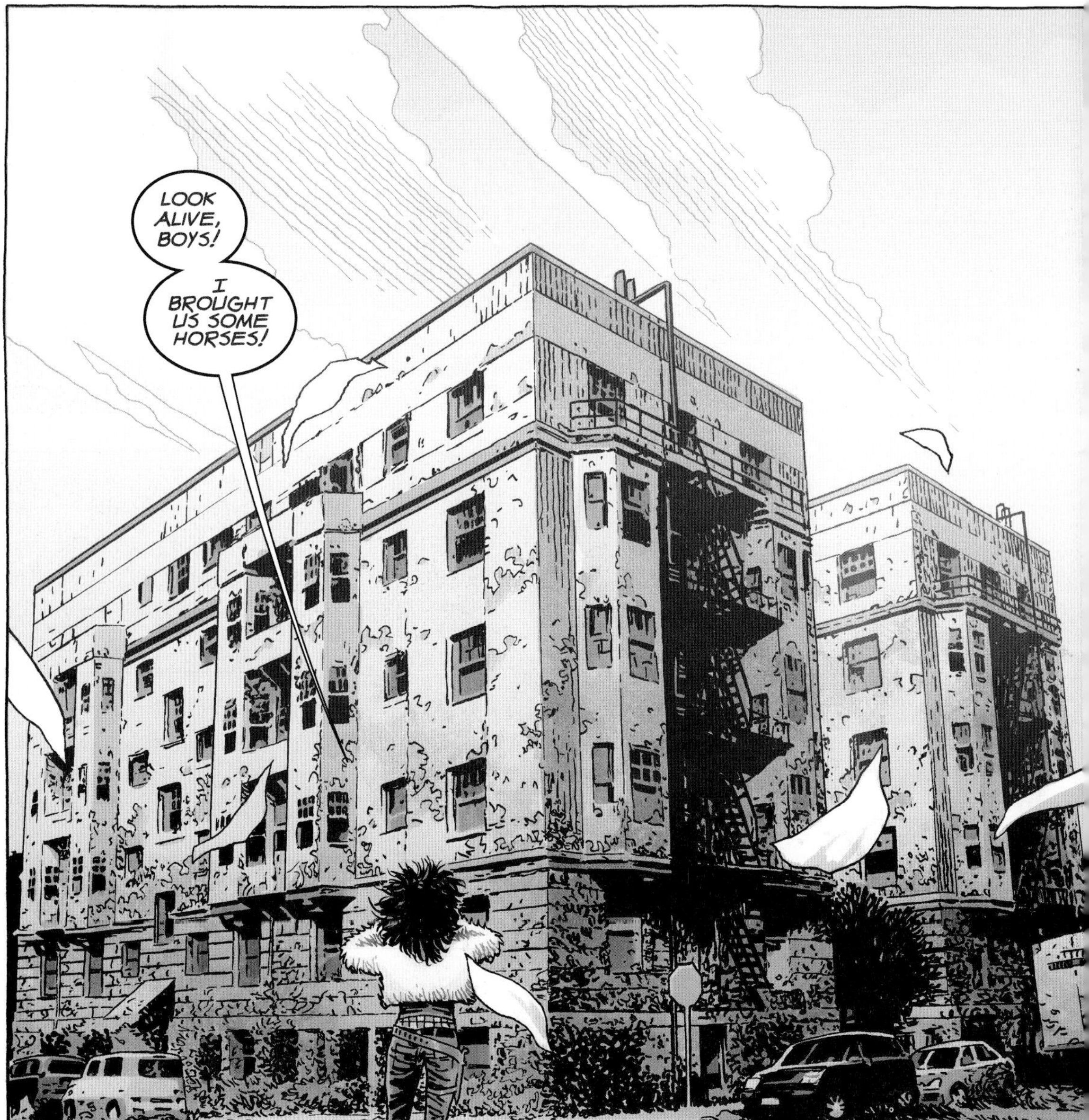
LOOK ALIVE, BOYS!
I BROUGHT US SOME HORSES!

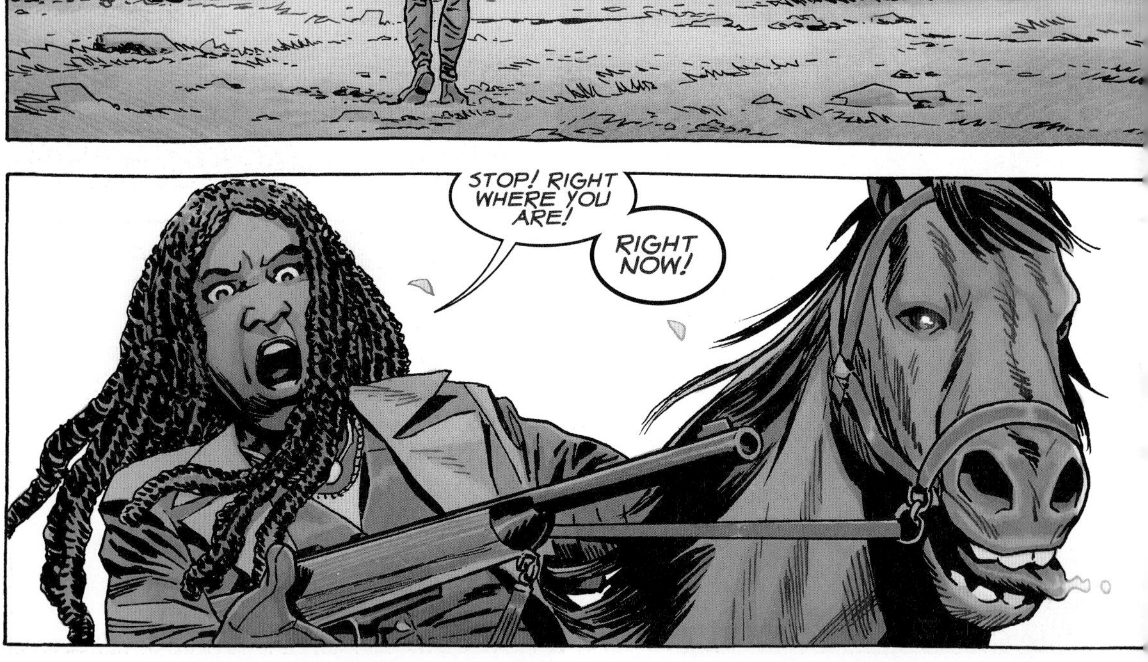
STOP! RIGHT WHERE YOU ARE!
RIGHT NOW!

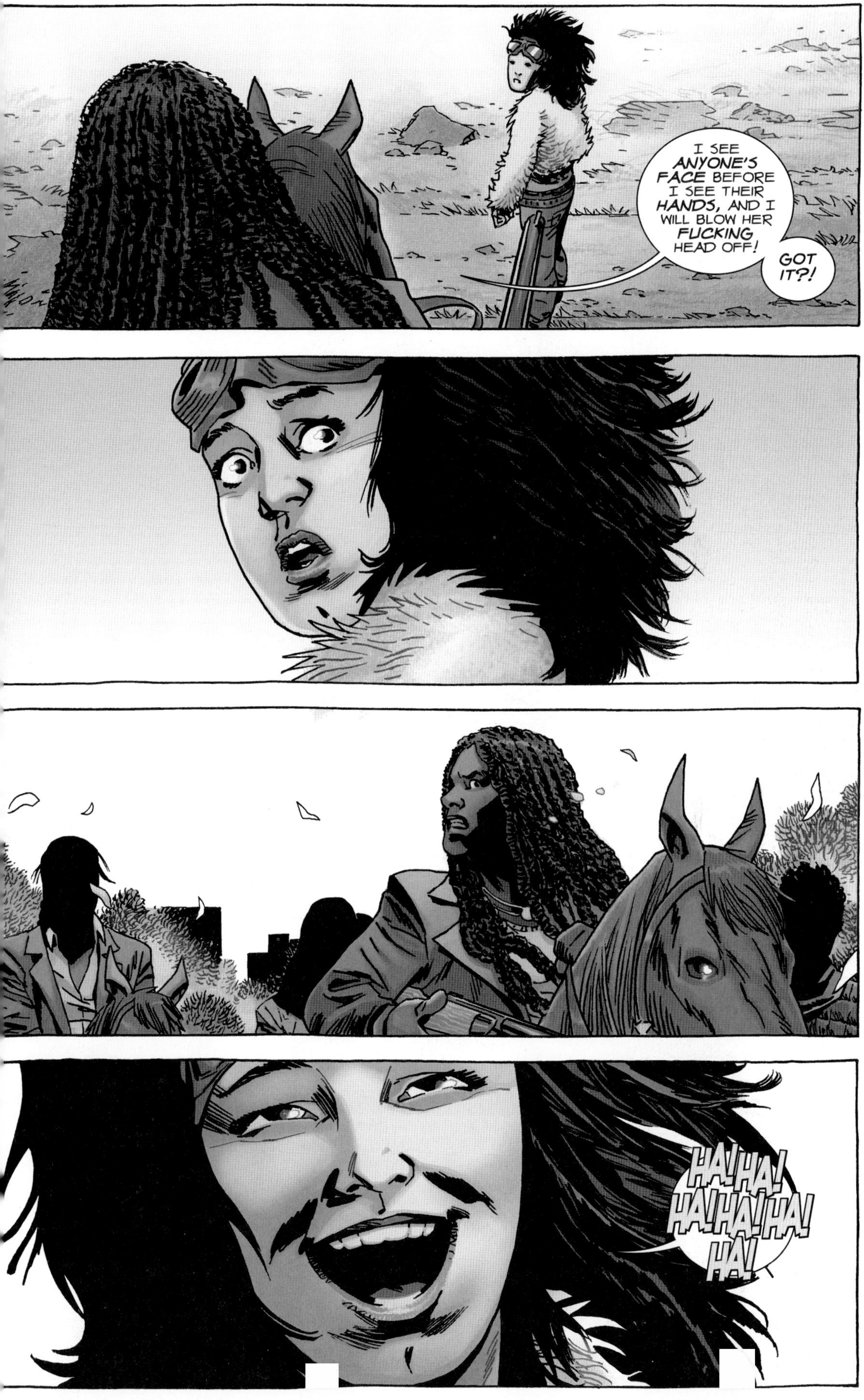
I SEE ANYONE'S FACE BEFORE I SEE THEIR HANDS, AND I WILL BLOW HER FUCKING HEAD OFF!
GOT IT?!
HA! HA! HA! HA! HA! HA!

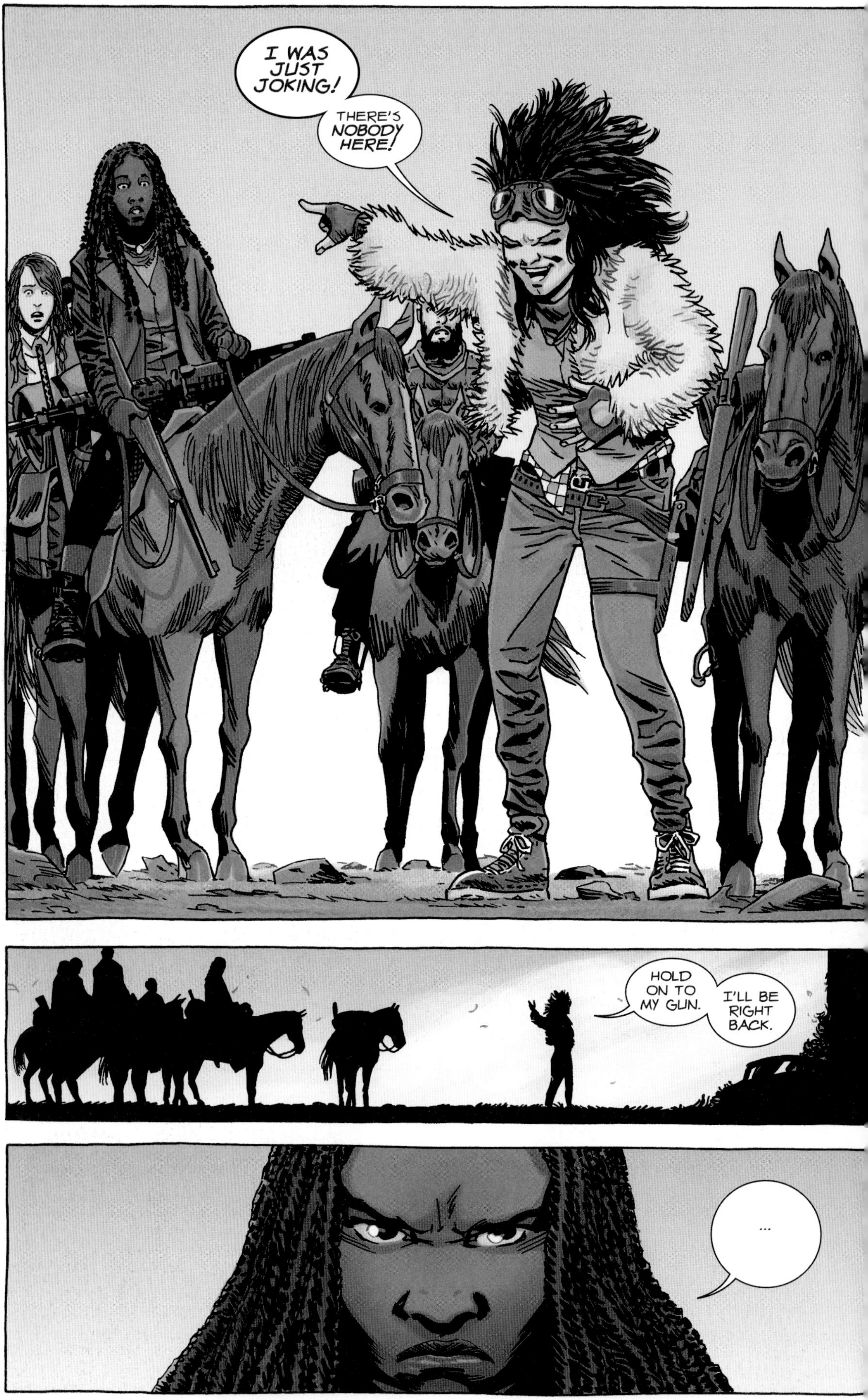
I WAS JUST JOKING!
THERE'S NOBODY HERE!
HOLD ON TO MY GUN.
I'LL BE RIGHT BACK.
...

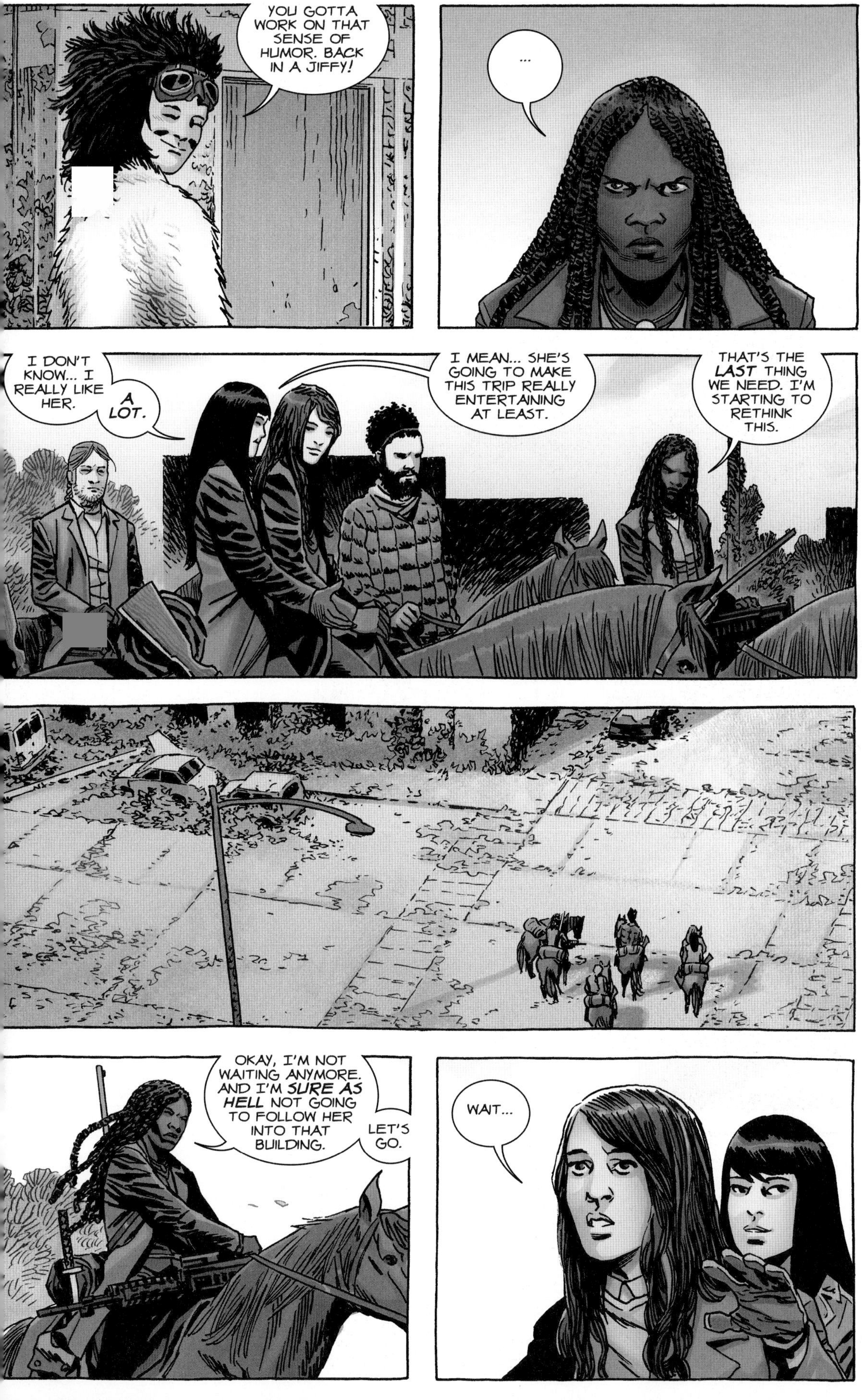
YOU GOTTA WORK ON THAT SENSE OF HUMOR. BACK IN A JIFFY!
...
I DON'T KNOW... I REALLY LIKE HER.
A LOT.
I MEAN... SHE'S GOING TO MAKE THIS TRIP REALLY ENTERTAINING AT LEAST.
THAT'S THE LAST THING WE NEED. I'M STARTING TO RETHINK THIS.
OKAY, I'M NOT WAITING ANYMORE. AND I'M SURE AS HELL NOT GOING TO FOLLOW HER INTO THAT BUILDING.
LET'S GO.
WAIT...

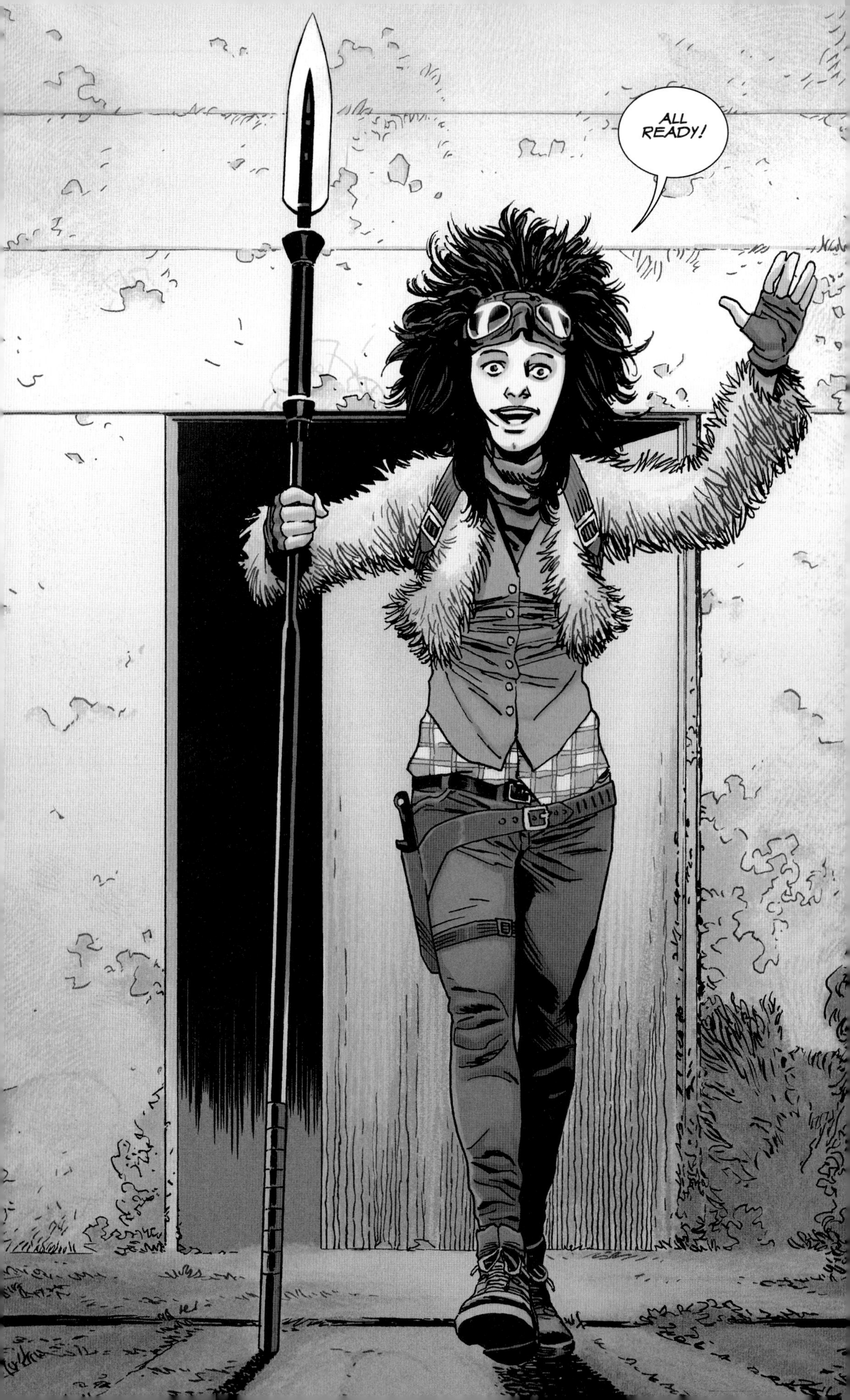
ALL READY!

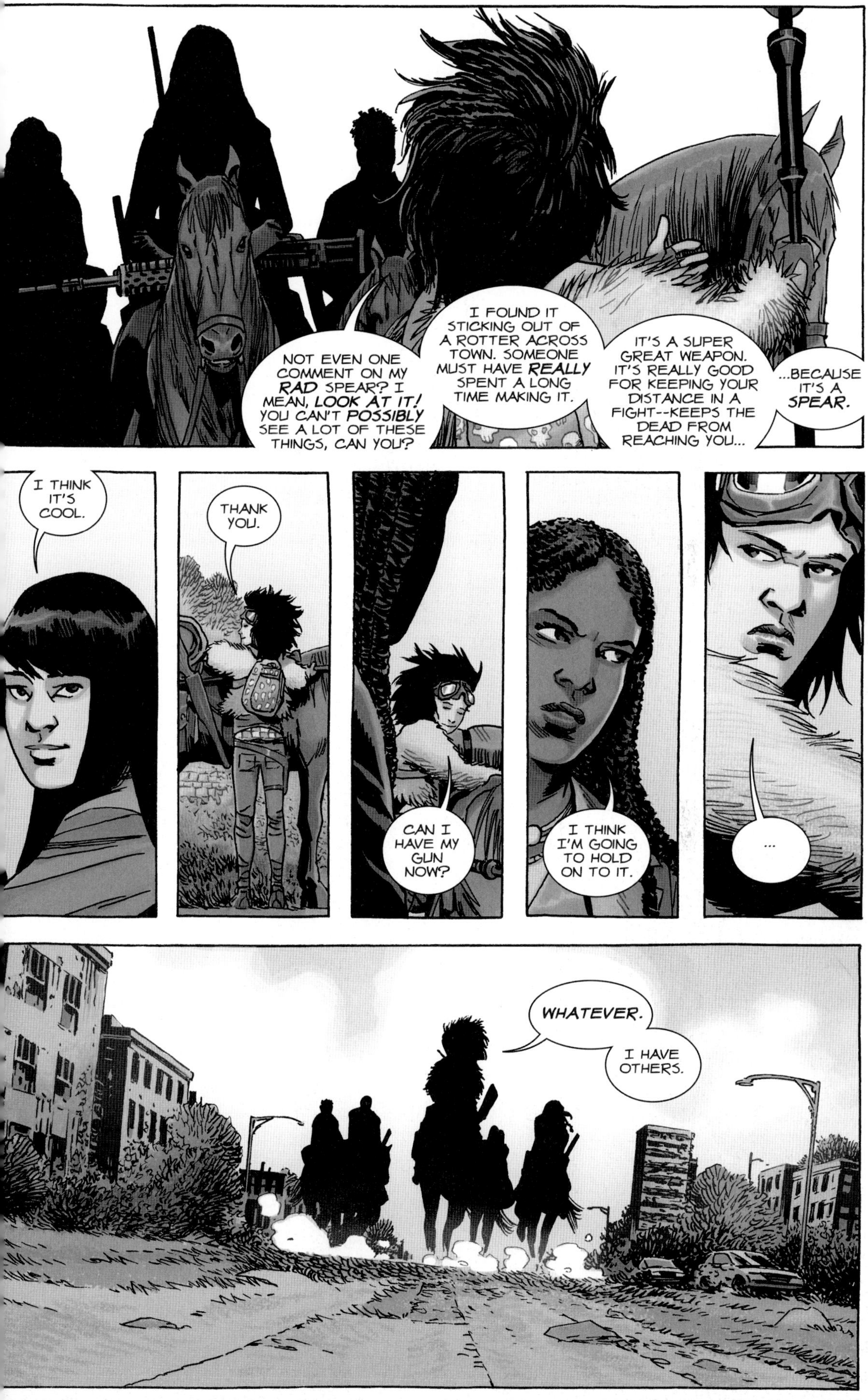
NOT EVEN ONE COMMENT ON MY RAD SPEAR? I MEAN, LOOK AT IT! YOU CAN'T POSSIBLY SEE A LOT OF THESE THINGS, CAN YOU?
I FOUND IT STICKING OUT OF A ROTTER ACROSS TOWN. SOMEONE MUST HAVE REALLY SPENT A LONG TIME MAKING IT.
IT'S A SUPER GREAT WEAPON. IT'S REALLY GOOD FOR KEEPING YOUR DISTANCE IN A FIGHT--KEEPS THE DEAD FROM REACHING YOU...
...BECAUSE IT'S A SPEAR.
I THINK IT'S COOL.
THANK YOU.
CAN I HAVE MY GUN NOW?
I THINK I'M GOING TO HOLD ON TO IT.
...
WHATEVER.
I HAVE OTHERS.

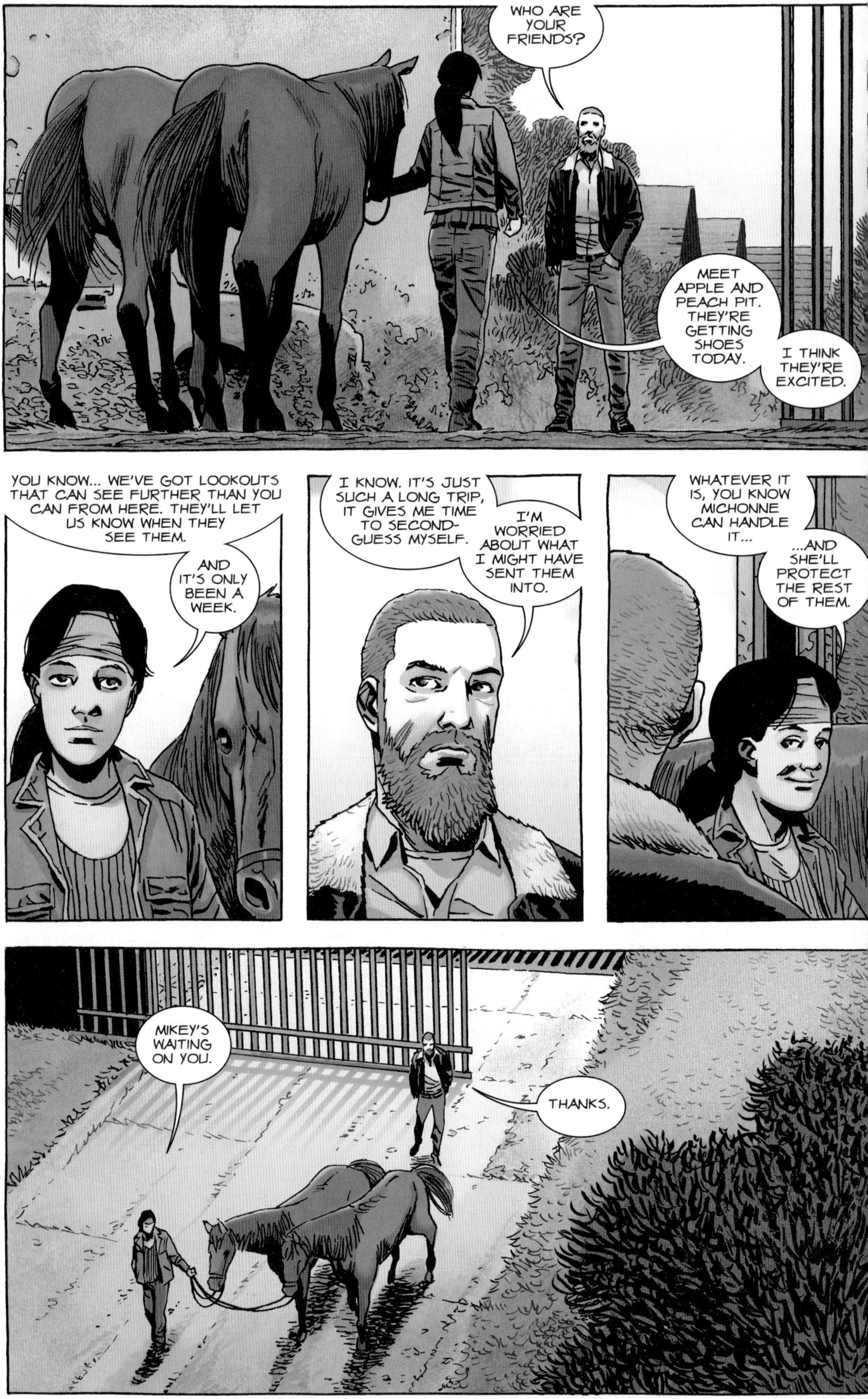
WHO ARE YOUR FRIENDS?
MEET APPLE AND PEACH PIT. THEY'RE GETTING SHOES TODAY.
I THINK THEY'RE EXCITED.
YOU KNOW... WE'VE GOT LOOKOUTS THAT CAN SEE FURTHER THAN YOU CAN FROM HERE. THEY'LL LET US KNOW WHEN THEY SEE THEM.
AND IT'S ONLY BEEN A WEEK.
I KNOW. IT'S JUST SUCH A LONG TRIP, IT GIVES ME TIME TO SECOND-GUESS MYSELF.
I'M WORRIED ABOUT WHAT I MIGHT HAVE SENT THEM INTO.
WHATEVER IT IS, YOU KNOW MICHONNE CAN HANDLE IT...
...AND SHE'LL PROTECT THE REST OF THEM.
MIKEY'S WAITING ON YOU.
THANKS.

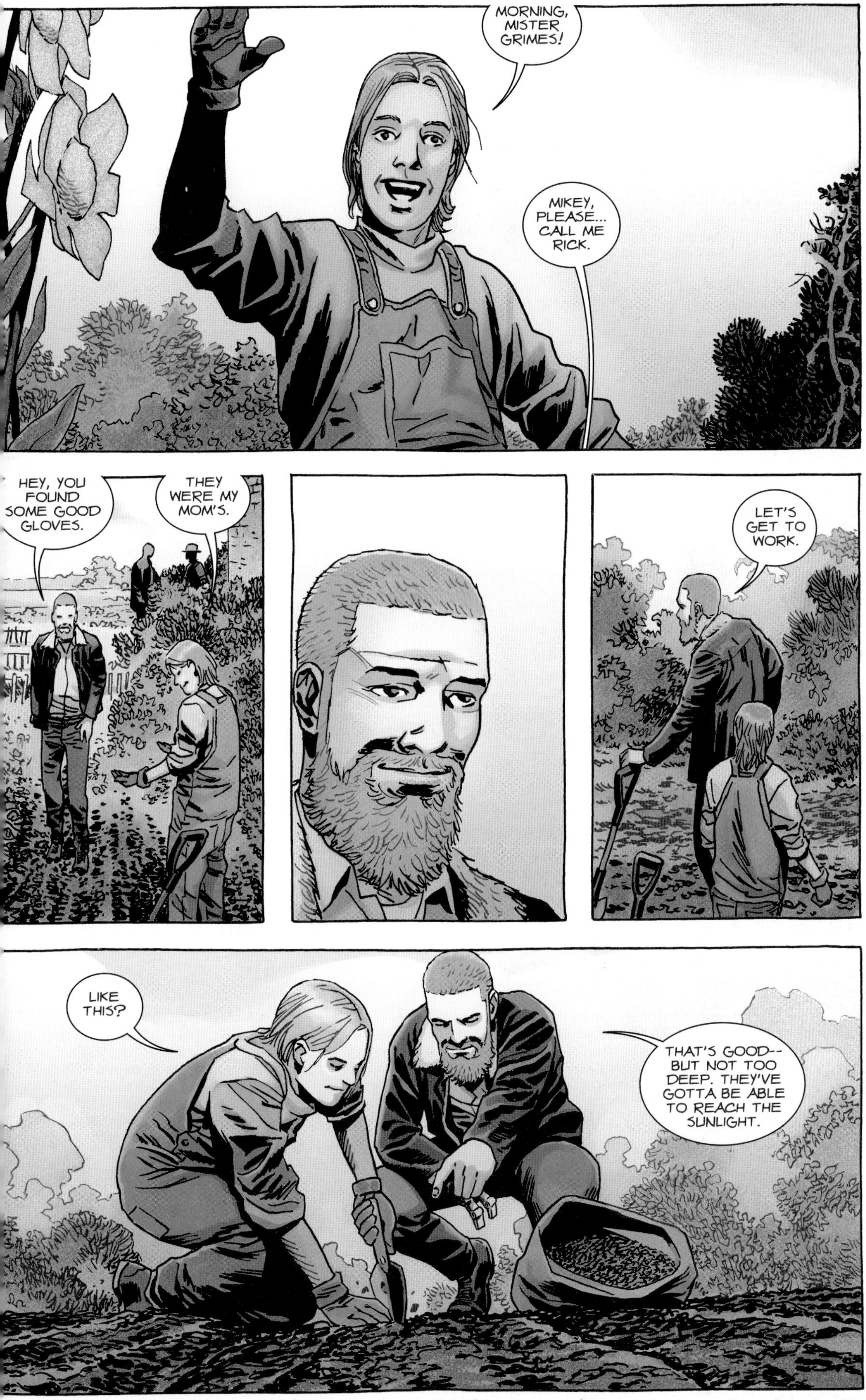
MORNING, MISTER GRIMES!
MIKEY, PLEASE... CALL ME RICK.
HEY, YOU FOUND SOME GOOD GLOVES.
THEY WERE MY MOM'S.
LET'S GET TO WORK.
LIKE THIS?
THAT'S GOOD-- BUT NOT TOO DEEP. THEY'VE GOTTA BE ABLE TO REACH THE SUNLIGHT.

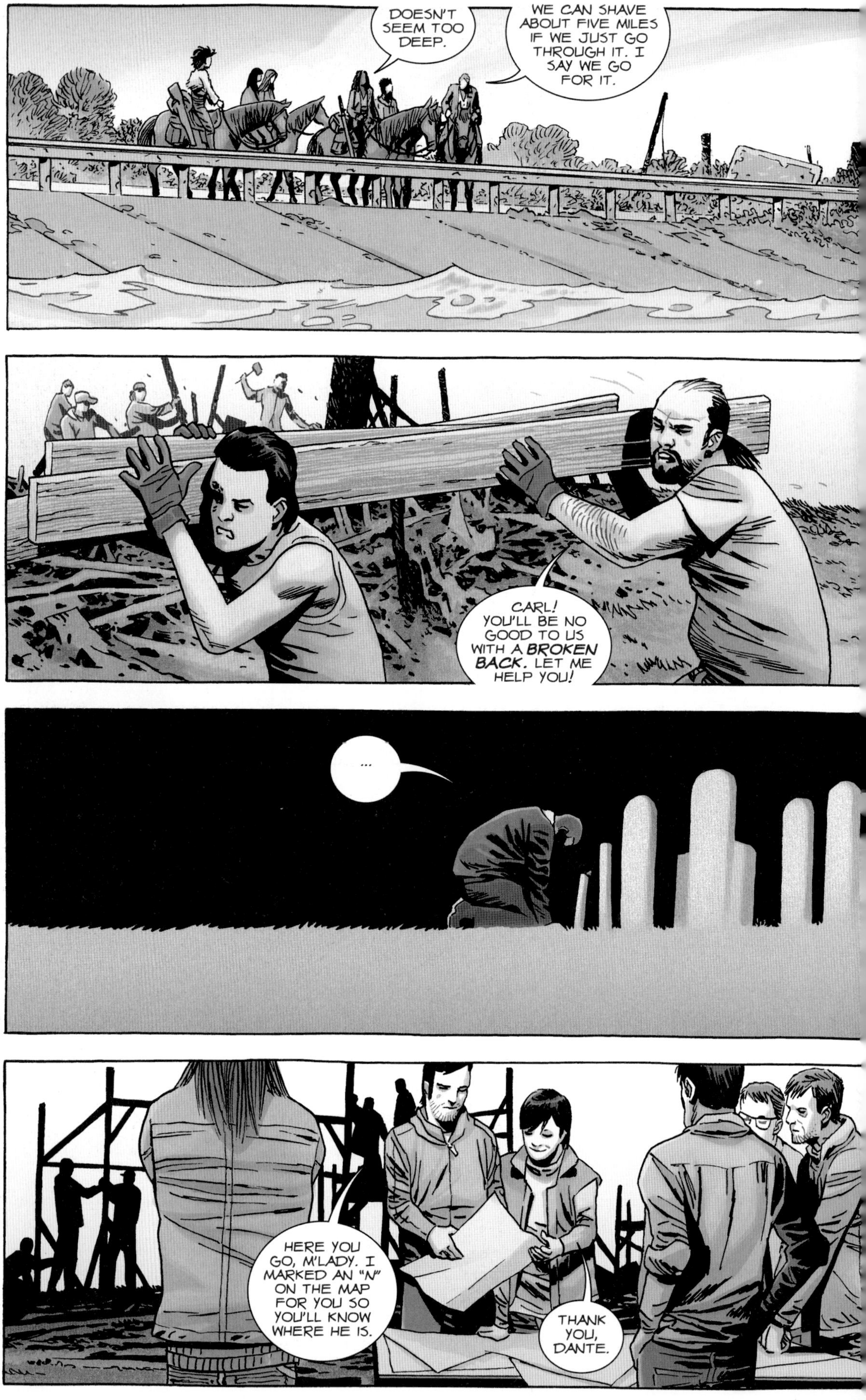
DOESN'T SEEM TOO DEEP.
WE CAN SHAVE ABOUT FIVE MILES IF WE JUST GO THROUGH IT. I SAY WE GO FOR IT.
CARL! YOU'LL BE NO GOOD TO US WITH A BROKEN BACK. LET ME HELP YOU!
...
HERE YOU GO, M'LADY. I MARKED AN "N" ON THE MAP FOR YOU SO YOU'LL KNOW WHERE HE IS.
THANK YOU, DANTE.

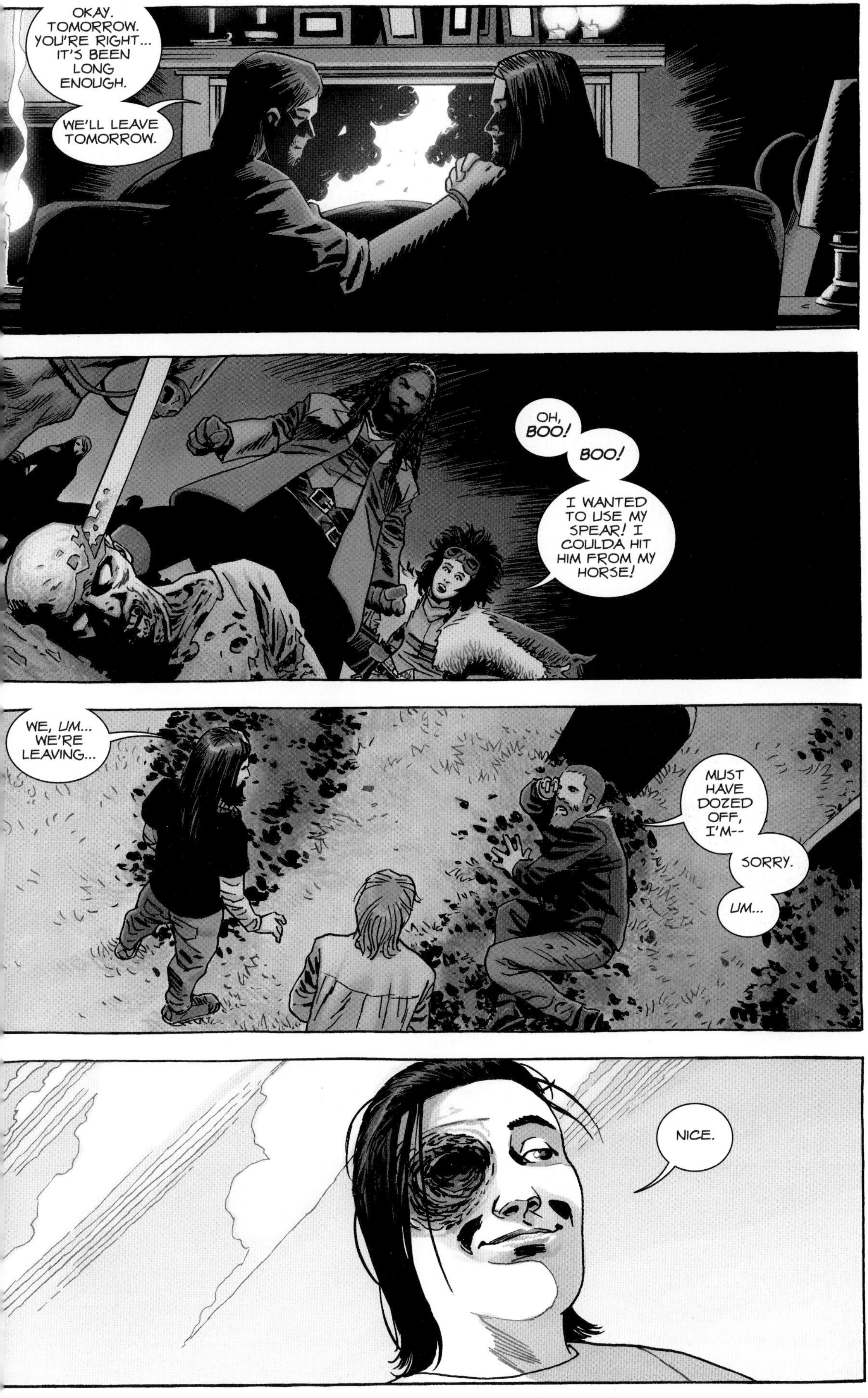
OKAY. TOMORROW. YOU'RE RIGHT... IT'S BEEN LONG ENOUGH.
WE'LL LEAVE TOMORROW.
OH, *BOO!*
BOO!
I WANTED TO USE MY SPEAR! I COULDA HIT HIM FROM MY HORSE!
WE, *UM*... WE'RE LEAVING...
MUST HAVE DOZED OFF, I'M--
SORRY.
UM...
NICE.

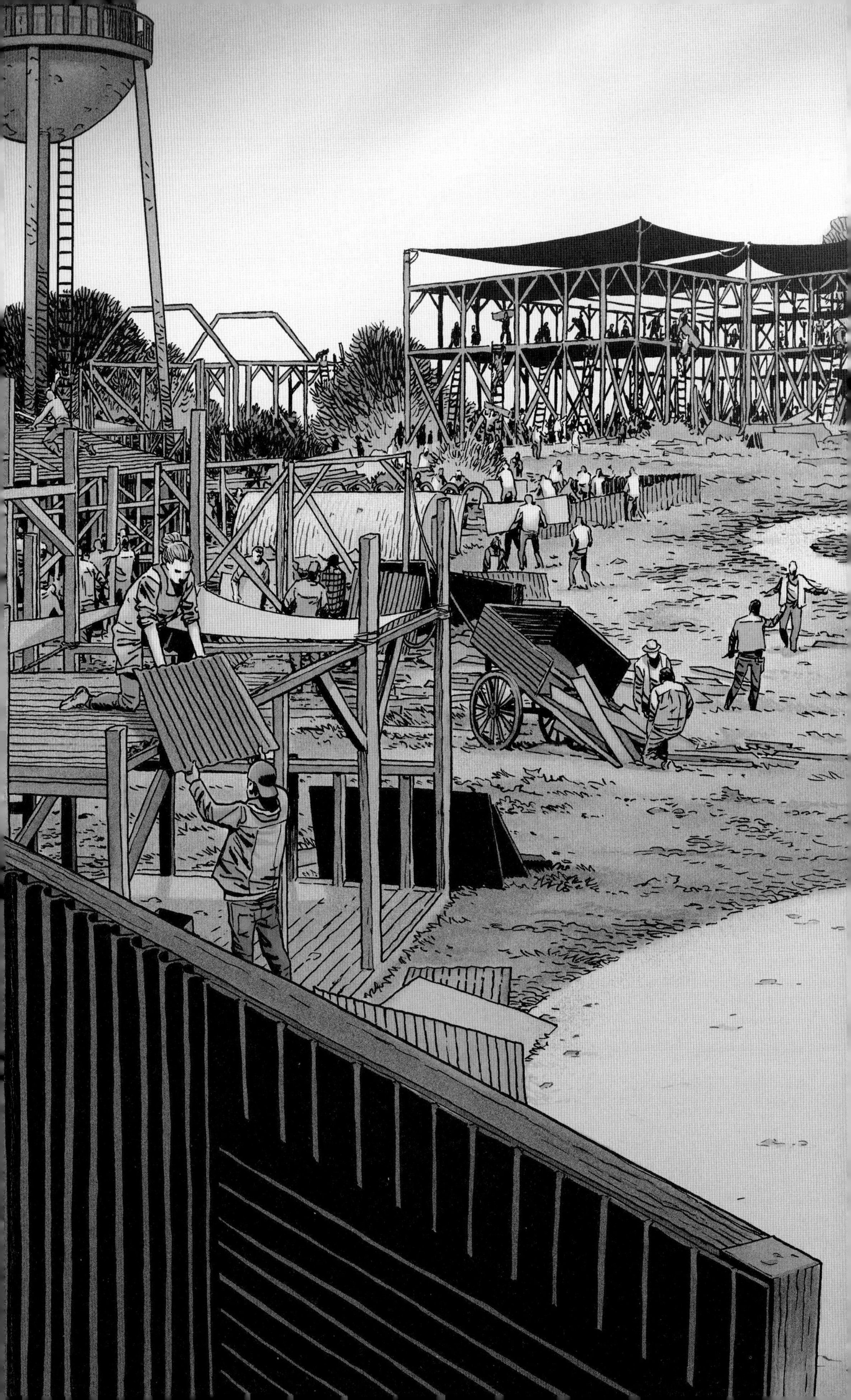

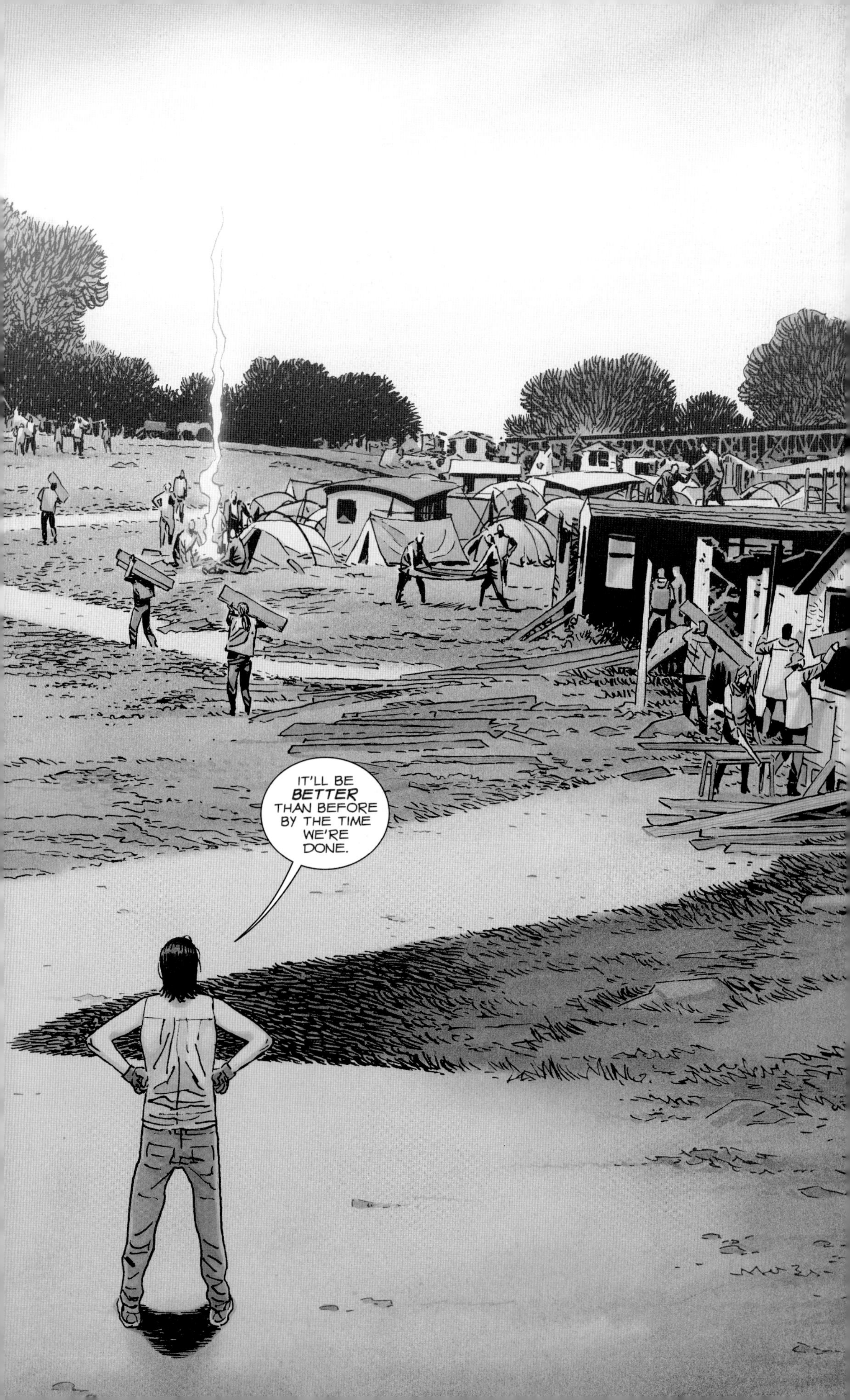
IT'LL BE BETTER THAN BEFORE BY THE TIME WE'RE DONE.

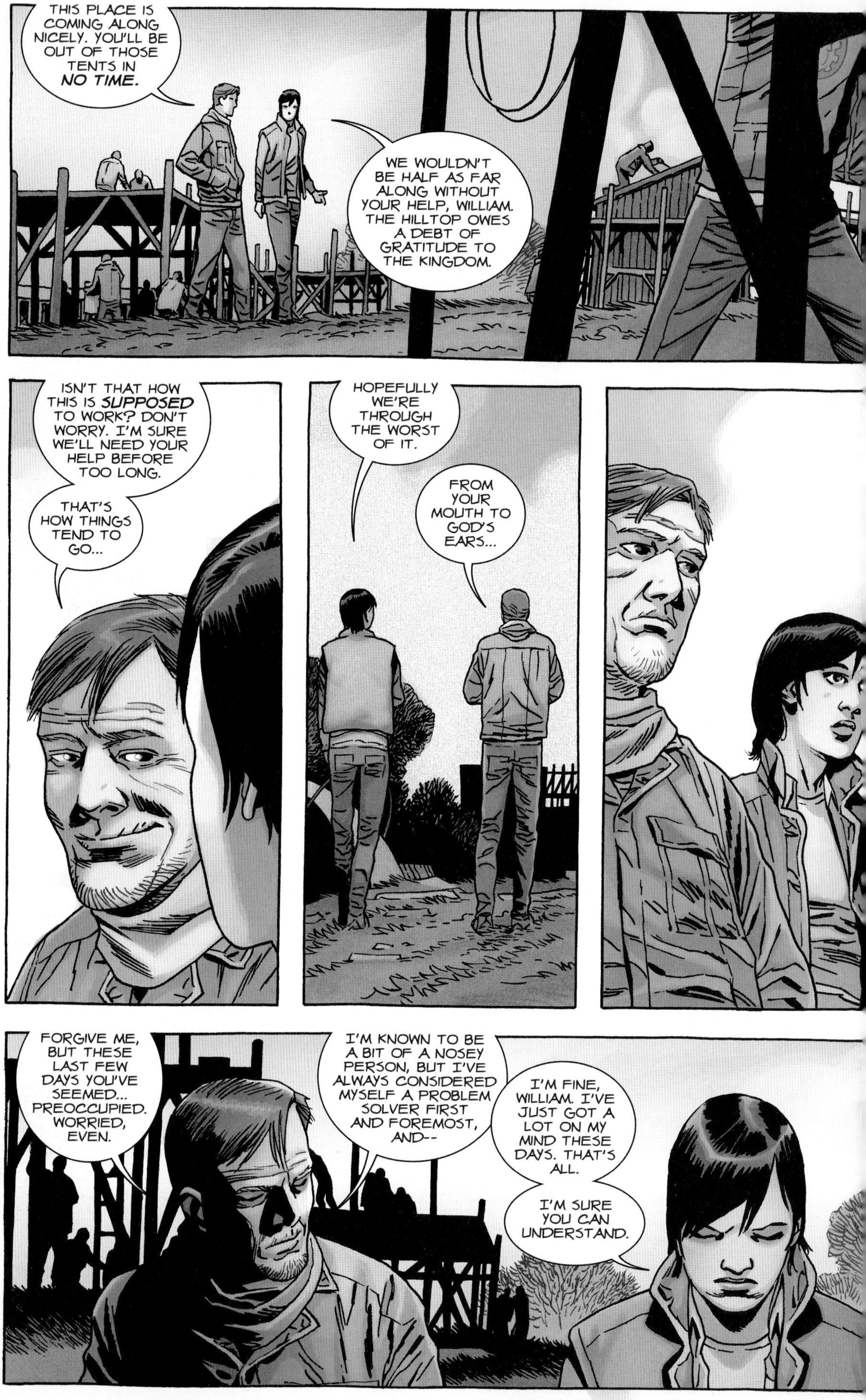

THIS PLACE IS COMING ALONG NICELY. YOU'LL BE OUT OF THOSE TENTS IN NO TIME.
WE WOULDN'T BE HALF AS FAR ALONG WITHOUT YOUR HELP, WILLIAM. THE HILLTOP OWES A DEBT OF GRATITUDE TO THE KINGDOM.
ISN'T THAT HOW THIS IS SUPPOSED TO WORK? DON'T WORRY. I'M SURE WE'LL NEED YOUR HELP BEFORE TOO LONG.
THAT'S HOW THINGS TEND TO GO...
HOPEFULLY WE'RE THROUGH THE WORST OF IT.
FROM YOUR MOUTH TO GOD'S EARS...
FORGIVE ME, BUT THESE LAST FEW DAYS YOU'VE SEEMED... PREOCCUPIED. WORRIED, EVEN.
I'M KNOWN TO BE A BIT OF A NOSEY PERSON, BUT I'VE ALWAYS CONSIDERED MYSELF A PROBLEM SOLVER FIRST AND FOREMOST, AND--
I'M FINE, WILLIAM. I'VE JUST GOT A LOT ON MY MIND THESE DAYS. THAT'S ALL.
I'M SURE YOU CAN UNDERSTAND.

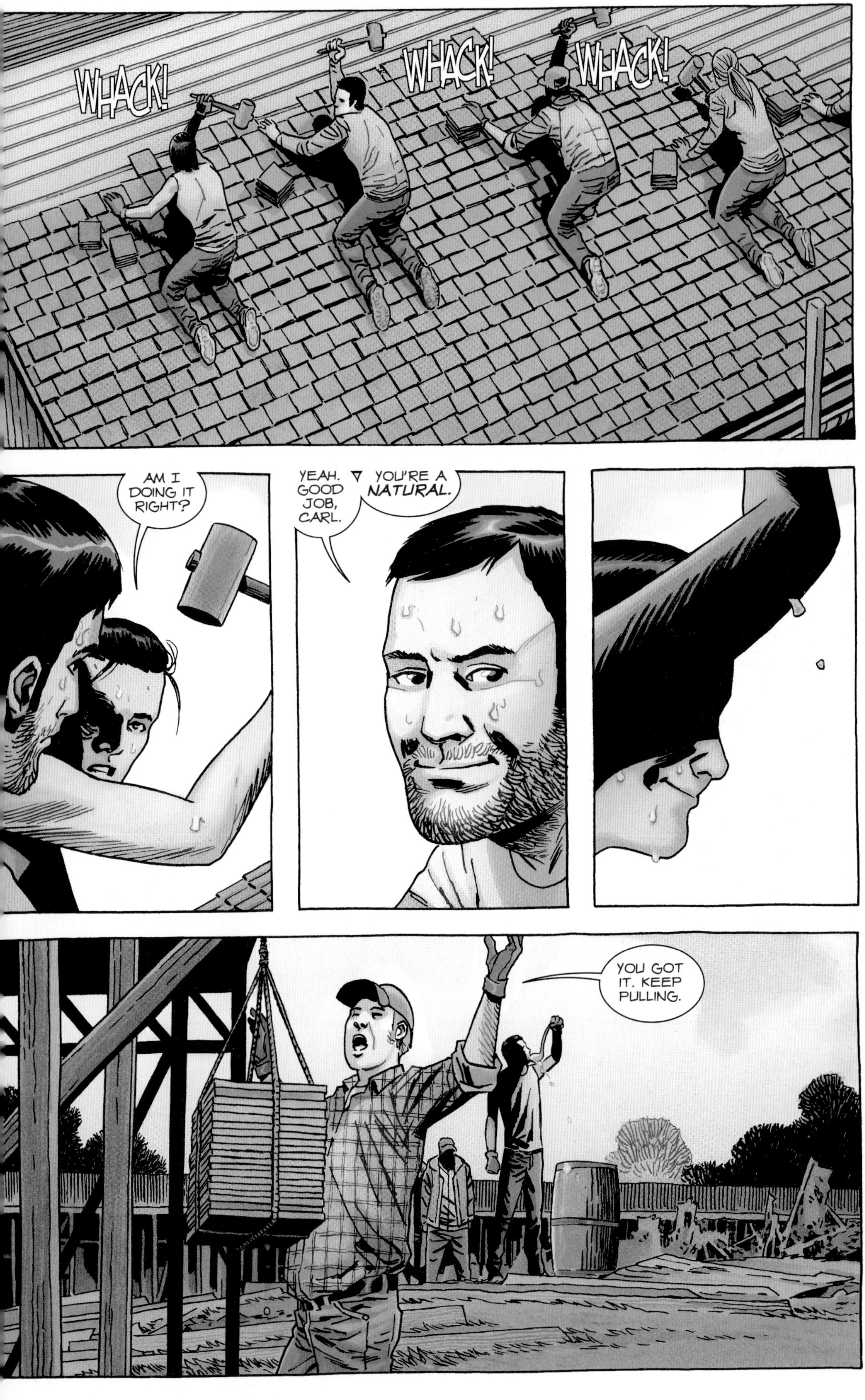
WHACK!
WHACK!
WHACK!
AM I DOING IT RIGHT?
YEAH. GOOD JOB, CARL.
YOU'RE A *NATURAL.*
YOU GOT IT. KEEP PULLING.

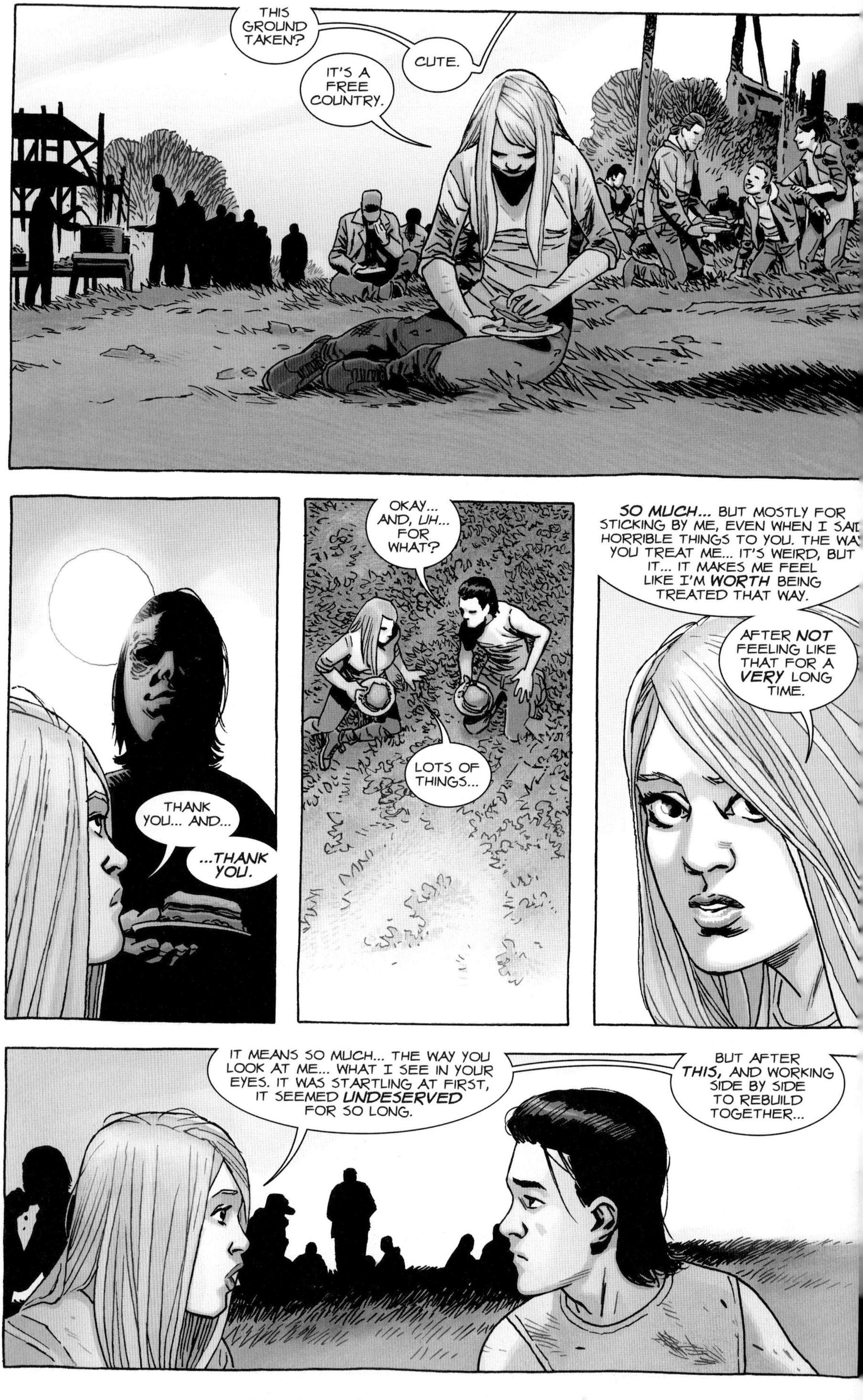
THIS GROUND TAKEN?
IT'S A FREE COUNTRY.
CUTE.
THANK YOU... AND...
...THANK YOU.
OKAY... AND, UH... FOR WHAT?
LOTS OF THINGS...
SO MUCH... BUT MOSTLY FOR STICKING BY ME, EVEN WHEN I SAI HORRIBLE THINGS TO YOU. THE WA YOU TREAT ME... IT'S WEIRD, BUT IT... IT MAKES ME FEEL LIKE I'M WORTH BEING TREATED THAT WAY.
AFTER NOT FEELING LIKE THAT FOR A VERY LONG TIME.
IT MEANS SO MUCH... THE WAY YOU LOOK AT ME... WHAT I SEE IN YOUR EYES. IT WAS STARTLING AT FIRST, IT SEEMED UNDESERVED FOR SO LONG.
BUT AFTER THIS, AND WORKING SIDE BY SIDE TO REBUILD TOGETHER...

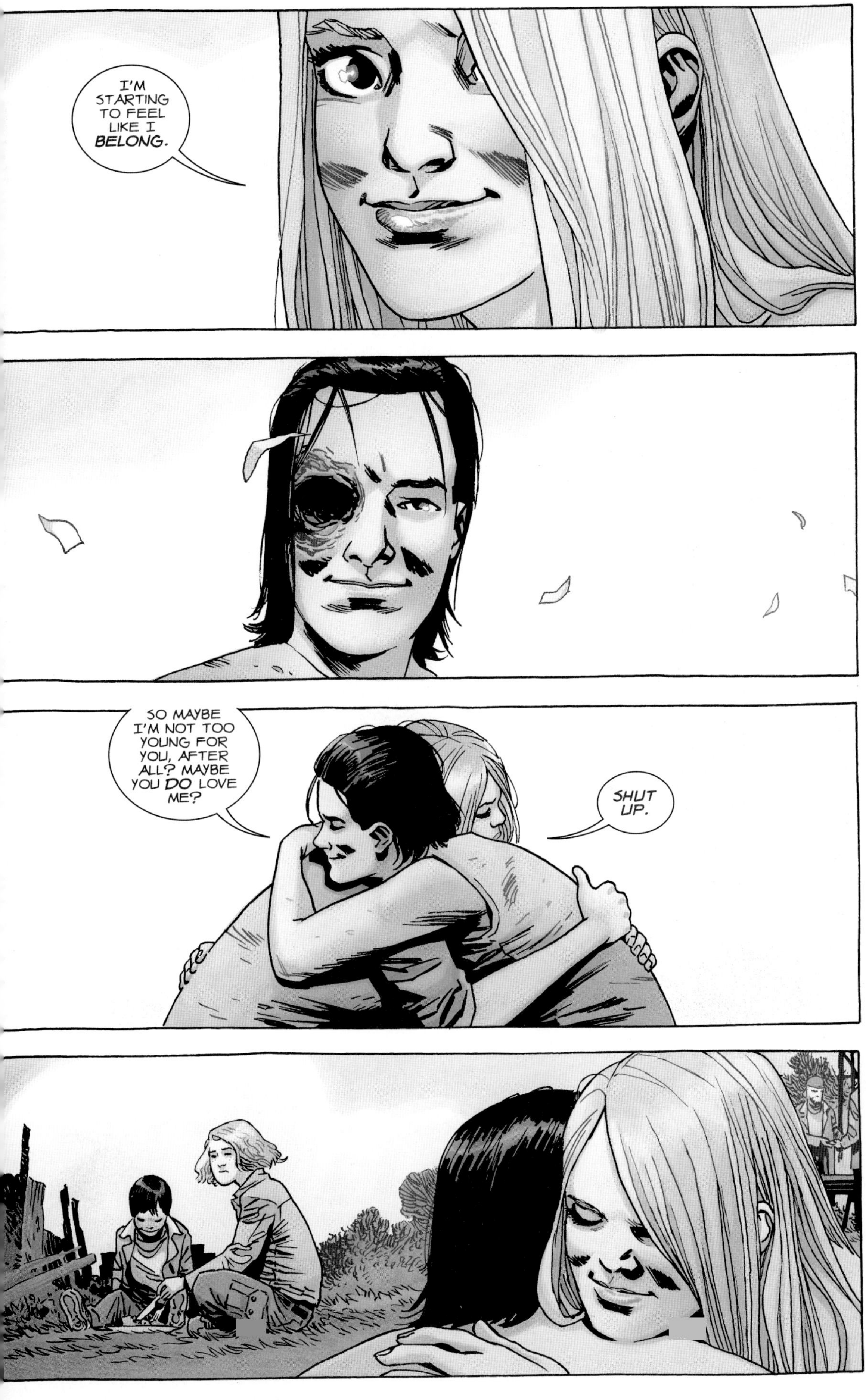
I'M STARTING TO FEEL LIKE I BELONG.
SO MAYBE I'M NOT TOO YOUNG FOR YOU, AFTER ALL? MAYBE YOU DO LOVE ME?
SHUT UP.

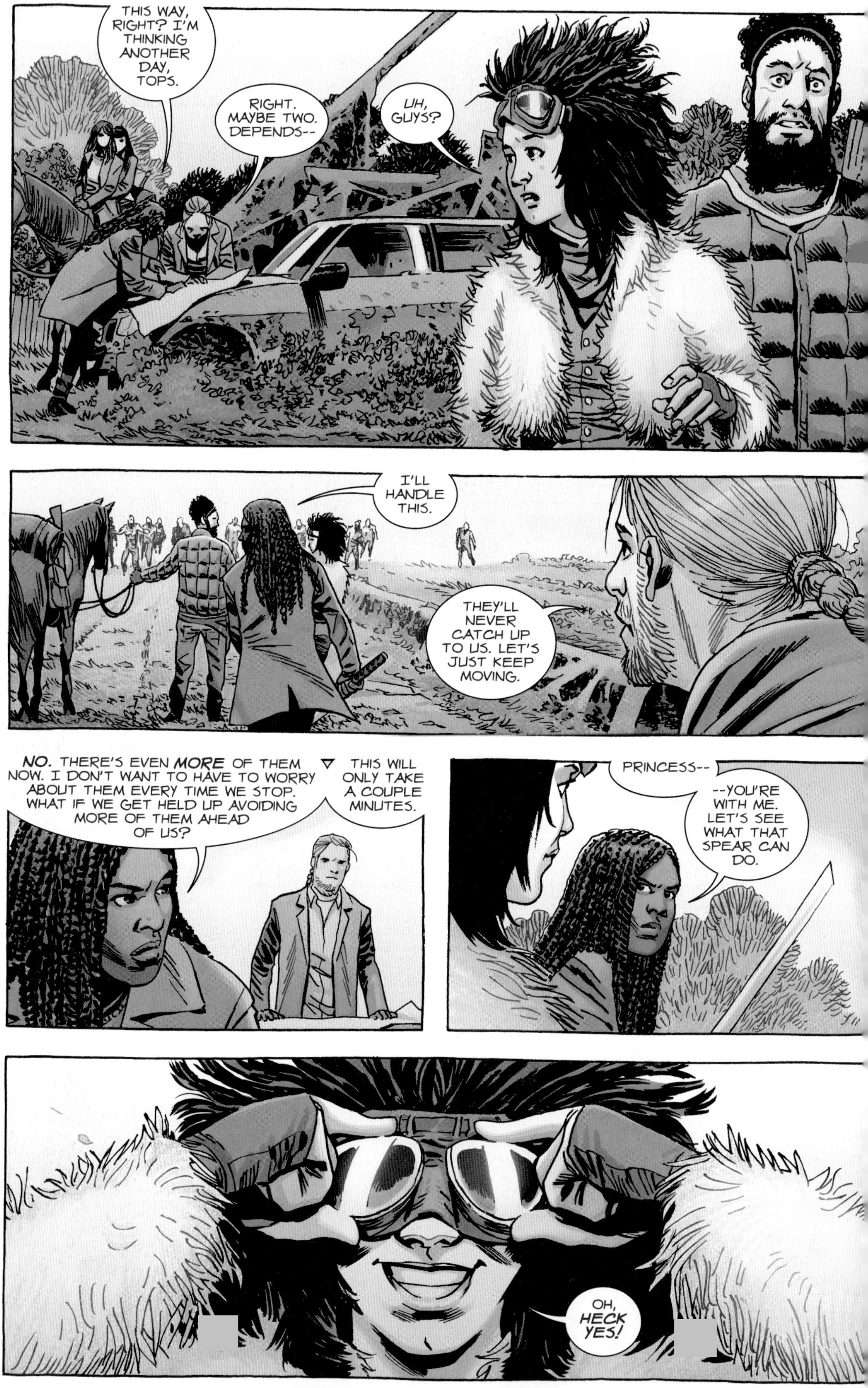
THIS WAY, RIGHT? I'M THINKING ANOTHER DAY, TOPS.
RIGHT. MAYBE TWO. DEPENDS--
UH, GUYS?
I'LL HANDLE THIS.
THEY'LL NEVER CATCH UP TO US. LET'S JUST KEEP MOVING.
NO. THERE'S EVEN MORE OF THEM NOW. I DON'T WANT TO HAVE TO WORRY ABOUT THEM EVERY TIME WE STOP. WHAT IF WE GET HELD UP AVOIDING MORE OF THEM AHEAD OF US?
THIS WILL ONLY TAKE A COUPLE MINUTES.
PRINCESS--
--YOU'RE WITH ME. LET'S SEE WHAT THAT SPEAR CAN DO.
OH, HECK YES!

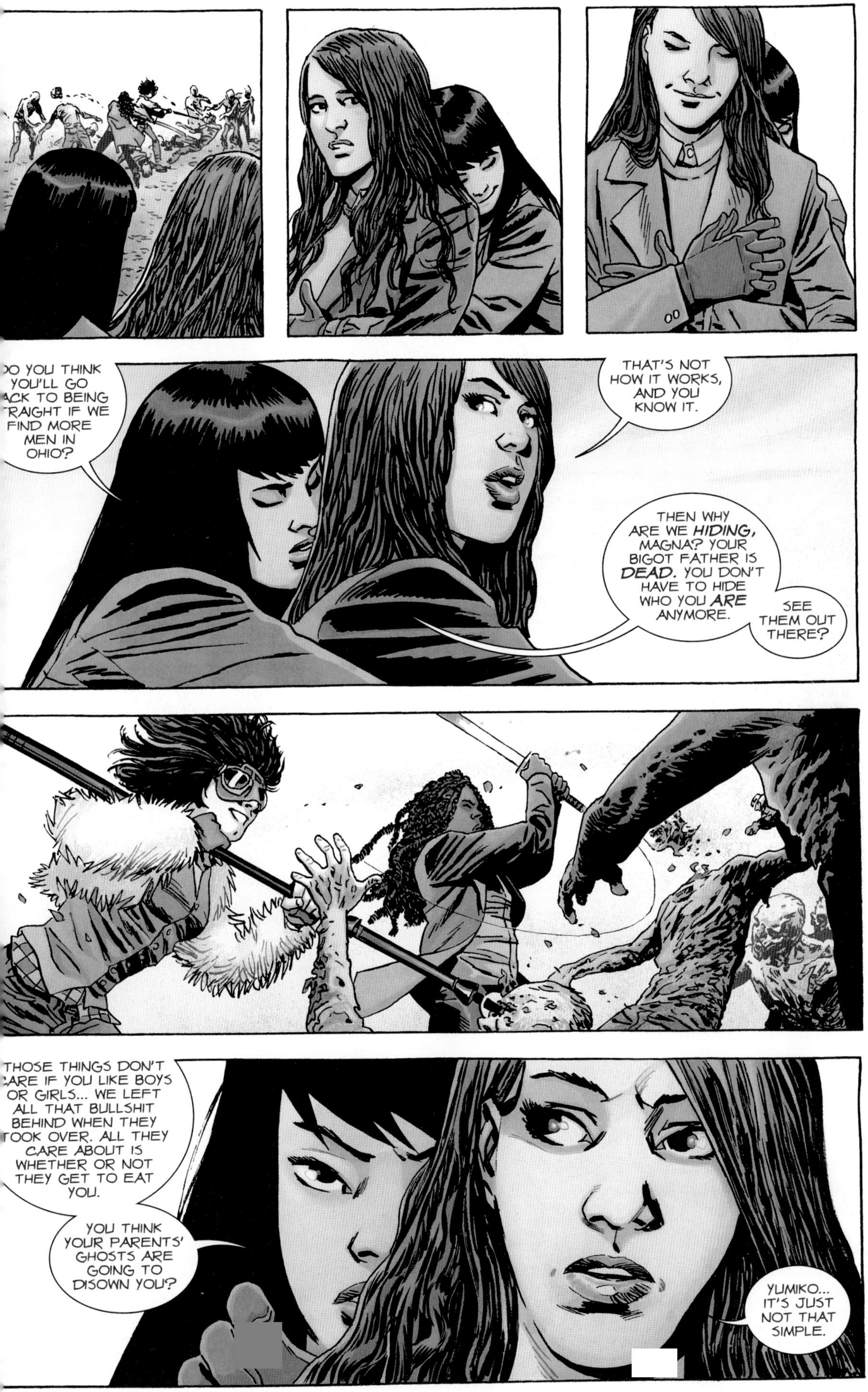

DO YOU THINK YOU'LL GO ACK TO BEING TRAIGHT IF WE FIND MORE MEN IN OHIO?
THAT'S NOT HOW IT WORKS, AND YOU KNOW IT.
THEN WHY ARE WE HIDING, MAGNA? YOUR BIGOT FATHER IS DEAD. YOU DON'T HAVE TO HIDE WHO YOU ARE ANYMORE.
SEE THEM OUT THERE?
THOSE THINGS DON'T CARE IF YOU LIKE BOYS OR GIRLS... WE LEFT ALL THAT BULLSHIT BEHIND WHEN THEY TOOK OVER. ALL THEY CARE ABOUT IS WHETHER OR NOT THEY GET TO EAT YOU.
YOU THINK YOUR PARENTS' GHOSTS ARE GOING TO DISOWN YOU?
YUMIKO... IT'S JUST NOT THAT SIMPLE.

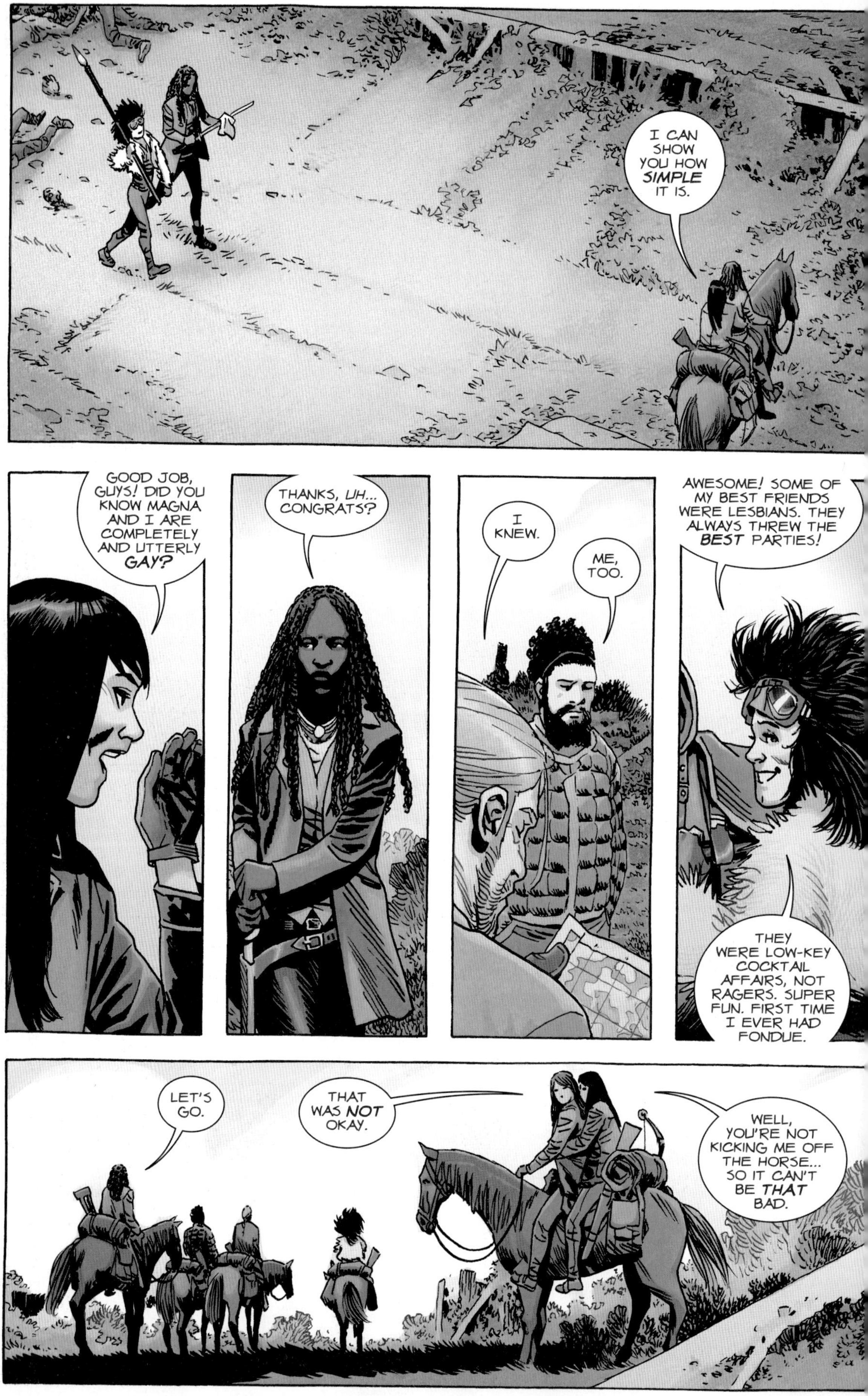
I CAN SHOW YOU HOW SIMPLE IT IS.
GOOD JOB, GUYS! DID YOU KNOW MAGNA AND I ARE COMPLETELY AND UTTERLY GAY?
THANKS, UH... CONGRATS?
I KNEW.
ME, TOO.
AWESOME! SOME OF MY BEST FRIENDS WERE LESBIANS. THEY ALWAYS THREW THE BEST PARTIES!
THEY WERE LOW-KEY COCKTAIL AFFAIRS, NOT RAGERS. SUPER FUN. FIRST TIME I EVER HAD FONDUE.
LET'S GO.
THAT WAS NOT OKAY.
WELL, YOU'RE NOT KICKING ME OFF THE HORSE... SO IT CAN'T BE THAT BAD.

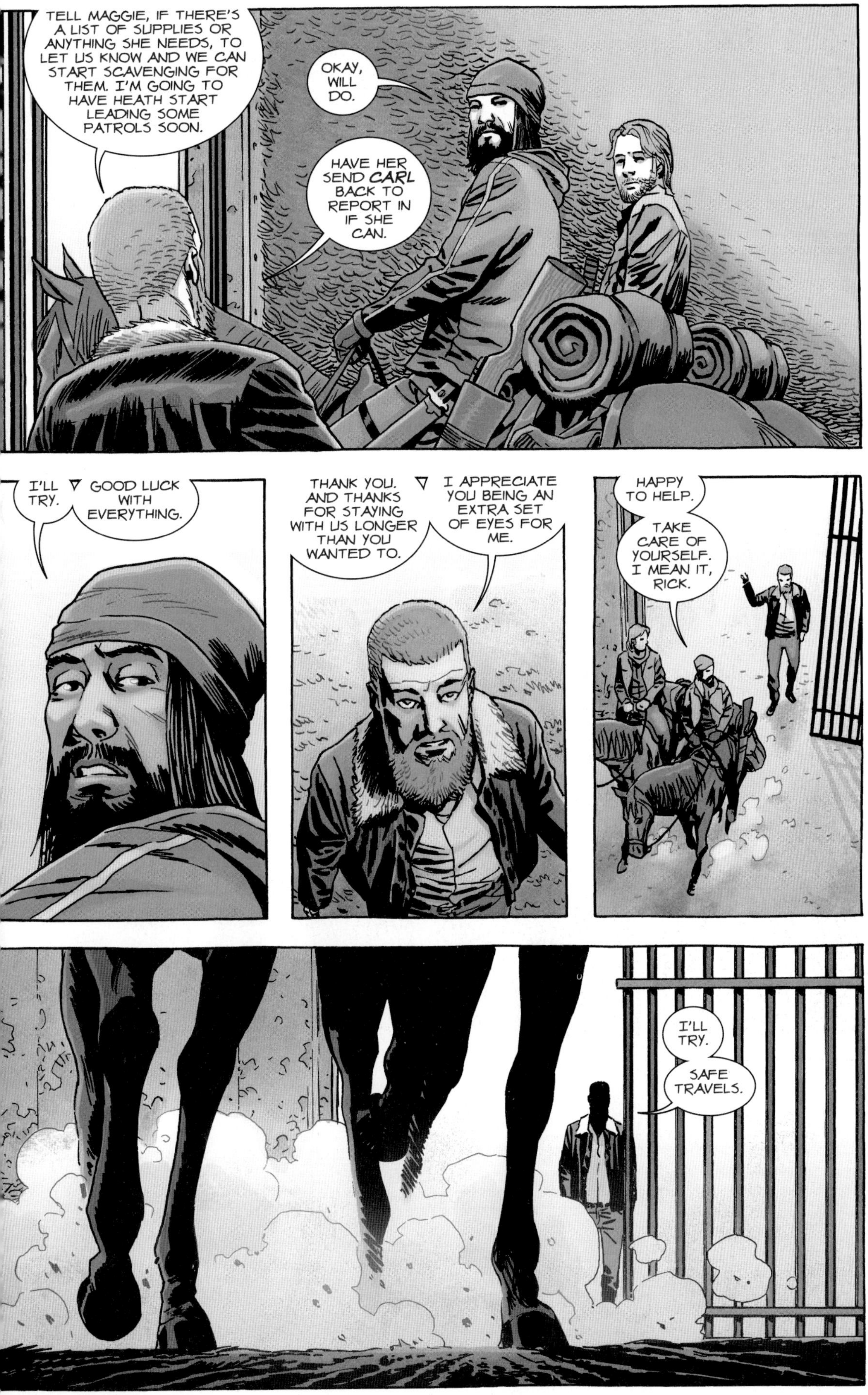
TELL MAGGIE, IF THERE'S A LIST OF SUPPLIES OR ANYTHING SHE NEEDS, TO LET US KNOW AND WE CAN START SCAVENGING FOR THEM. I'M GOING TO HAVE HEATH START LEADING SOME PATROLS SOON.
OKAY, WILL DO.
HAVE HER SEND CARL BACK TO REPORT IN IF SHE CAN.
I'LL TRY.
GOOD LUCK WITH EVERYTHING.
THANK YOU. AND THANKS FOR STAYING WITH US LONGER THAN YOU WANTED TO.
I APPRECIATE YOU BEING AN EXTRA SET OF EYES FOR ME.
HAPPY TO HELP.
TAKE CARE OF YOURSELF. I MEAN IT, RICK.
I'LL TRY.
SAFE TRAVELS.

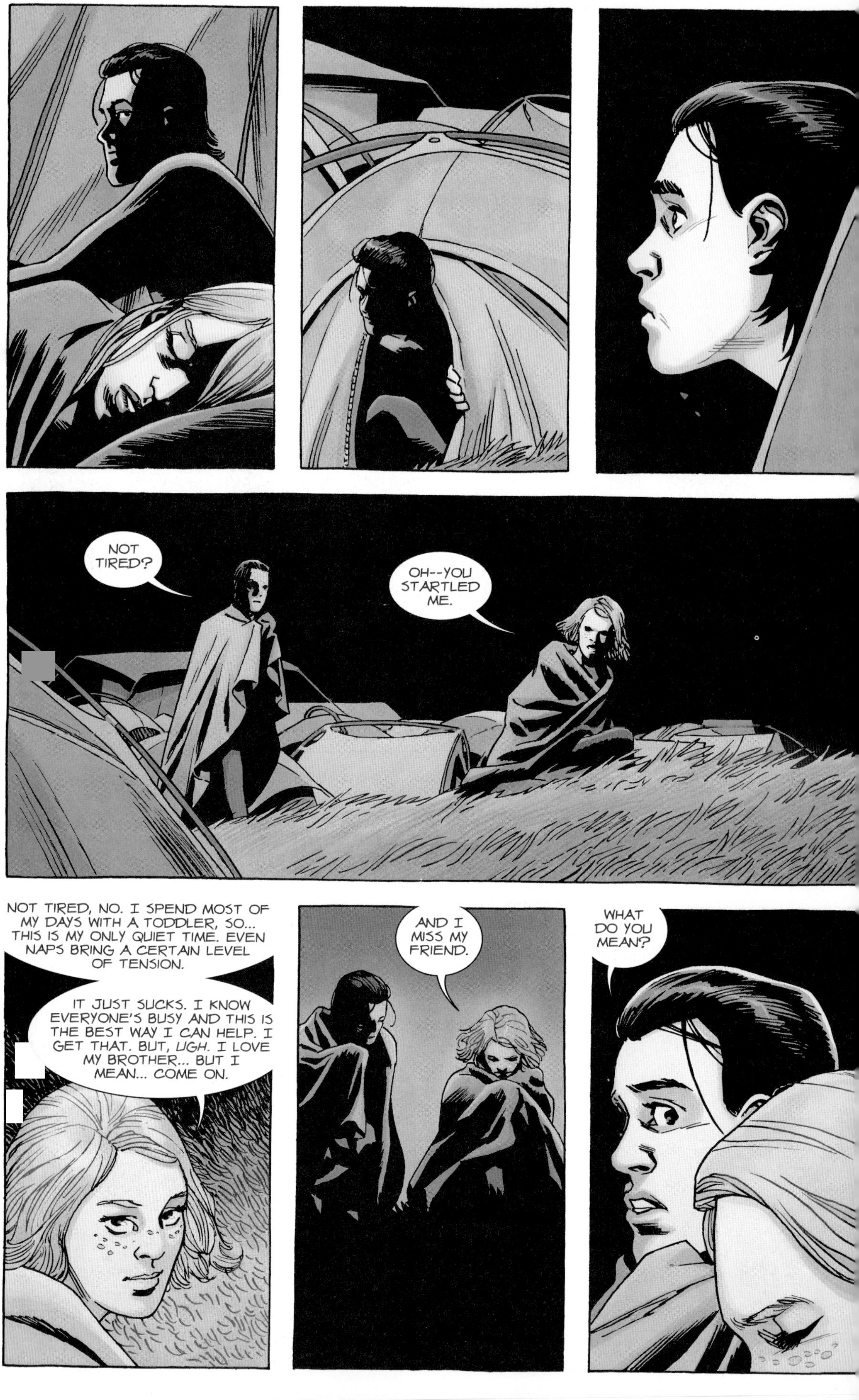
NOT TIRED?
OH--YOU STARTLED ME.
NOT TIRED, NO. I SPEND MOST OF MY DAYS WITH A TODDLER, SO... THIS IS MY ONLY QUIET TIME. EVEN NAPS BRING A CERTAIN LEVEL OF TENSION.
IT JUST SUCKS. I KNOW EVERYONE'S BUSY AND THIS IS THE BEST WAY I CAN HELP. I GET THAT. BUT, *UGH*. I LOVE MY BROTHER... BUT I MEAN... COME ON.
AND I MISS MY FRIEND.
WHAT DO YOU MEAN?

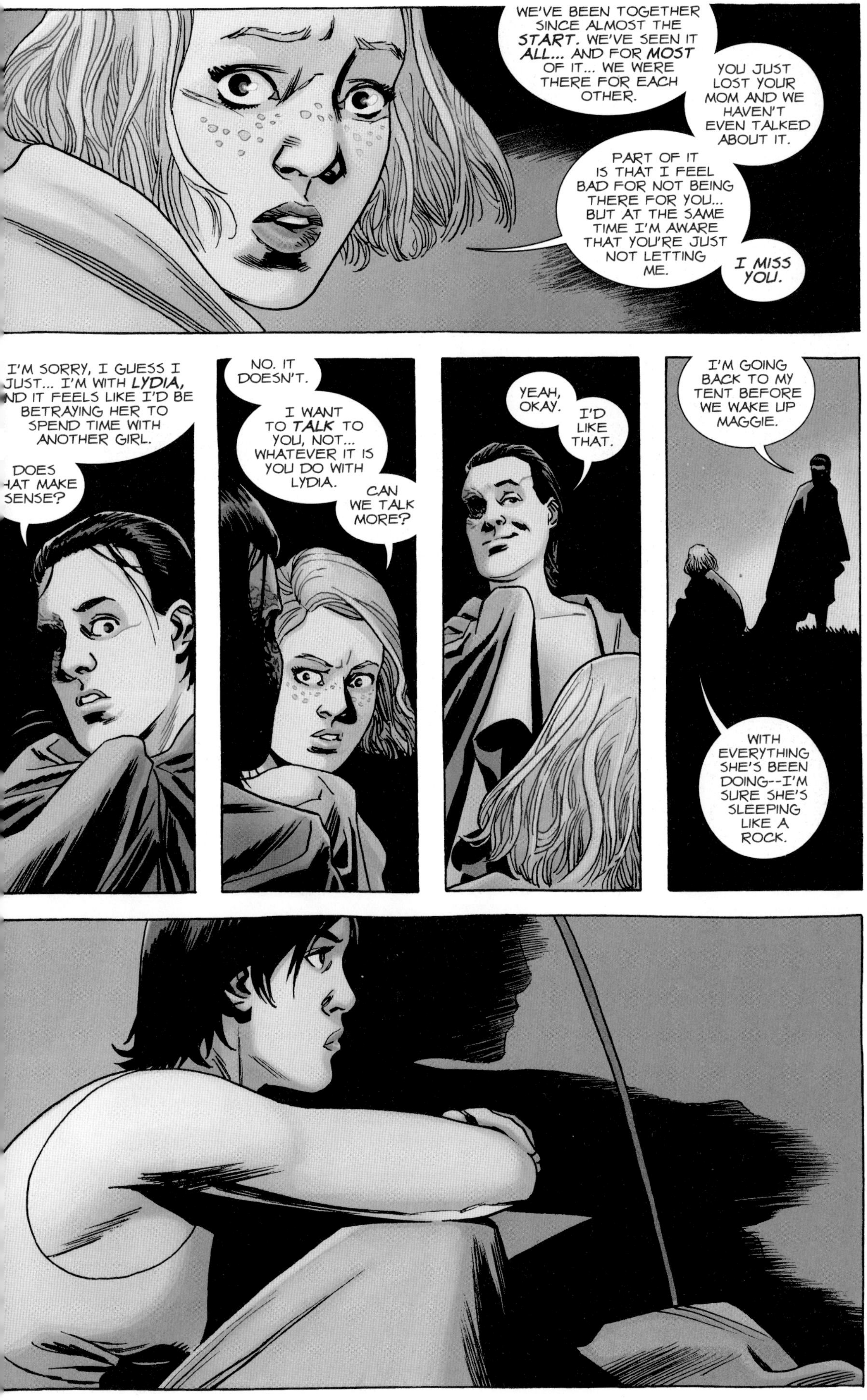
WE'VE BEEN TOGETHER SINCE ALMOST THE START. WE'VE SEEN IT ALL... AND FOR MOST OF IT... WE WERE THERE FOR EACH OTHER.
YOU JUST LOST YOUR MOM AND WE HAVEN'T EVEN TALKED ABOUT IT.
PART OF IT IS THAT I FEEL BAD FOR NOT BEING THERE FOR YOU... BUT AT THE SAME TIME I'M AWARE THAT YOU'RE JUST NOT LETTING ME.
I MISS YOU.
I'M SORRY, I GUESS I JUST... I'M WITH LYDIA, ND IT FEELS LIKE I'D BE BETRAYING HER TO SPEND TIME WITH ANOTHER GIRL.
DOES HAT MAKE SENSE?
NO. IT DOESN'T.
I WANT TO TALK TO YOU, NOT... WHATEVER IT IS YOU DO WITH LYDIA.
CAN WE TALK MORE?
YEAH, OKAY.
I'D LIKE THAT.
I'M GOING BACK TO MY TENT BEFORE WE WAKE UP MAGGIE.
WITH EVERYTHING SHE'S BEEN DOING--I'M SURE SHE'S SLEEPING LIKE A ROCK.

IN CASE YOU'RE WONDERING, THINGS ARE ALMOST BACK TO NORMAL HERE. CAN'T SAY THE SAME JUST YET FOR THE OTHER COMMUNITIES, BUT WE'LL GET THERE.

OUR PEOPLE HAVE BECOME STRONG... IT'S AMAZING HOW WELL THEY WORK TOGETHER.

YOU'D BE SO...

YOU'D BE...

I MISS YOU SO MUCH.

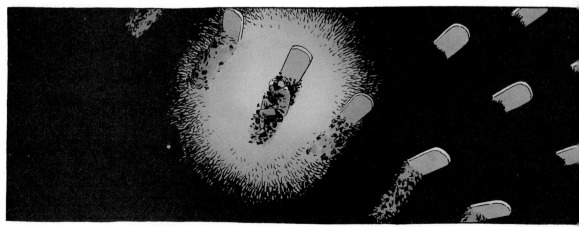

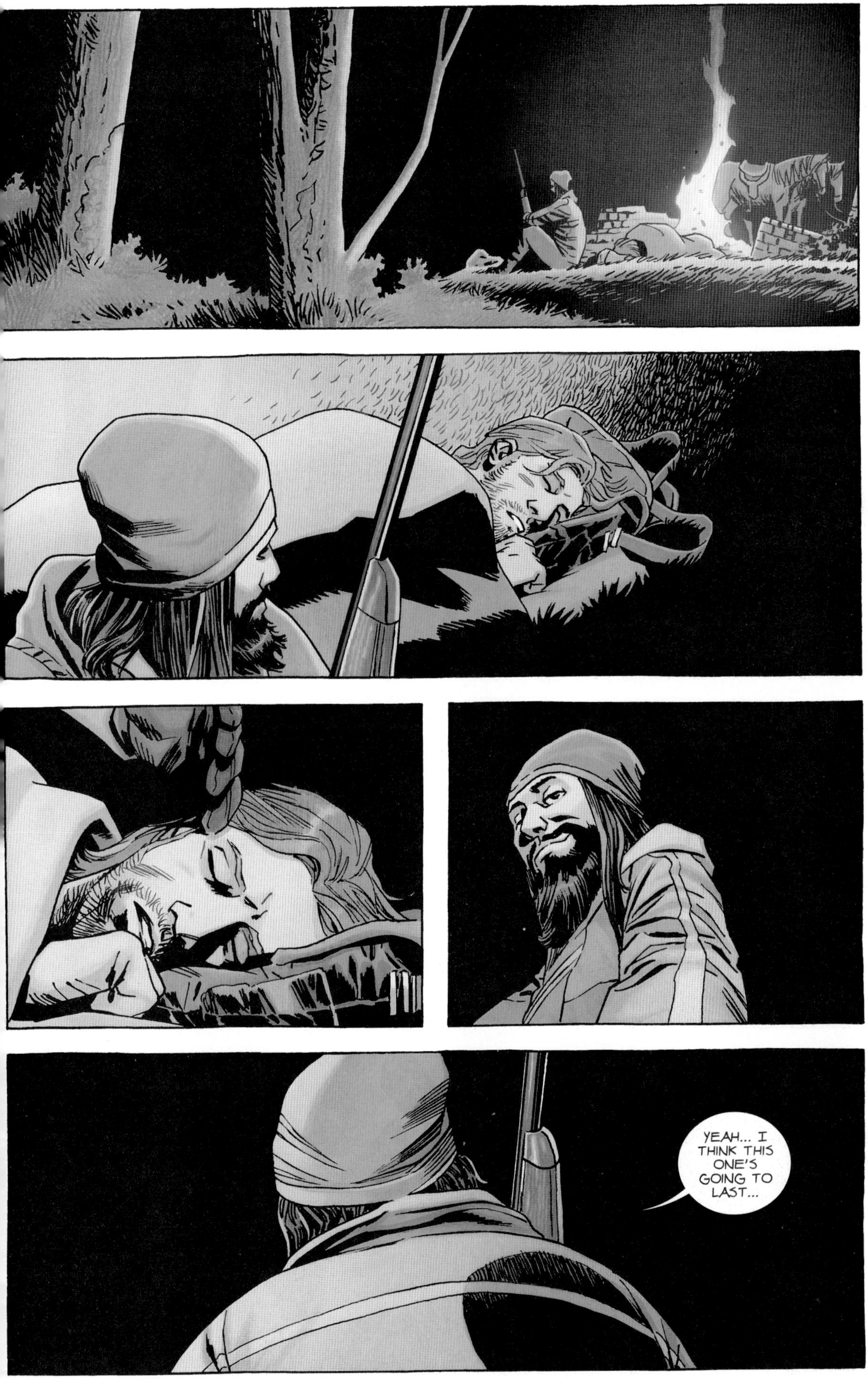
YEAH... I THINK THIS ONE'S GOING TO LAST...

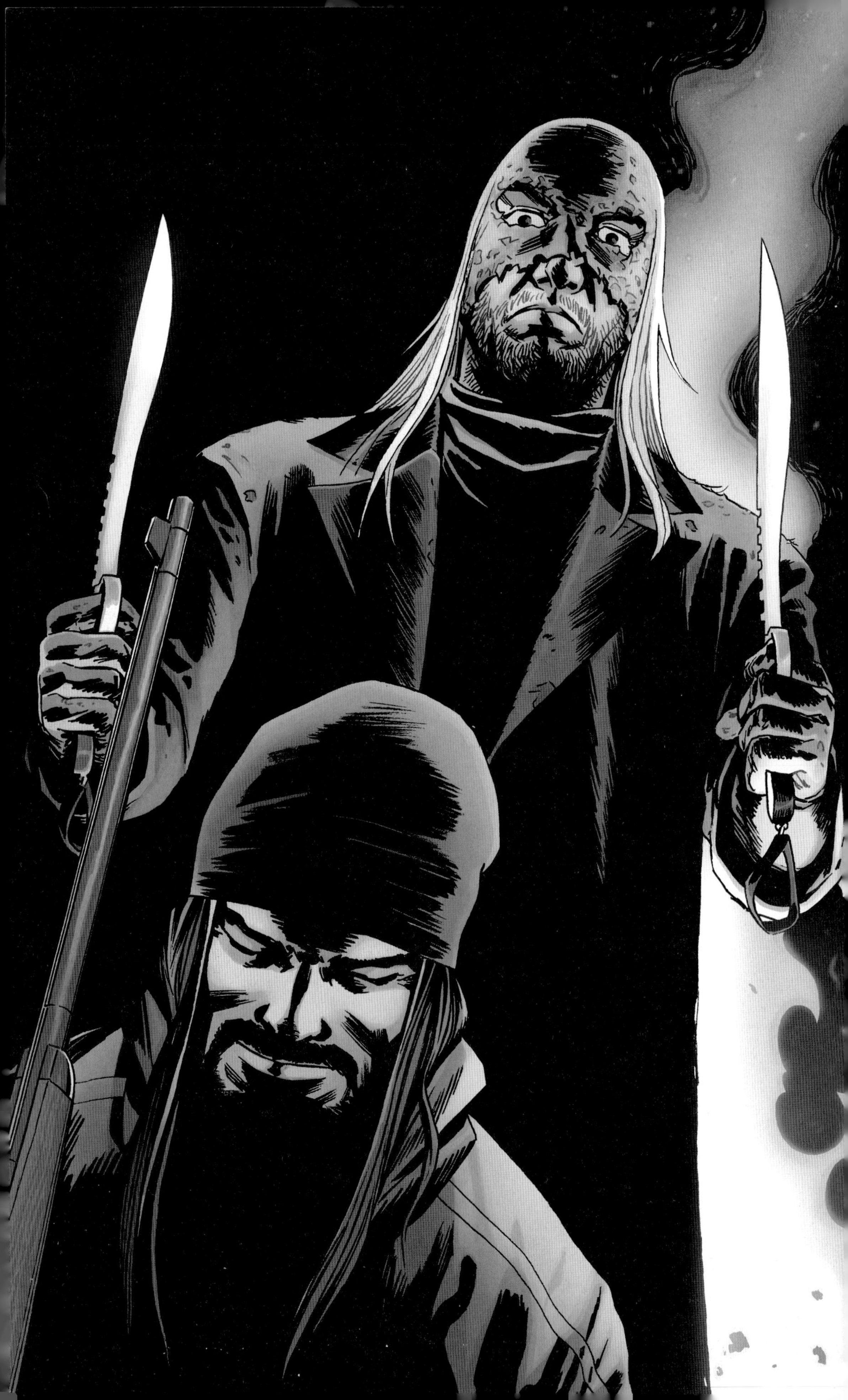

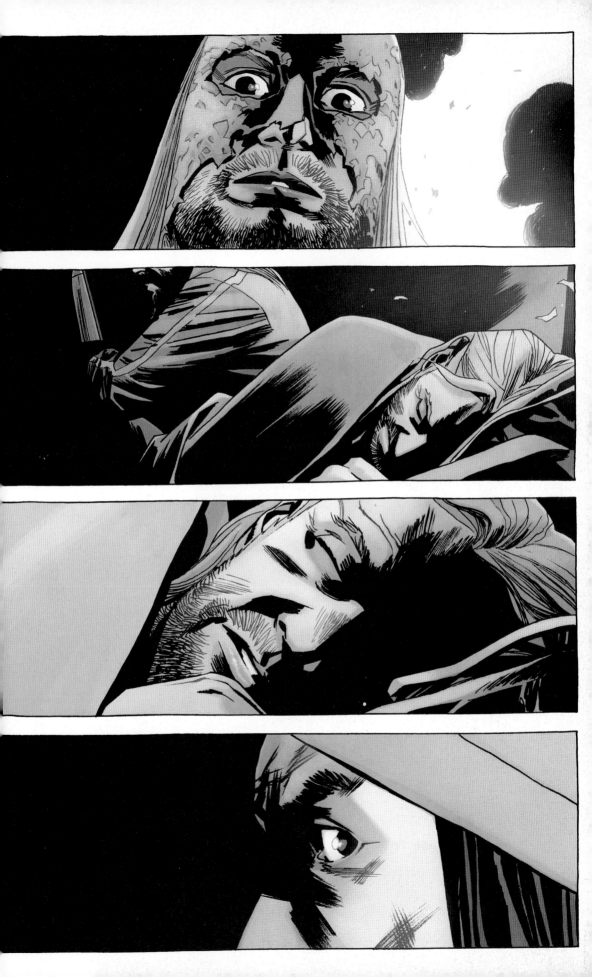

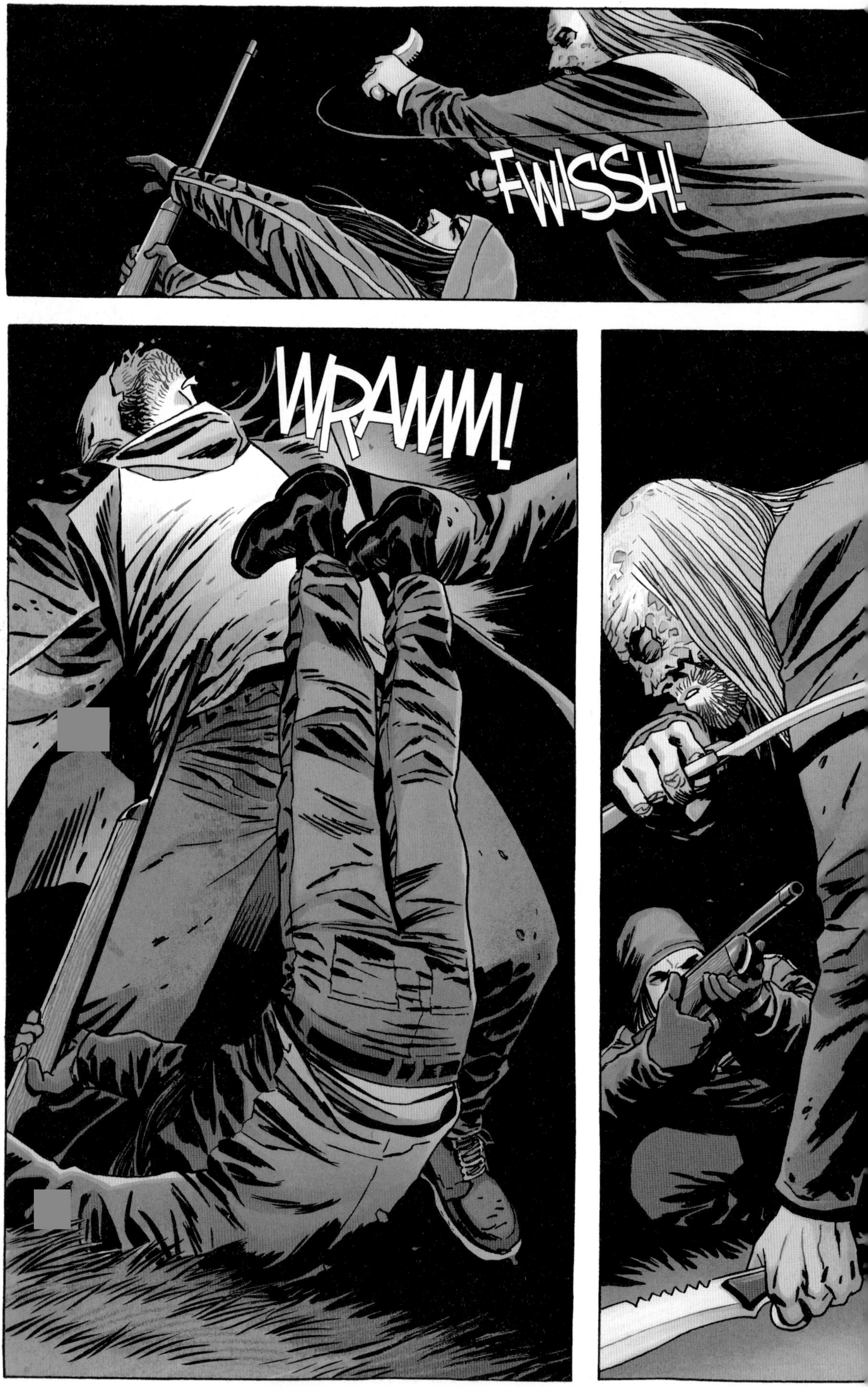
FWISSH!
WRAMM!

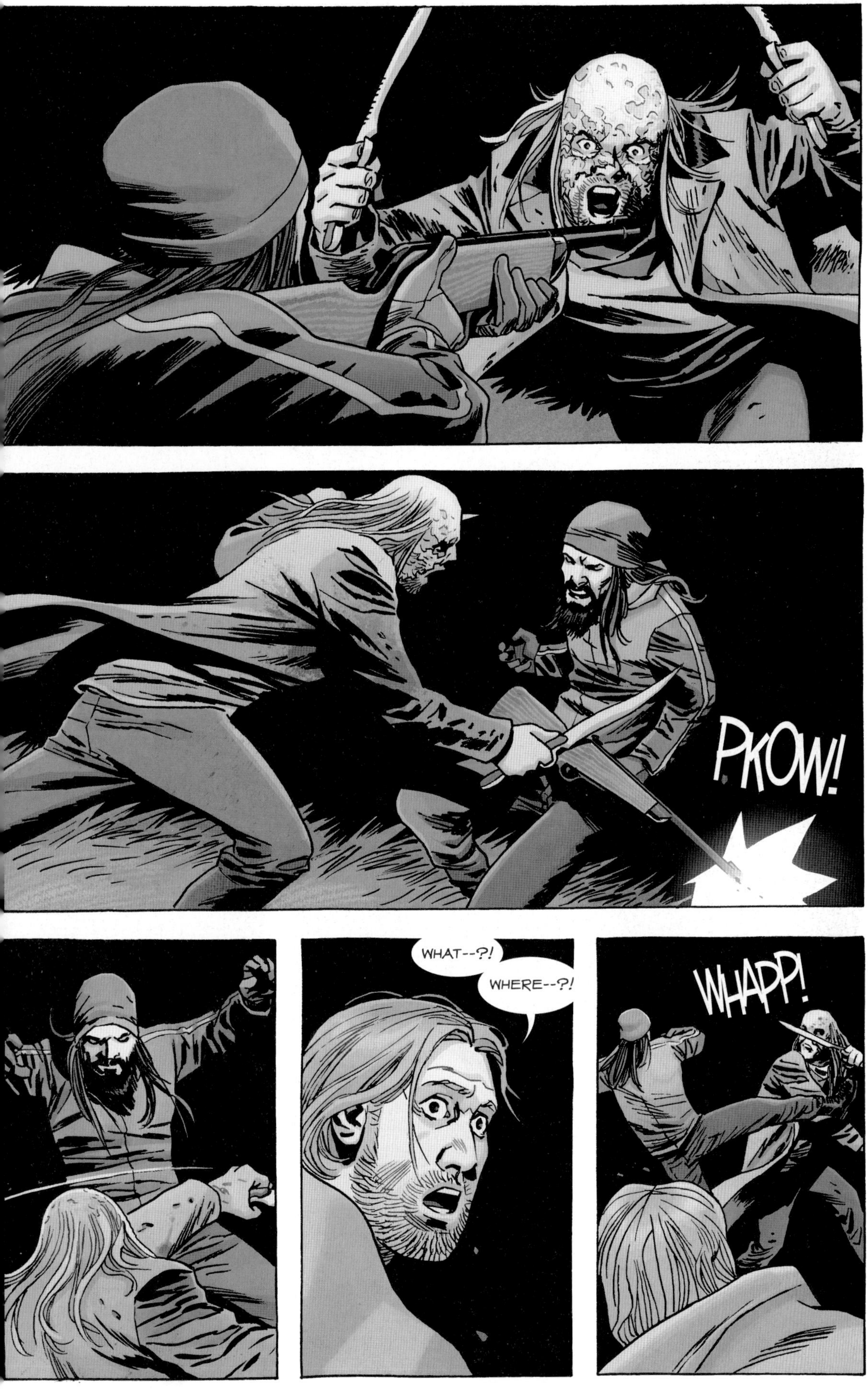
PKOW!
WHAT--?!
WHERE--?!
WHAPP!

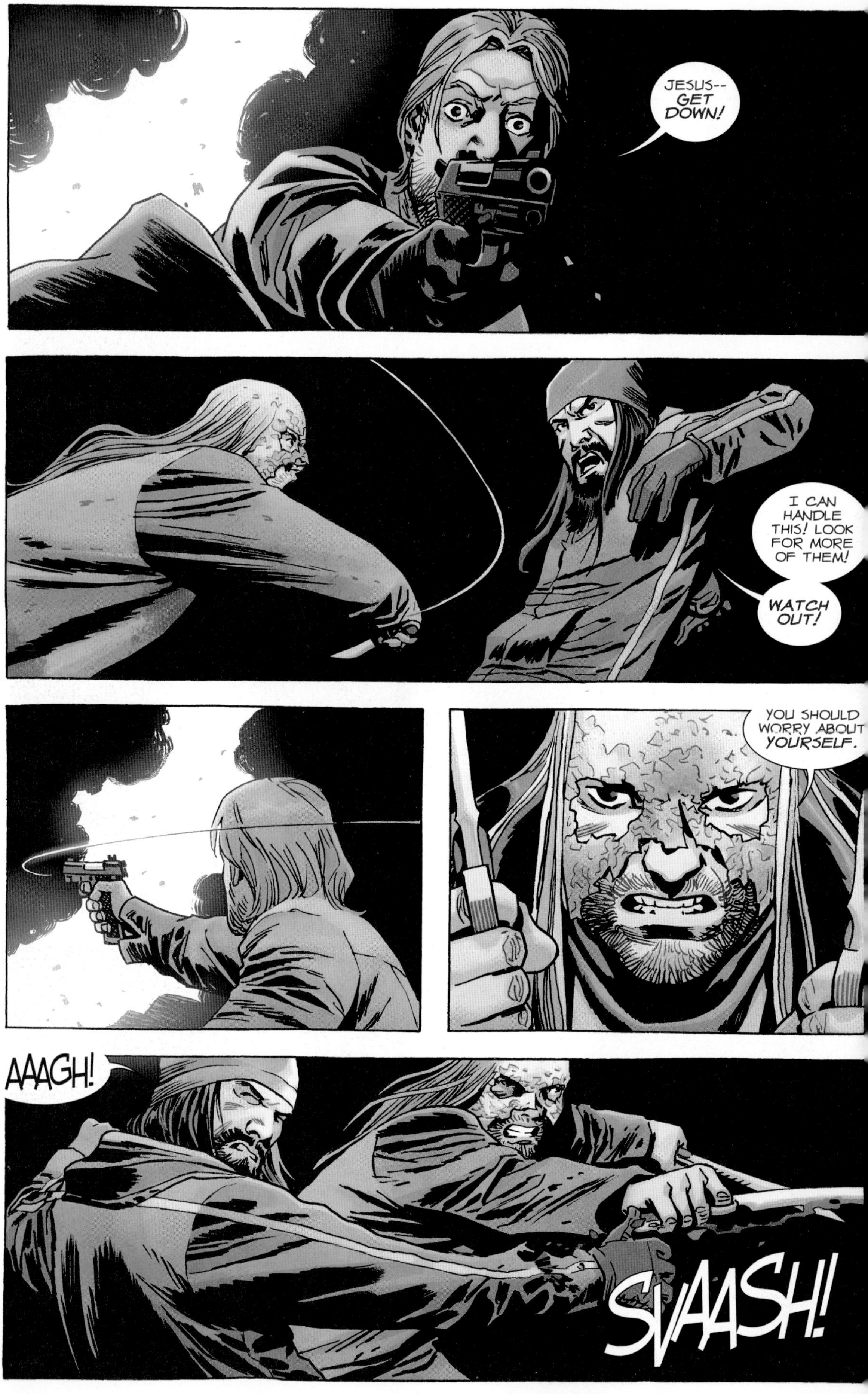
JESUS-- GET DOWN!
I CAN HANDLE THIS! LOOK FOR MORE OF THEM!
WATCH OUT!
YOU SHOULD WORRY ABOUT YOURSELF.
AAAGH!
SVAASH!

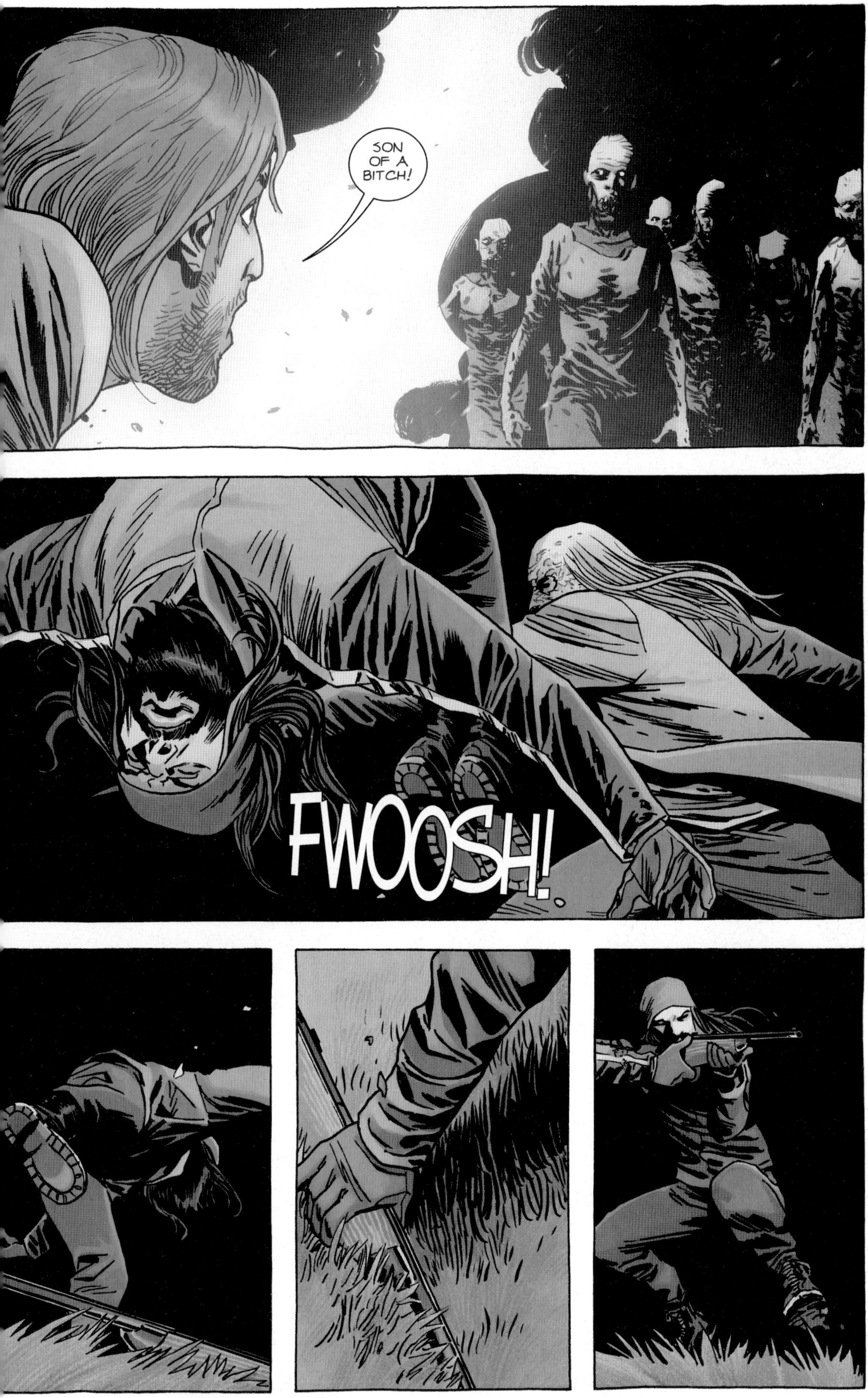
SON OF A BITCH!
FWOOSH!

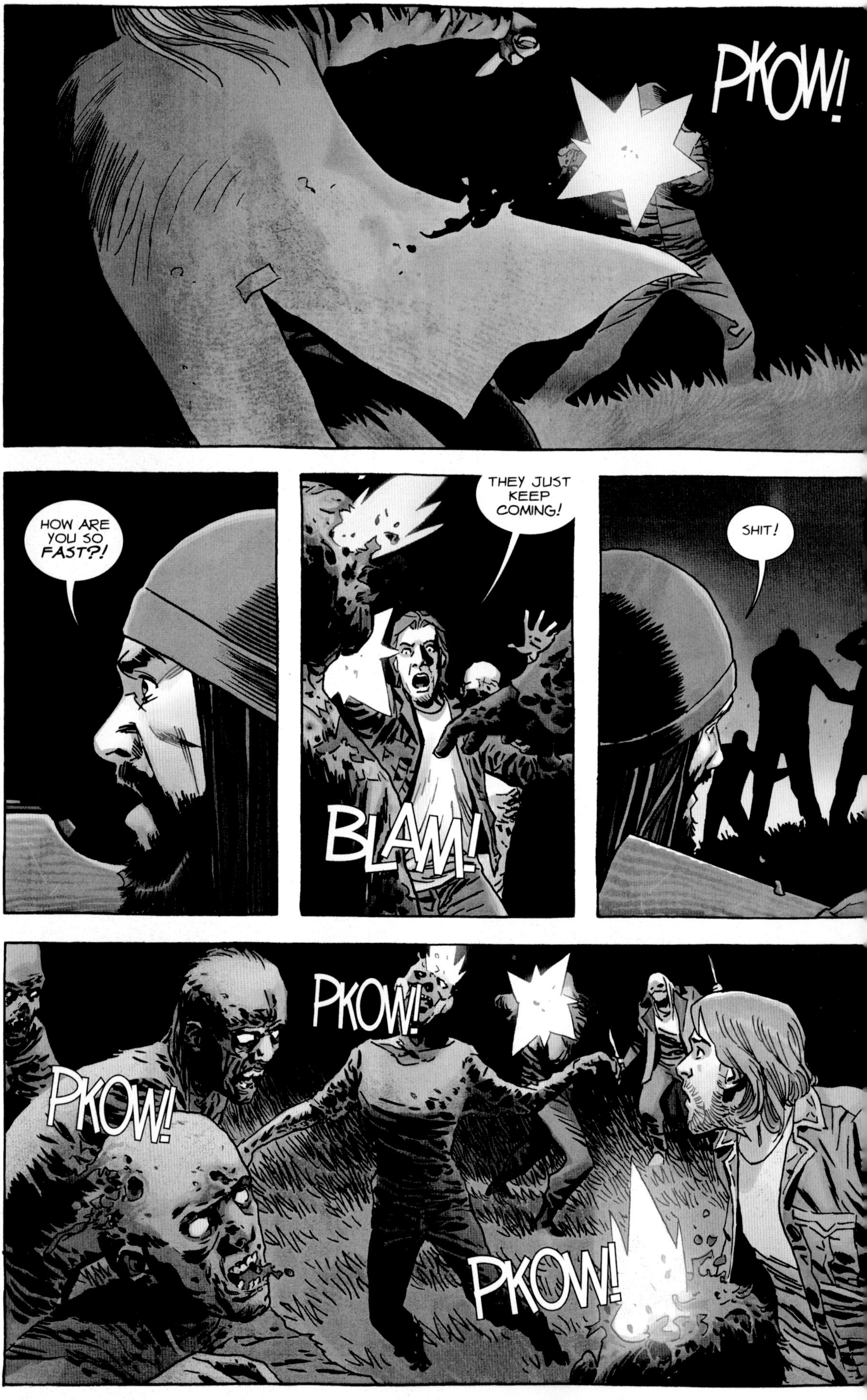
PKOW!
HOW ARE YOU SO FAST?!
THEY JUST KEEP COMING!
BLAM!
SHIT!
PKOW!
PKOW!
PKOW!

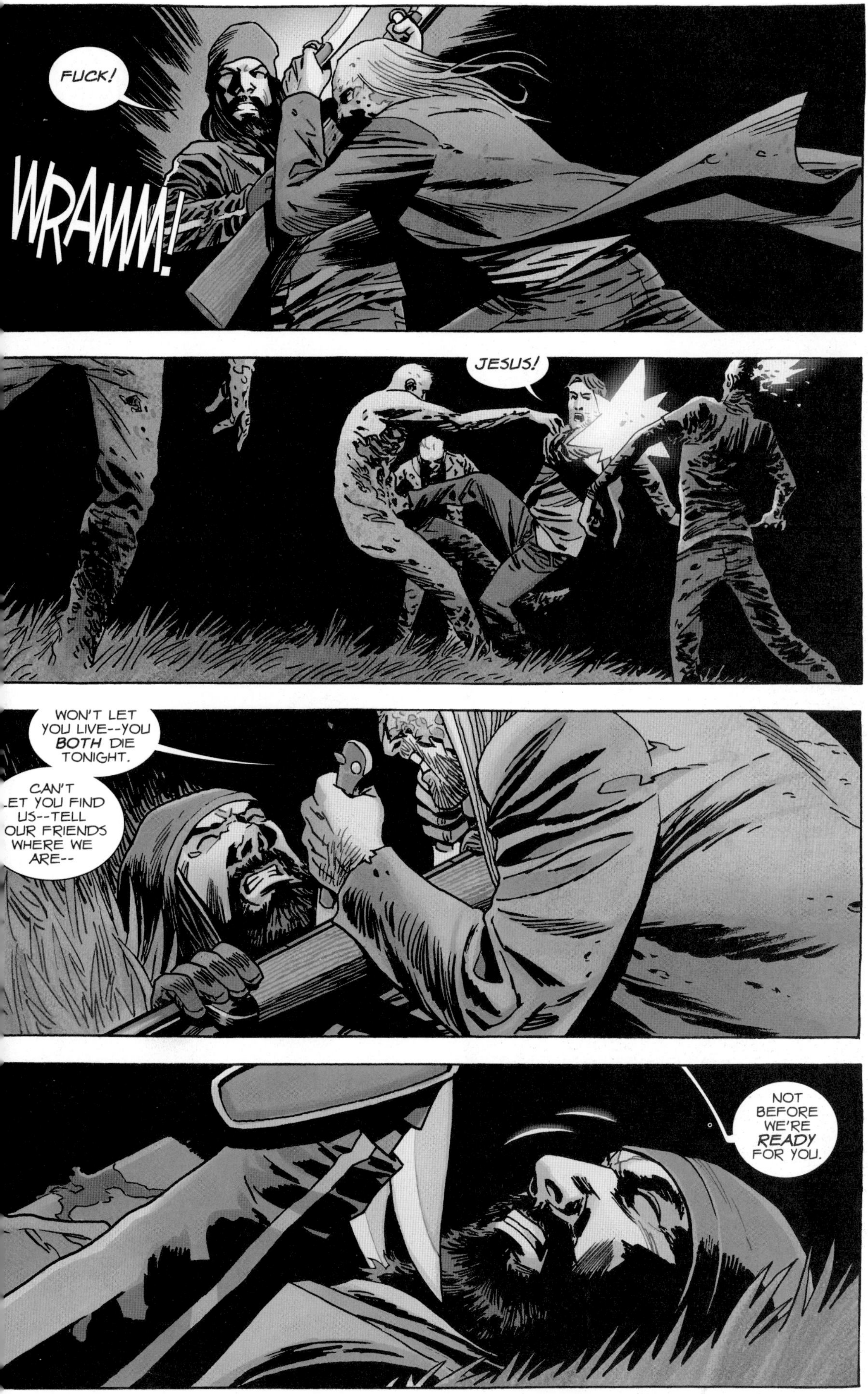
FUCK!
WRAMM!
JESUS!
WON'T LET YOU LIVE--YOU BOTH DIE TONIGHT.
CAN'T LET YOU FIND US--TELL OUR FRIENDS WHERE WE ARE--
NOT BEFORE WE'RE READY FOR YOU.

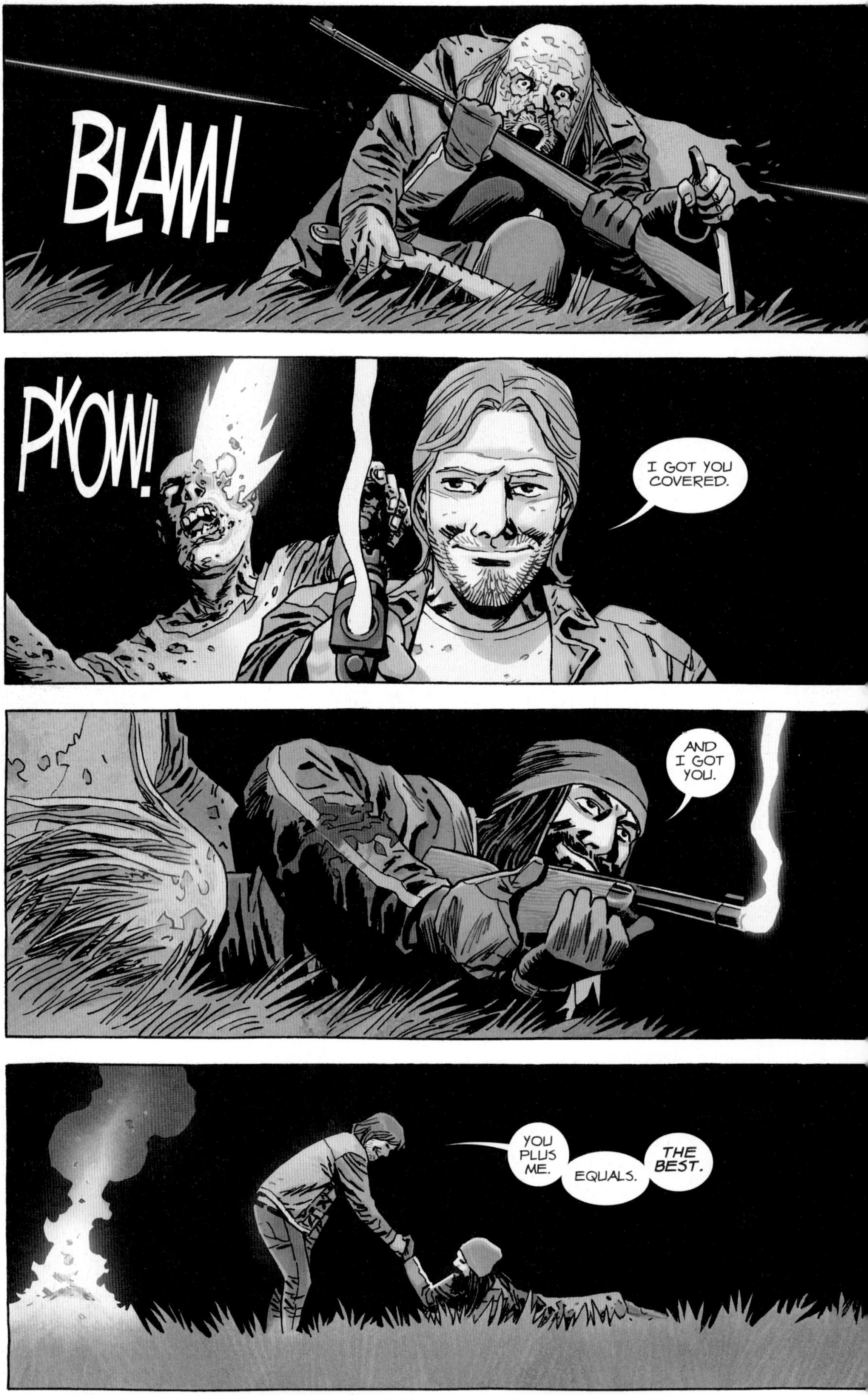
BLAM!
PKOW!
I GOT YOU COVERED.
AND I GOT YOU.
YOU PLUS ME.
EQUALS.
THE BEST.

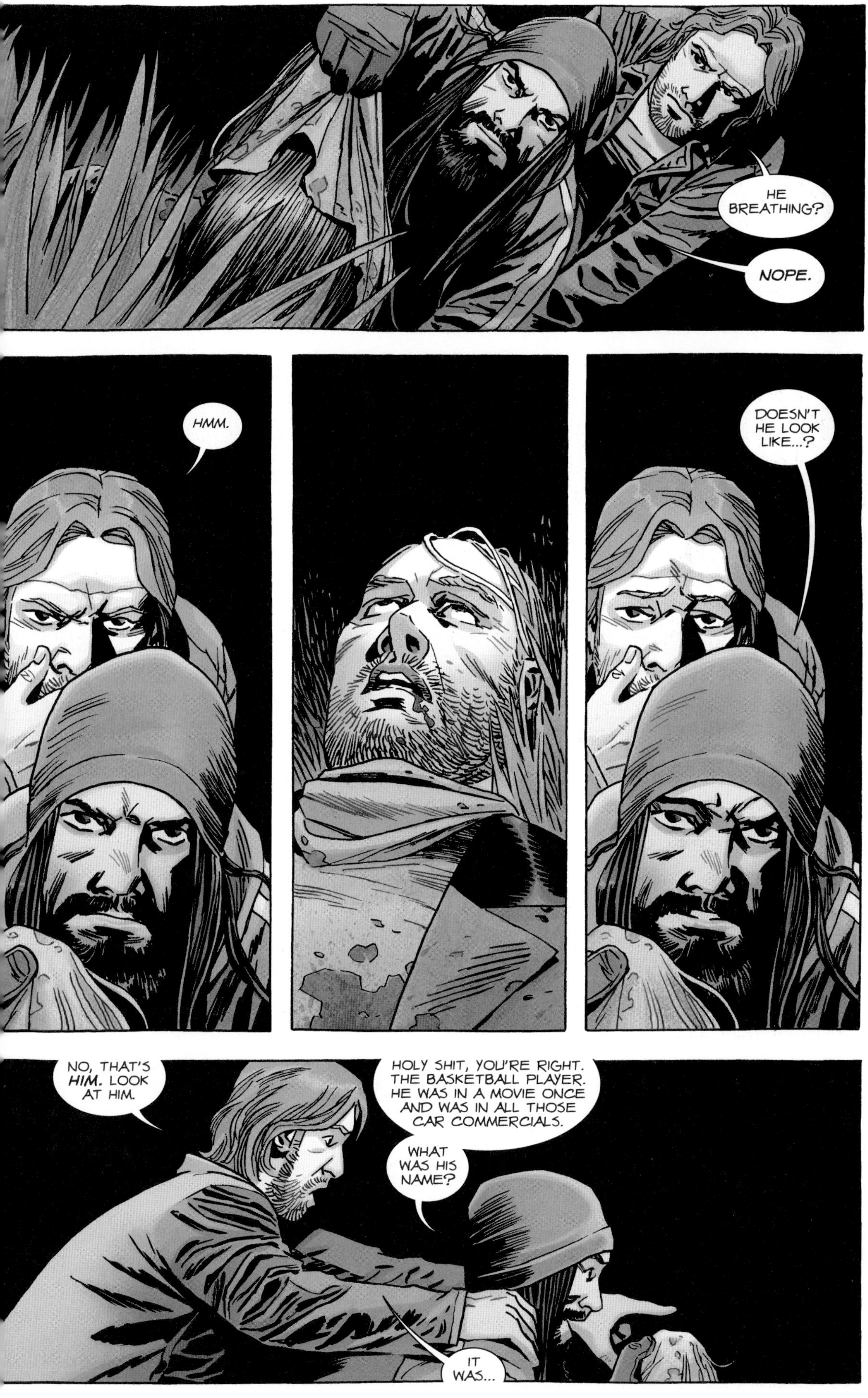
HE BREATHING?
NOPE.
HMM.
DOESN'T HE LOOK LIKE...?
NO, THAT'S HIM. LOOK AT HIM.
HOLY SHIT, YOU'RE RIGHT. THE BASKETBALL PLAYER. HE WAS IN A MOVIE ONCE AND WAS IN ALL THOSE CAR COMMERCIALS.
WHAT WAS HIS NAME?
IT WAS...

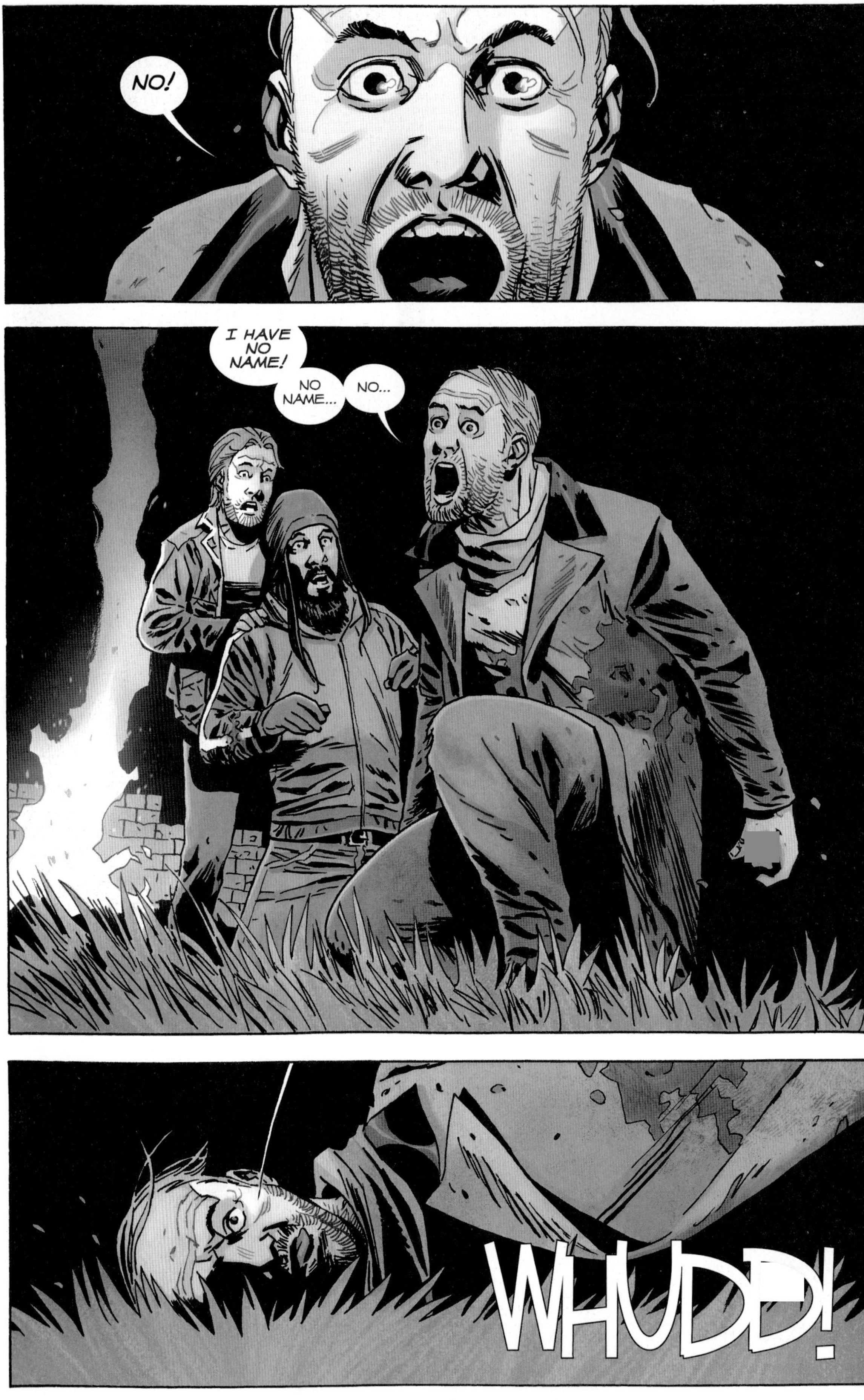
NO!
I HAVE NO NAME!
NO NAME...
NO...
WHUDD!

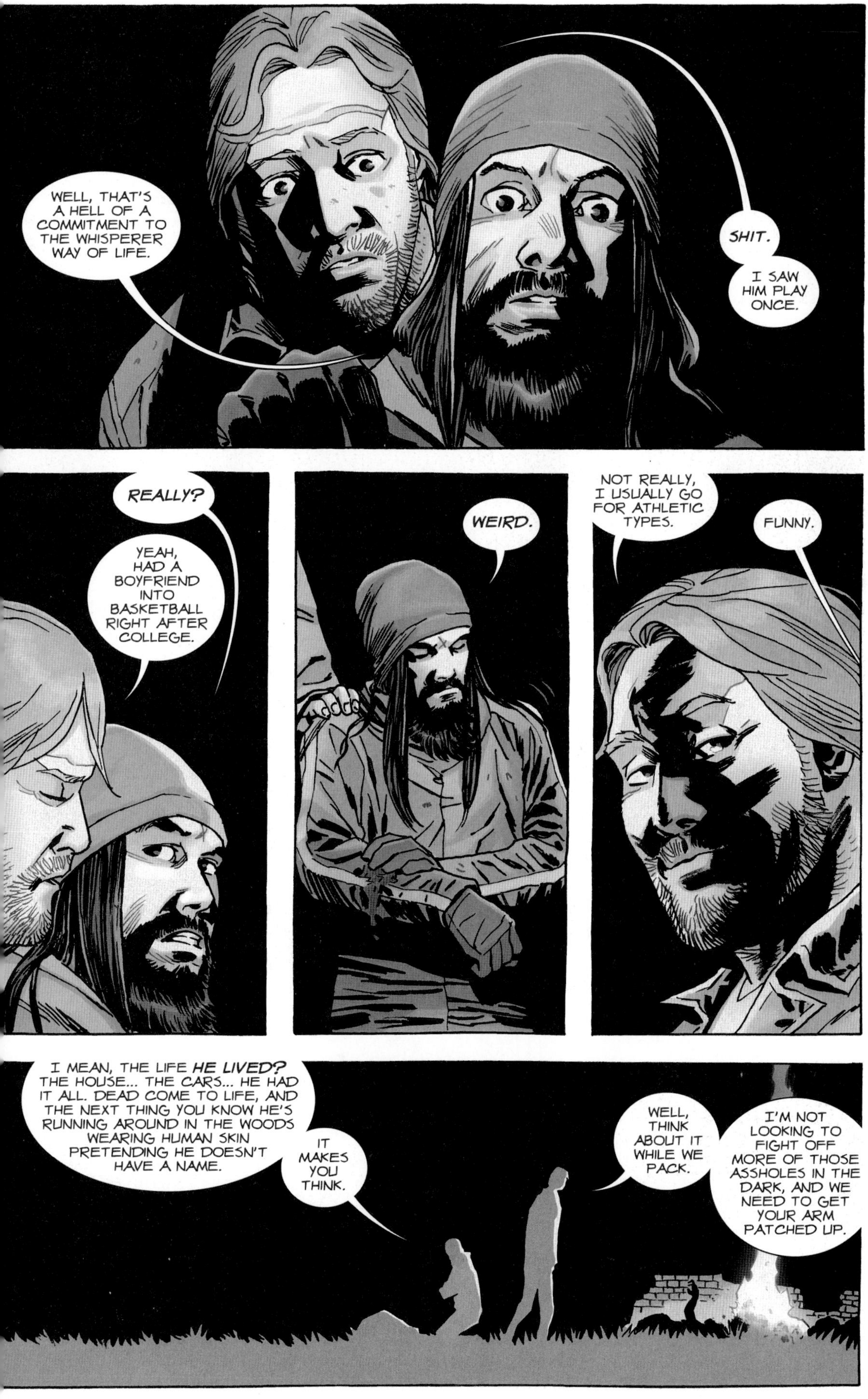
WELL, THAT'S A HELL OF A COMMITMENT TO THE WHISPERER WAY OF LIFE.
SHIT.
I SAW HIM PLAY ONCE.
REALLY?
YEAH, HAD A BOYFRIEND INTO BASKETBALL RIGHT AFTER COLLEGE.
WEIRD.
NOT REALLY, I USUALLY GO FOR ATHLETIC TYPES.
FUNNY.
I MEAN, THE LIFE HE LIVED? THE HOUSE... THE CARS... HE HAD IT ALL. DEAD COME TO LIFE, AND THE NEXT THING YOU KNOW HE'S RUNNING AROUND IN THE WOODS WEARING HUMAN SKIN PRETENDING HE DOESN'T HAVE A NAME.
IT MAKES YOU THINK.
WELL, THINK ABOUT IT WHILE WE PACK.
I'M NOT LOOKING TO FIGHT OFF MORE OF THOSE ASSHOLES IN THE DARK, AND WE NEED TO GET YOUR ARM PATCHED UP.

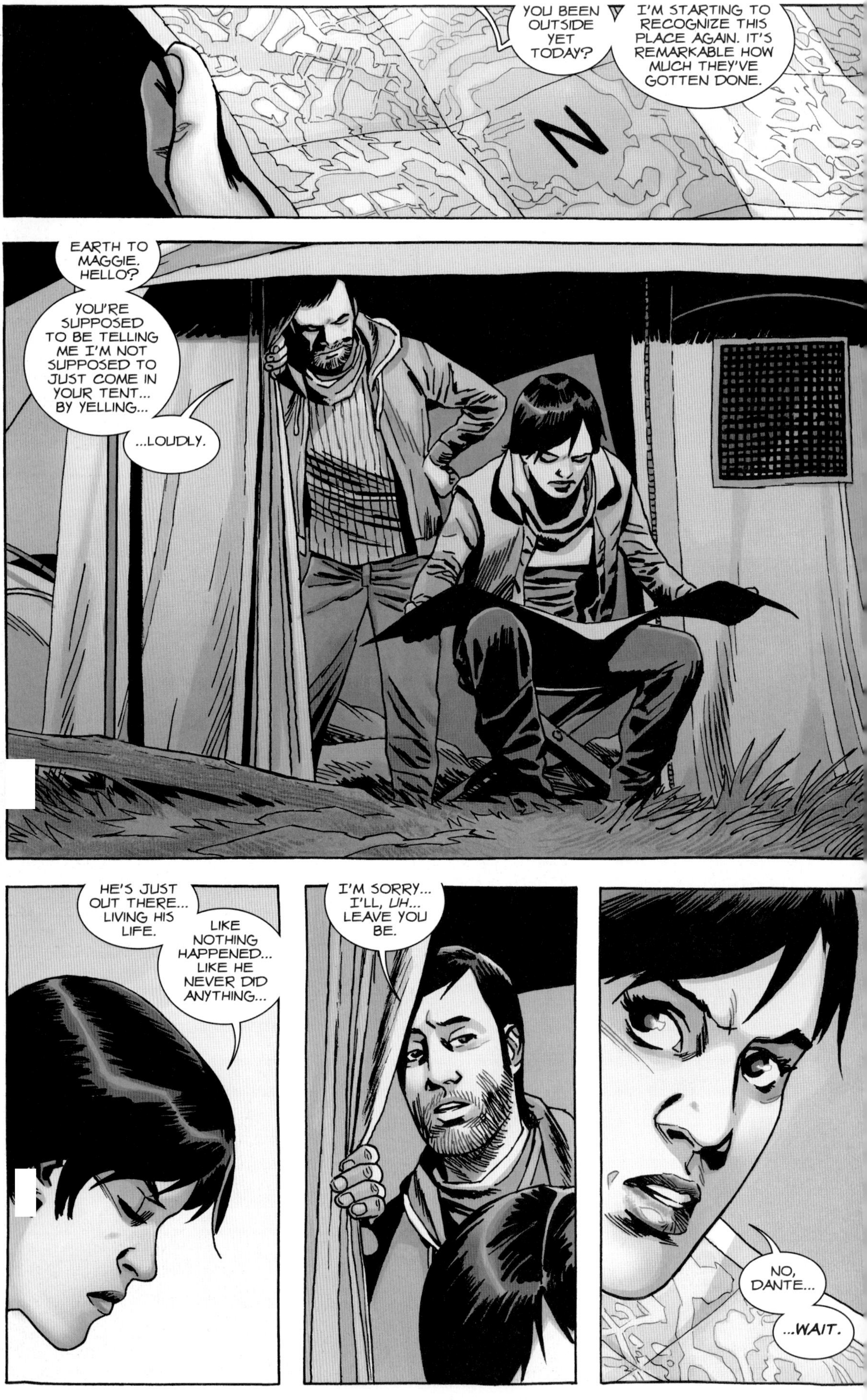
YOU BEEN OUTSIDE YET TODAY?
I'M STARTING TO RECOGNIZE THIS PLACE AGAIN. IT'S REMARKABLE HOW MUCH THEY'VE GOTTEN DONE.
EARTH TO MAGGIE. HELLO?
YOU'RE SUPPOSED TO BE TELLING ME I'M NOT SUPPOSED TO JUST COME IN YOUR TENT... BY YELLING...
...LOUDLY.
HE'S JUST OUT THERE... LIVING HIS LIFE.
LIKE NOTHING HAPPENED... LIKE HE NEVER DID ANYTHING...
I'M SORRY... I'LL, *UH*... LEAVE YOU BE.
NO, DANTE...
...*WAIT*.

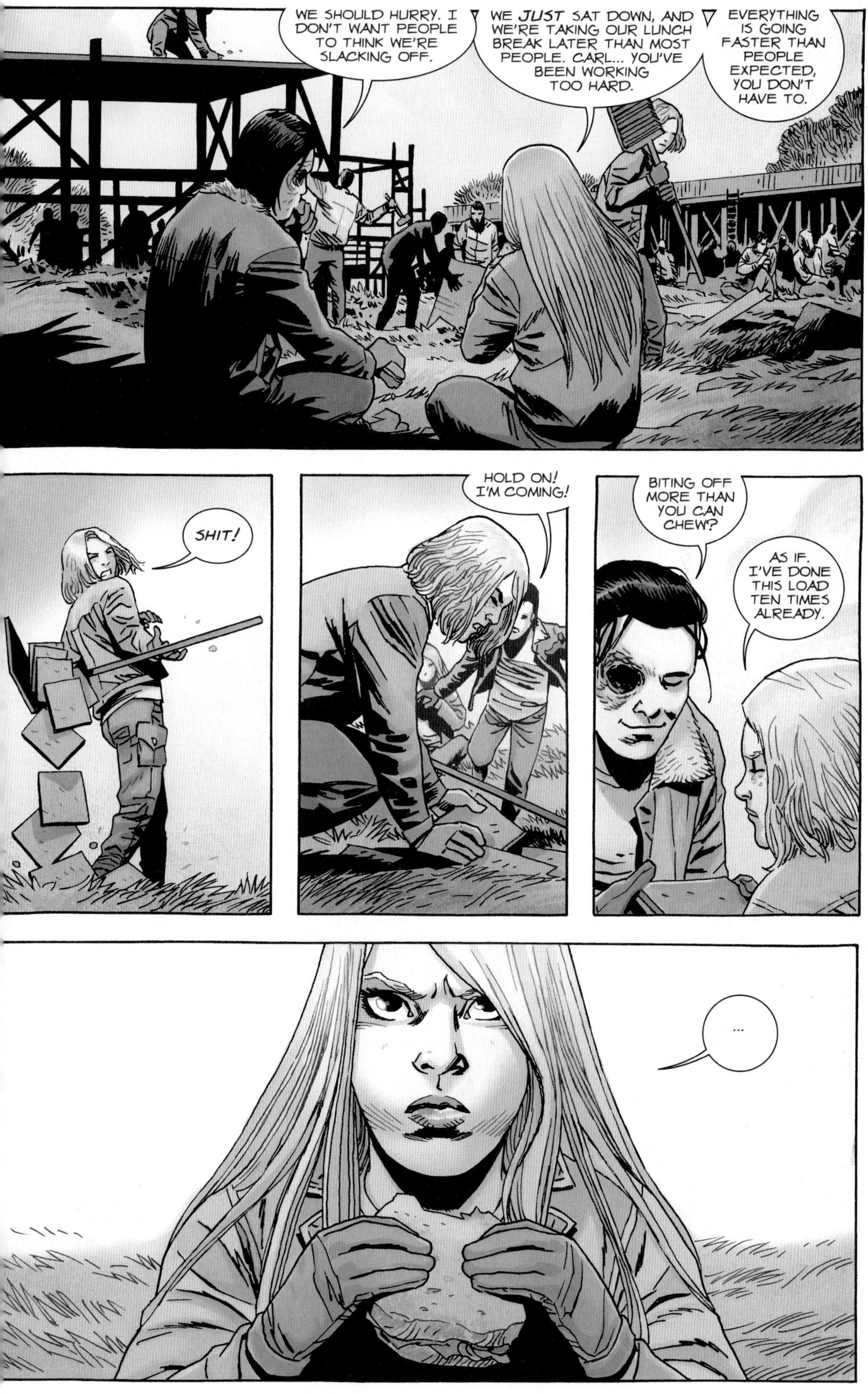
WE SHOULD HURRY. I DON'T WANT PEOPLE TO THINK WE'RE SLACKING OFF.
WE JUST SAT DOWN, AND WE'RE TAKING OUR LUNCH BREAK LATER THAN MOST PEOPLE. CARL... YOU'VE BEEN WORKING TOO HARD.
EVERYTHING IS GOING FASTER THAN PEOPLE EXPECTED, YOU DON'T HAVE TO.
SHIT!
HOLD ON! I'M COMING!
BITING OFF MORE THAN YOU CAN CHEW?
AS IF. I'VE DONE THIS LOAD TEN TIMES ALREADY.
...

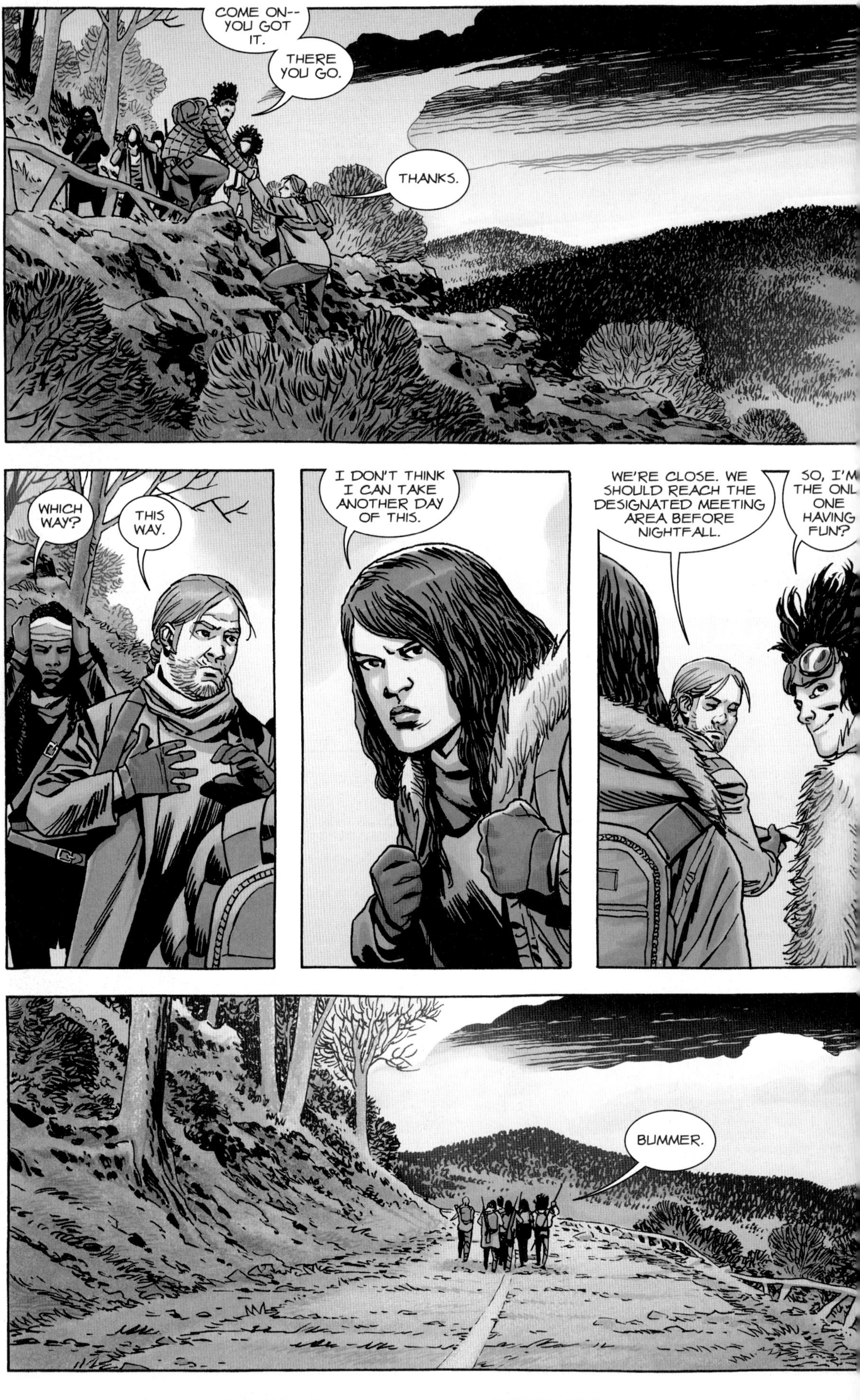
COME ON-- YOU GOT IT.
THERE YOU GO.
THANKS.
WHICH WAY?
THIS WAY.
I DON'T THINK I CAN TAKE ANOTHER DAY OF THIS.
WE'RE CLOSE. WE SHOULD REACH THE DESIGNATED MEETING AREA BEFORE NIGHTFALL.
SO, I'M THE ONL ONE HAVING FUN?
BUMMER.

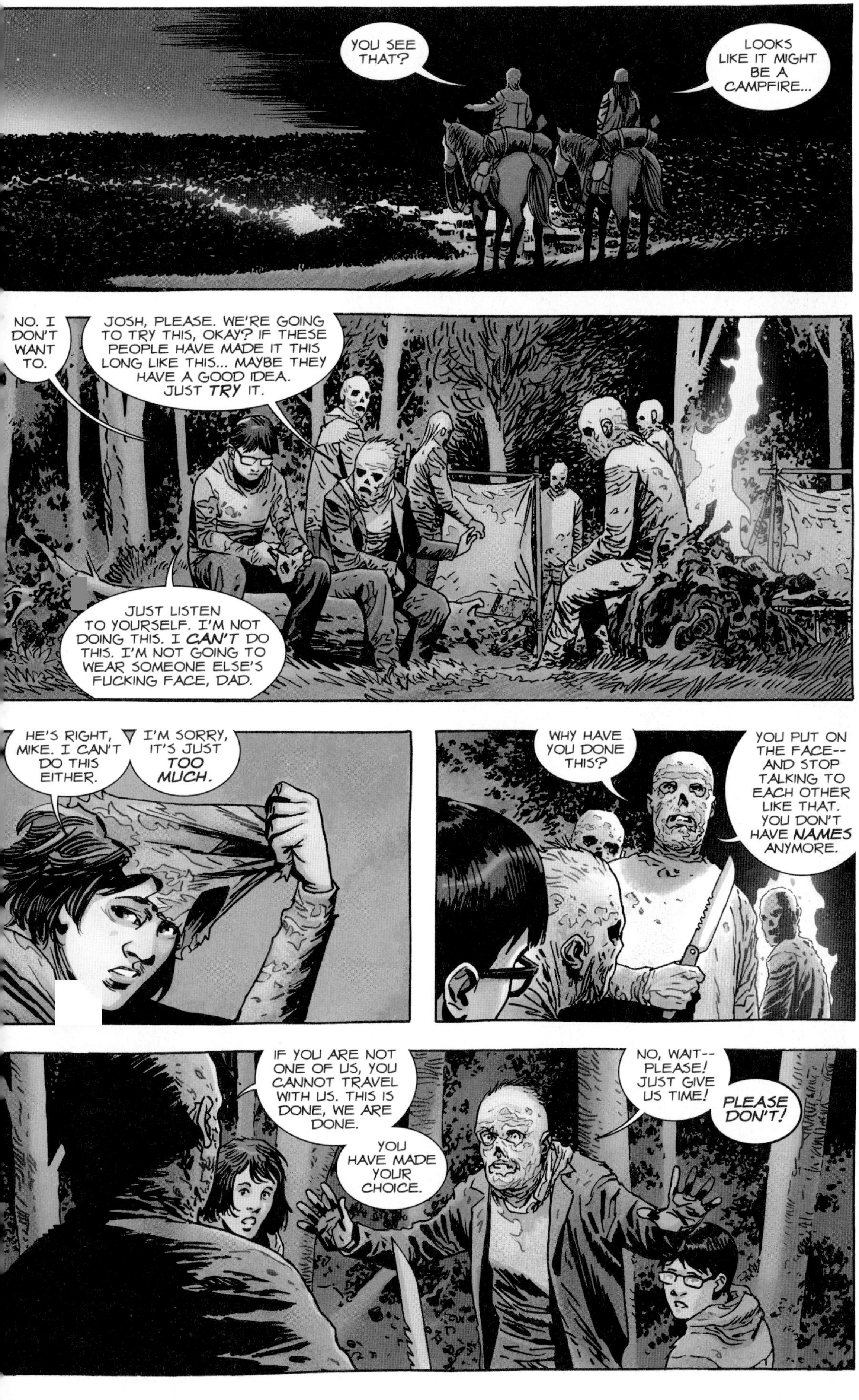
YOU SEE THAT?
LOOKS LIKE IT MIGHT BE A CAMPFIRE...
NO. I DON'T WANT TO.
JOSH, PLEASE. WE'RE GOING TO TRY THIS, OKAY? IF THESE PEOPLE HAVE MADE IT THIS LONG LIKE THIS... MAYBE THEY HAVE A GOOD IDEA. JUST TRY IT.
JUST LISTEN TO YOURSELF. I'M NOT DOING THIS. I CAN'T DO THIS. I'M NOT GOING TO WEAR SOMEONE ELSE'S FUCKING FACE, DAD.
HE'S RIGHT, MIKE. I CAN'T DO THIS EITHER.
I'M SORRY, IT'S JUST TOO MUCH.
WHY HAVE YOU DONE THIS?
YOU PUT ON THE FACE-- AND STOP TALKING TO EACH OTHER LIKE THAT. YOU DON'T HAVE NAMES ANYMORE.
IF YOU ARE NOT ONE OF US, YOU CANNOT TRAVEL WITH US. THIS IS DONE, WE ARE DONE.
YOU HAVE MADE YOUR CHOICE.
NO, WAIT-- PLEASE! JUST GIVE US TIME!
PLEASE DON'T!

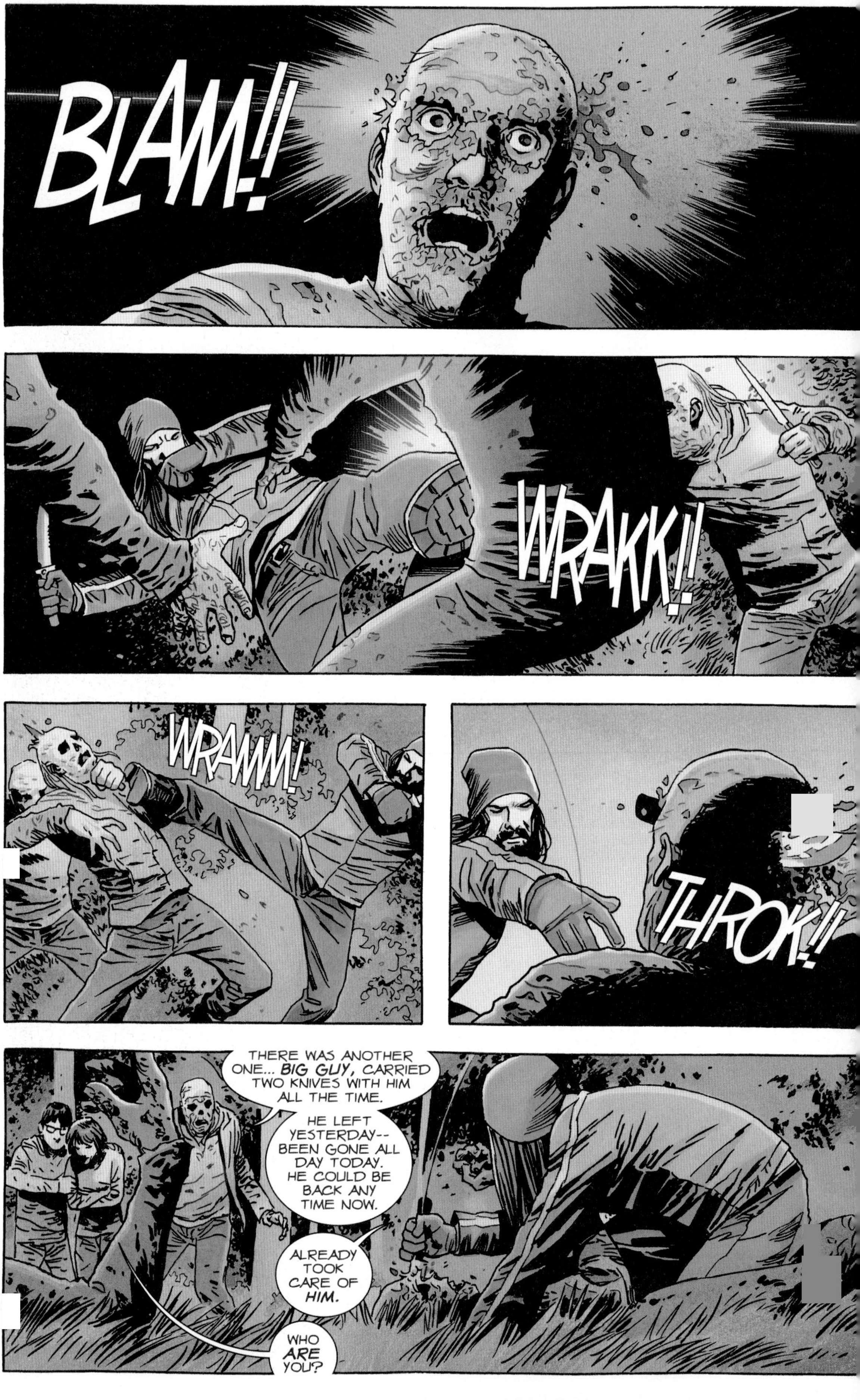
BLAM!!
WRAKK!!
WRAMM!
THROK!!
THERE WAS ANOTHER ONE... BIG GUY, CARRIED TWO KNIVES WITH HIM ALL THE TIME.
HE LEFT YESTERDAY-- BEEN GONE ALL DAY TODAY. HE COULD BE BACK ANY TIME NOW.
ALREADY TOOK CARE OF HIM.
WHO ARE YOU?

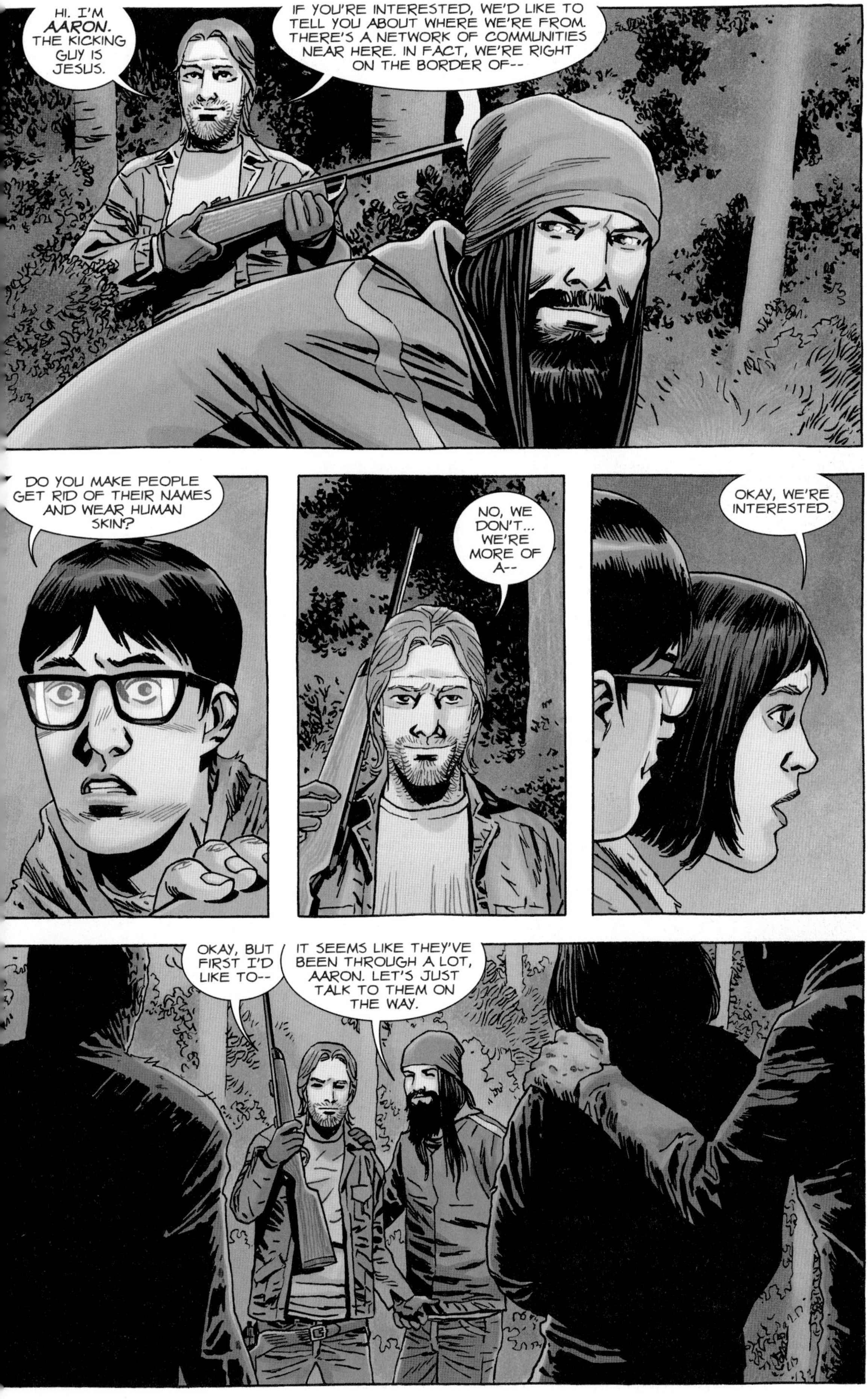
HI. I'M AARON. THE KICKING GUY IS JESUS.
IF YOU'RE INTERESTED, WE'D LIKE TO TELL YOU ABOUT WHERE WE'RE FROM. THERE'S A NETWORK OF COMMUNITIES NEAR HERE. IN FACT, WE'RE RIGHT ON THE BORDER OF--
DO YOU MAKE PEOPLE GET RID OF THEIR NAMES AND WEAR HUMAN SKIN?
NO, WE DON'T... WE'RE MORE OF A--
OKAY, WE'RE INTERESTED.
OKAY, BUT FIRST I'D LIKE TO--
IT SEEMS LIKE THEY'VE BEEN THROUGH A LOT, AARON. LET'S JUST TALK TO THEM ON THE WAY.

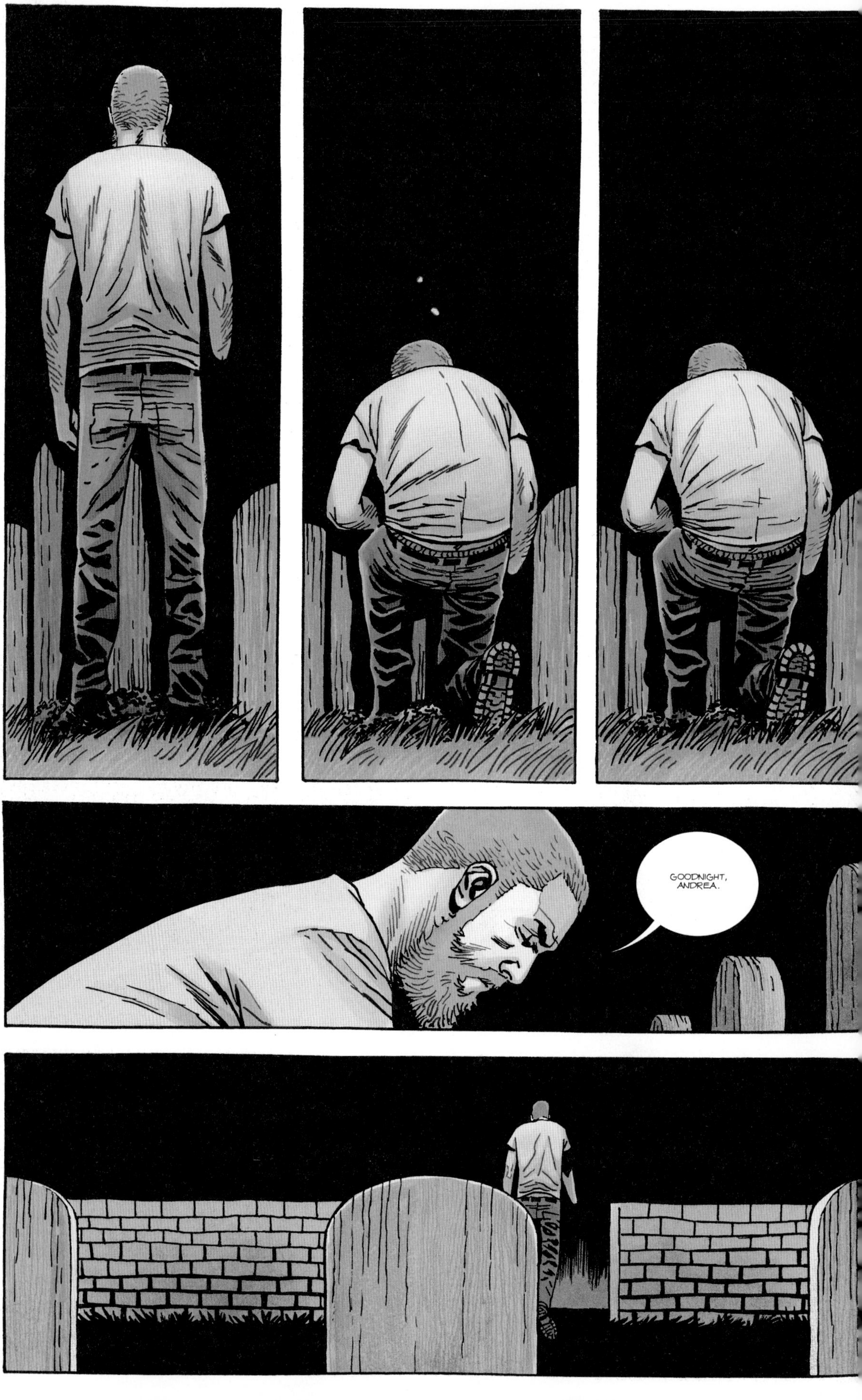
GOODNIGHT, ANDREA.

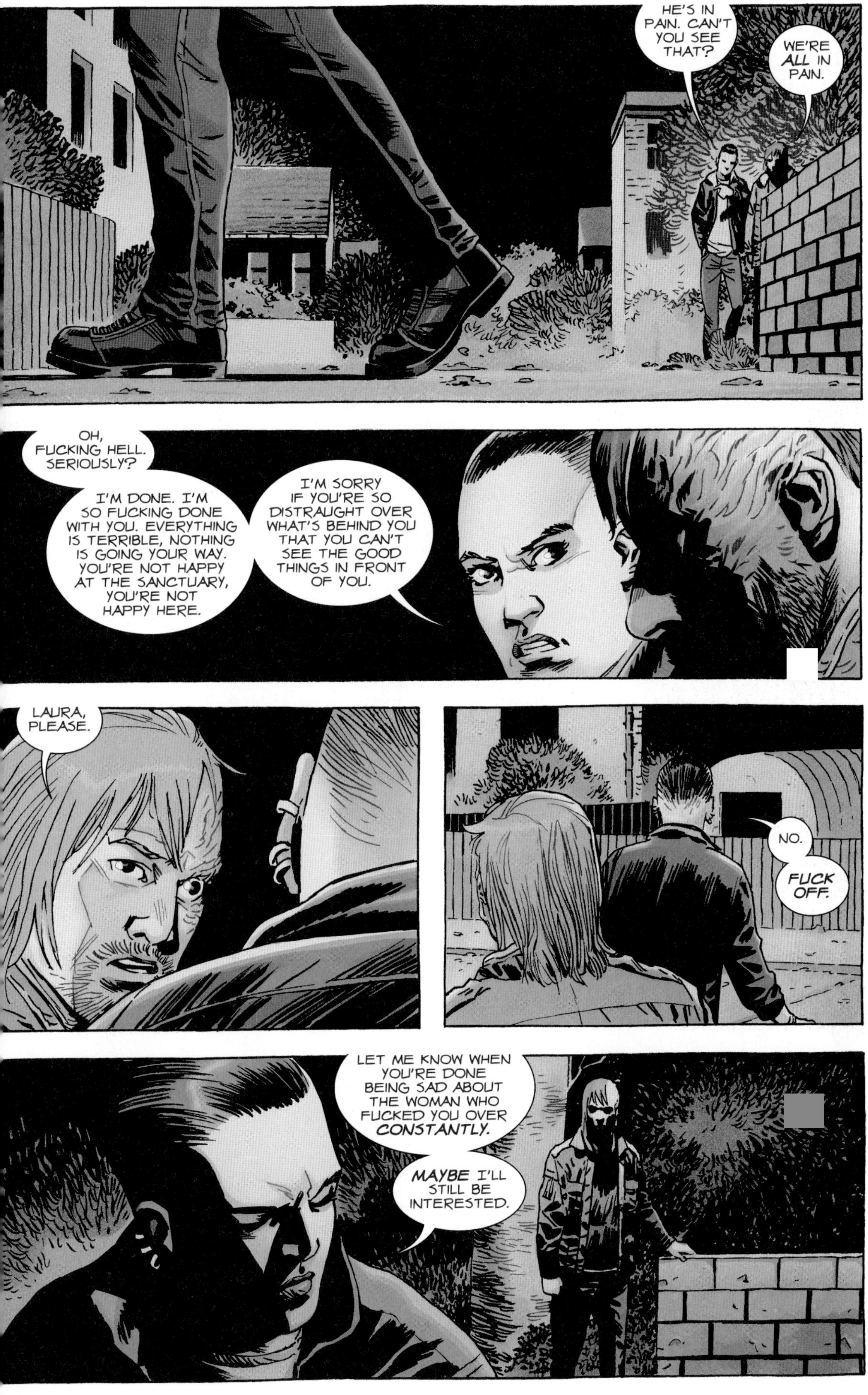
HE'S IN PAIN. CAN'T YOU SEE THAT?
WE'RE ALL IN PAIN.
OH, FUCKING HELL. SERIOUSLY?
I'M DONE. I'M SO FUCKING DONE WITH YOU. EVERYTHING IS TERRIBLE, NOTHING IS GOING YOUR WAY. YOU'RE NOT HAPPY AT THE SANCTUARY, YOU'RE NOT HAPPY HERE.
I'M SORRY IF YOU'RE SO DISTRAUGHT OVER WHAT'S BEHIND YOU THAT YOU CAN'T SEE THE GOOD THINGS IN FRONT OF YOU.
LAURA, PLEASE.
NO.
FUCK OFF.
LET ME KNOW WHEN YOU'RE DONE BEING SAD ABOUT THE WOMAN WHO FUCKED YOU OVER CONSTANTLY.
MAYBE I'LL STILL BE INTERESTED.

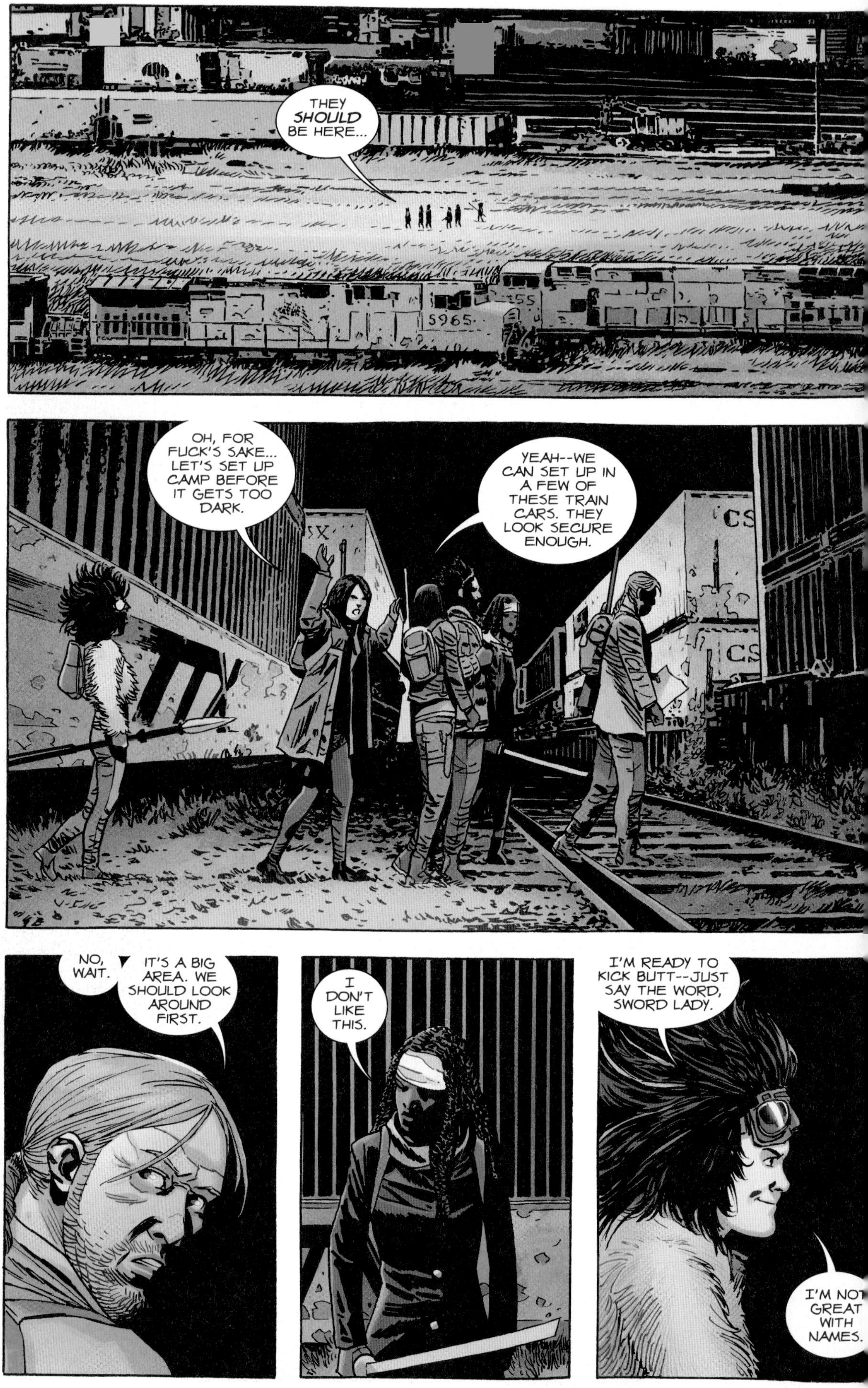
THEY SHOULD BE HERE...
OH, FOR FUCK'S SAKE... LET'S SET UP CAMP BEFORE IT GETS TOO DARK.
YEAH--WE CAN SET UP IN A FEW OF THESE TRAIN CARS. THEY LOOK SECURE ENOUGH.
NO, WAIT.
IT'S A BIG AREA. WE SHOULD LOOK AROUND FIRST.
I DON'T LIKE THIS.
I'M READY TO KICK BUTT--JUST SAY THE WORD, SWORD LADY.
I'M NOT GREAT WITH NAMES.

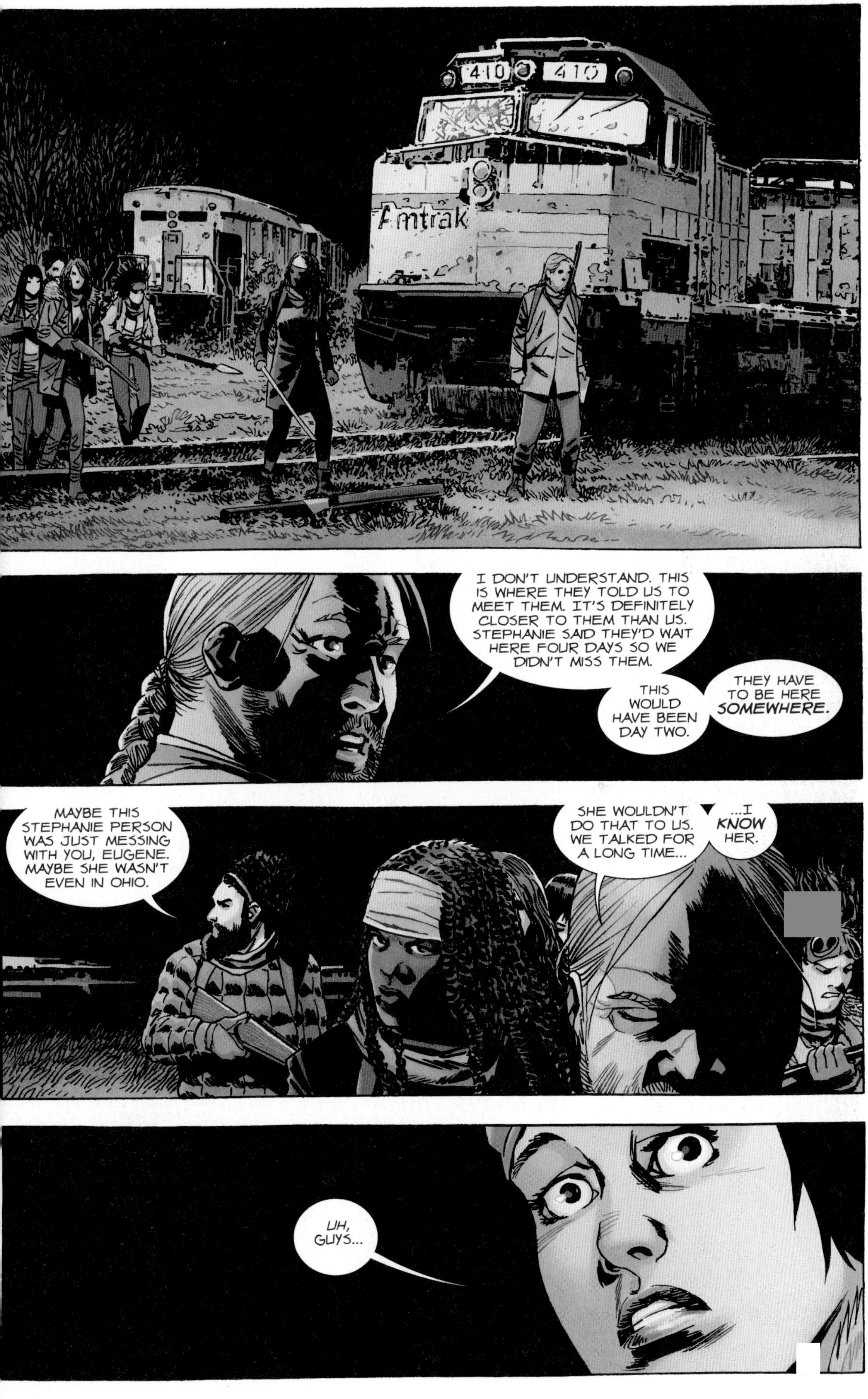
410
410
Amtrak
I DON'T UNDERSTAND. THIS IS WHERE THEY TOLD US TO MEET THEM. IT'S DEFINITELY CLOSER TO THEM THAN US. STEPHANIE SAID THEY'D WAIT HERE FOUR DAYS SO WE DIDN'T MISS THEM.
THIS WOULD HAVE BEEN DAY TWO.
THEY HAVE TO BE HERE *SOMEWHERE.*
MAYBE THIS STEPHANIE PERSON WAS JUST MESSING WITH YOU, EUGENE. MAYBE SHE WASN'T EVEN IN OHIO.
SHE WOULDN'T DO THAT TO US. WE TALKED FOR A LONG TIME...
...I *KNOW* HER.
UH, GUYS...

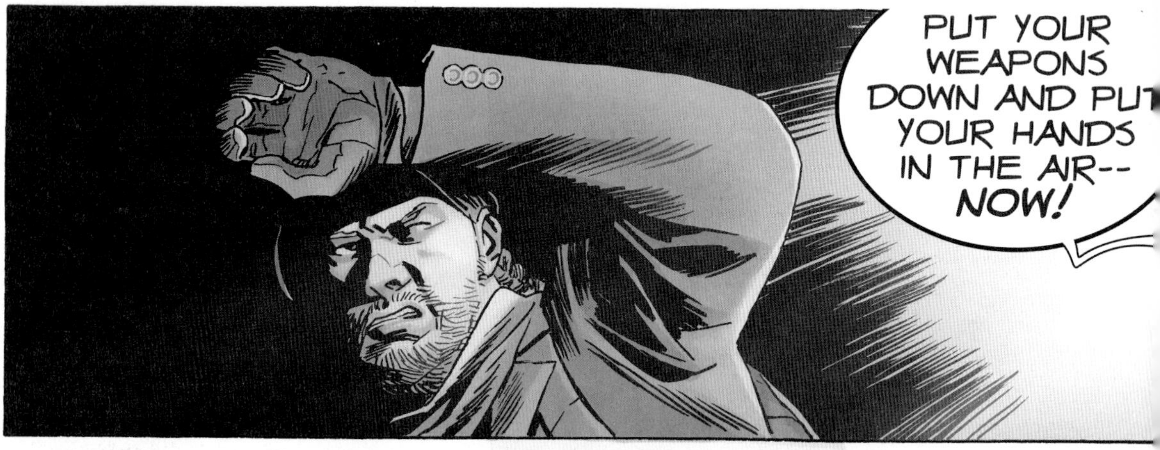
PUT YOUR WEAPONS DOWN AND PUT YOUR HANDS IN THE AIR-- NOW!

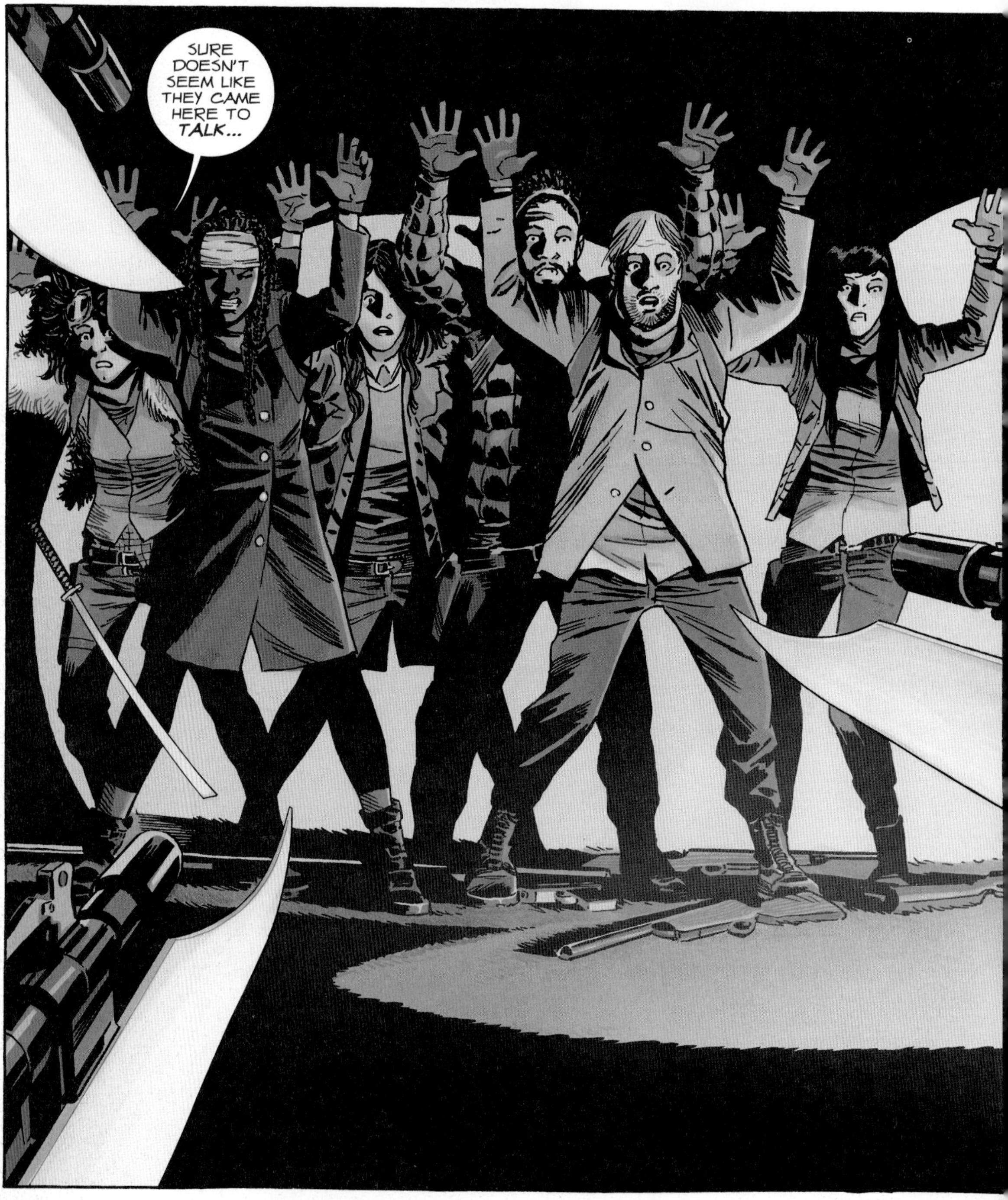
SURE DOESN'T SEEM LIKE THEY CAME HERE TO TALK...

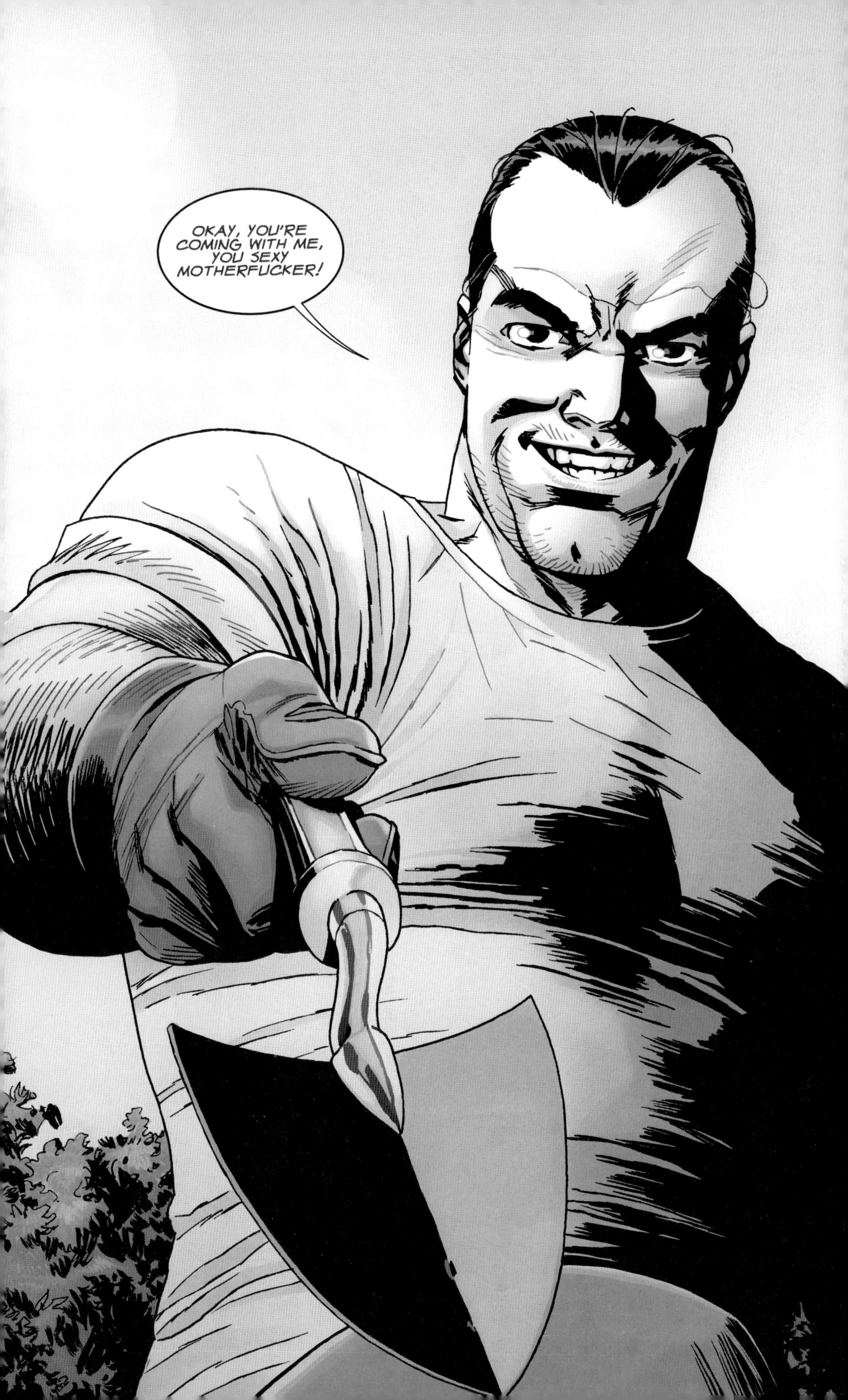
OKAY, YOU'RE COMING WITH ME, YOU SEXY MOTHERFUCKER!

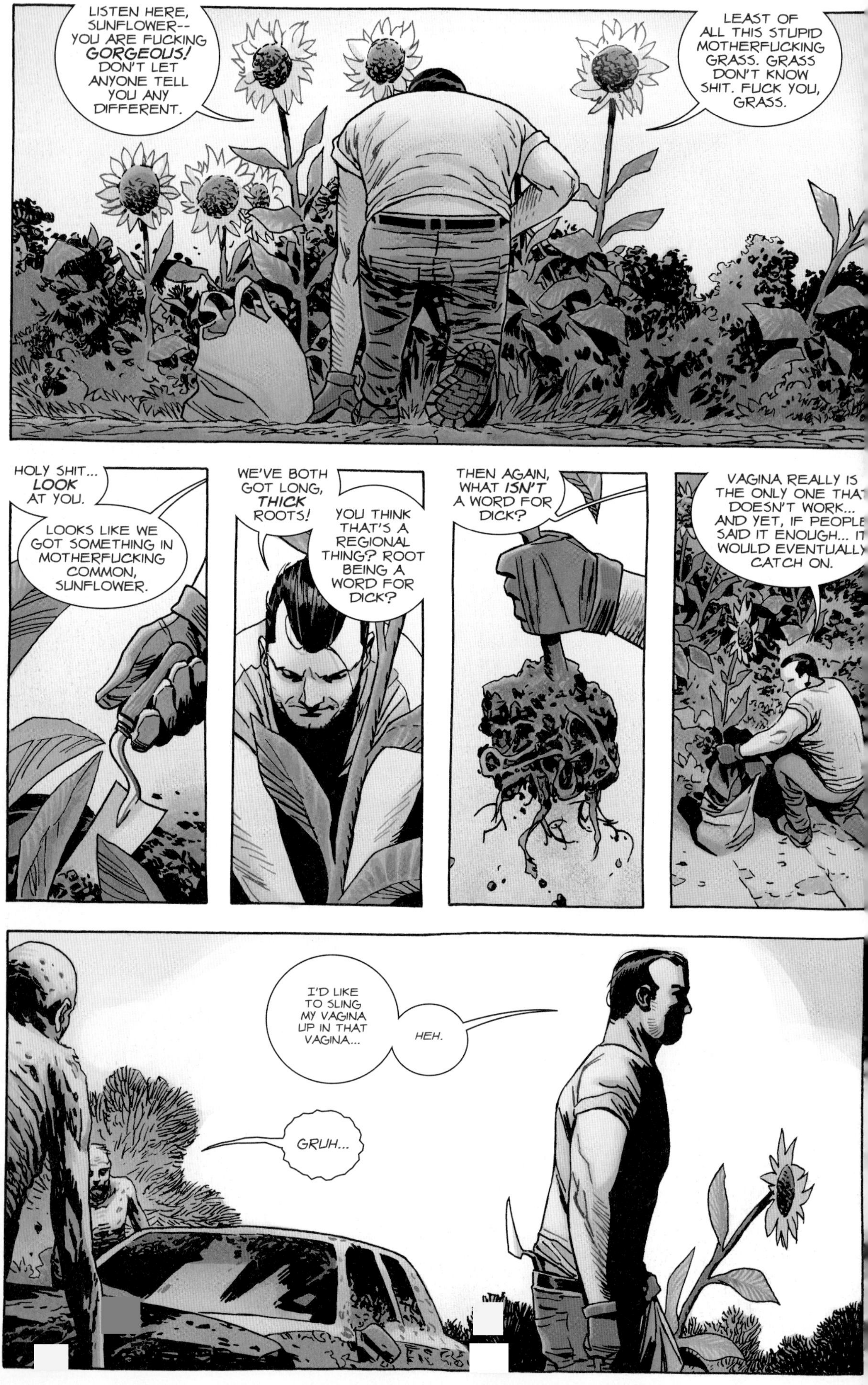
LISTEN HERE, SUNFLOWER-- YOU ARE FUCKING GORGEOUS! DON'T LET ANYONE TELL YOU ANY DIFFERENT.
LEAST OF ALL THIS STUPID MOTHERFUCKING GRASS. GRASS DON'T KNOW SHIT. FUCK YOU, GRASS.
HOLY SHIT... LOOK AT YOU.
LOOKS LIKE WE GOT SOMETHING IN MOTHERFUCKING COMMON, SUNFLOWER.
WE'VE BOTH GOT LONG, THICK ROOTS!
YOU THINK THAT'S A REGIONAL THING? ROOT BEING A WORD FOR DICK?
THEN AGAIN, WHAT ISN'T A WORD FOR DICK?
VAGINA REALLY IS THE ONLY ONE THAT DOESN'T WORK... AND YET, IF PEOPLE SAID IT ENOUGH... IT WOULD EVENTUALLY CATCH ON.
I'D LIKE TO SLING MY VAGINA UP IN THAT VAGINA...
HEH.
GRUH...

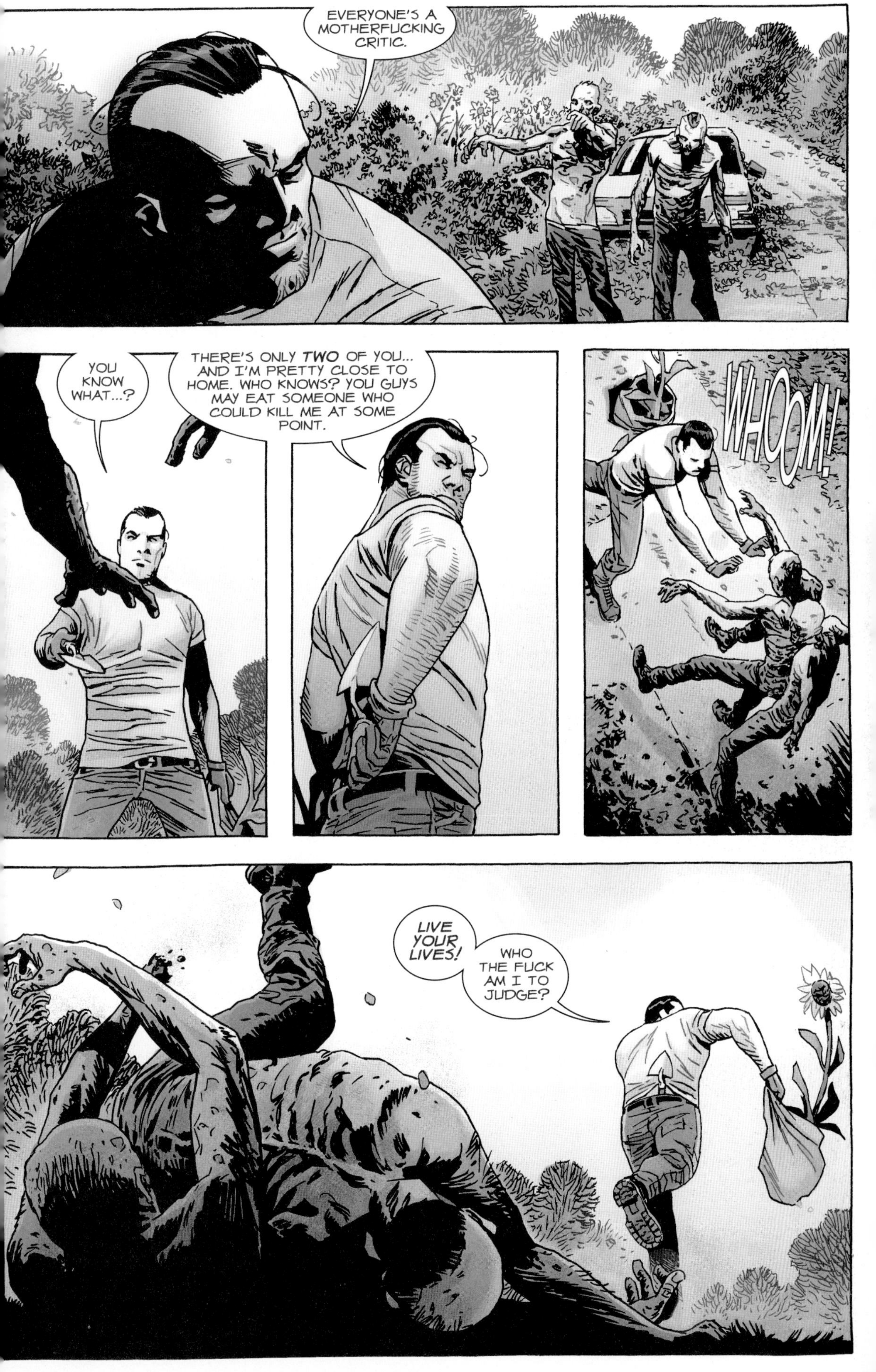
EVERYONE'S A MOTHERFUCKING CRITIC.
YOU KNOW WHAT...?
THERE'S ONLY TWO OF YOU... AND I'M PRETTY CLOSE TO HOME. WHO KNOWS? YOU GUYS MAY EAT SOMEONE WHO COULD KILL ME AT SOME POINT.
WHOOM!
LIVE YOUR LIVES!
WHO THE FUCK AM I TO JUDGE?

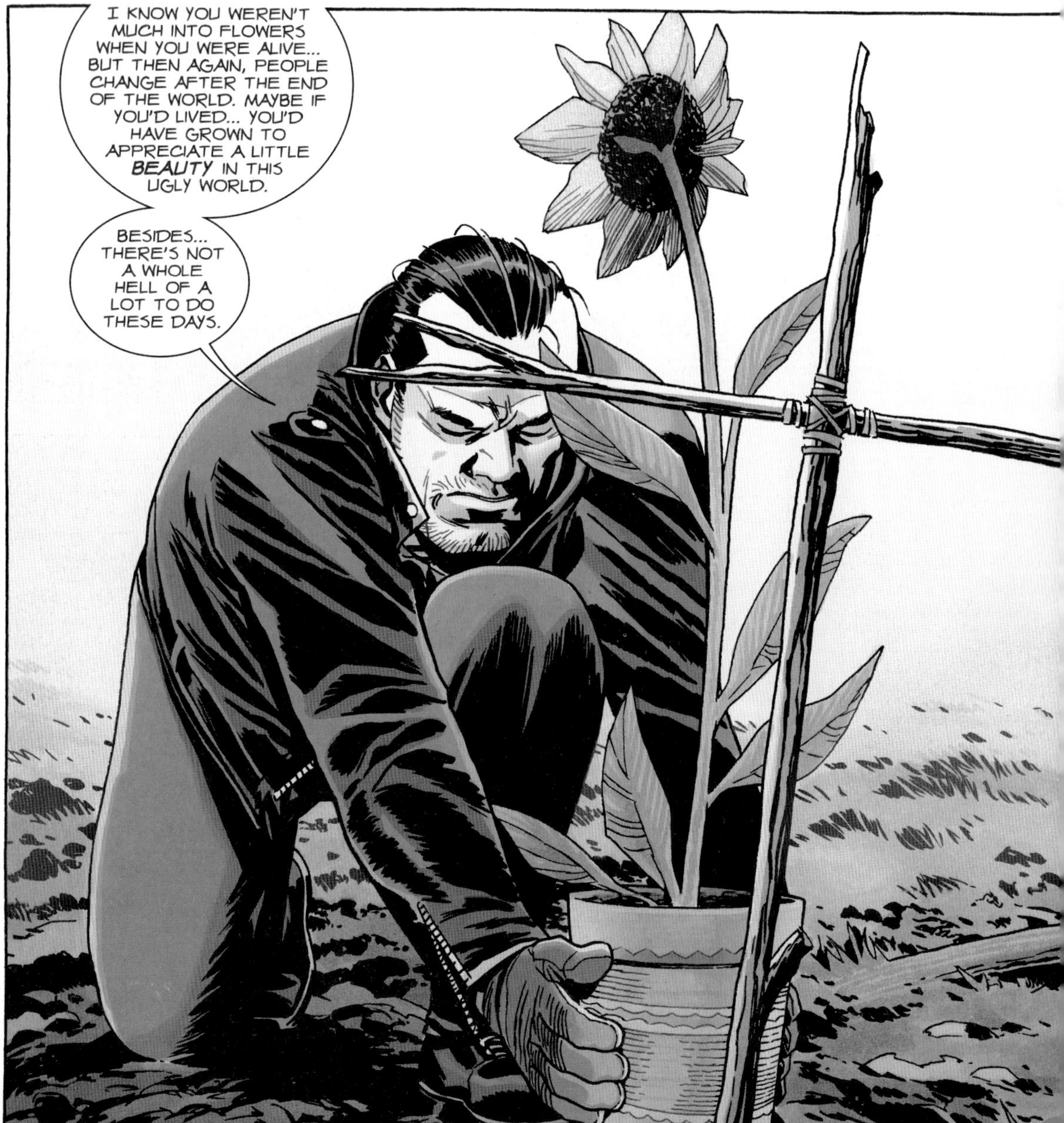
I KNOW YOU WEREN'T MUCH INTO FLOWERS WHEN YOU WERE ALIVE... BUT THEN AGAIN, PEOPLE CHANGE AFTER THE END OF THE WORLD. MAYBE IF YOU'D LIVED... YOU'D HAVE GROWN TO APPRECIATE A LITTLE *BEAUTY* IN THIS UGLY WORLD.
BESIDES... THERE'S NOT A WHOLE HELL OF A LOT TO DO THESE DAYS.

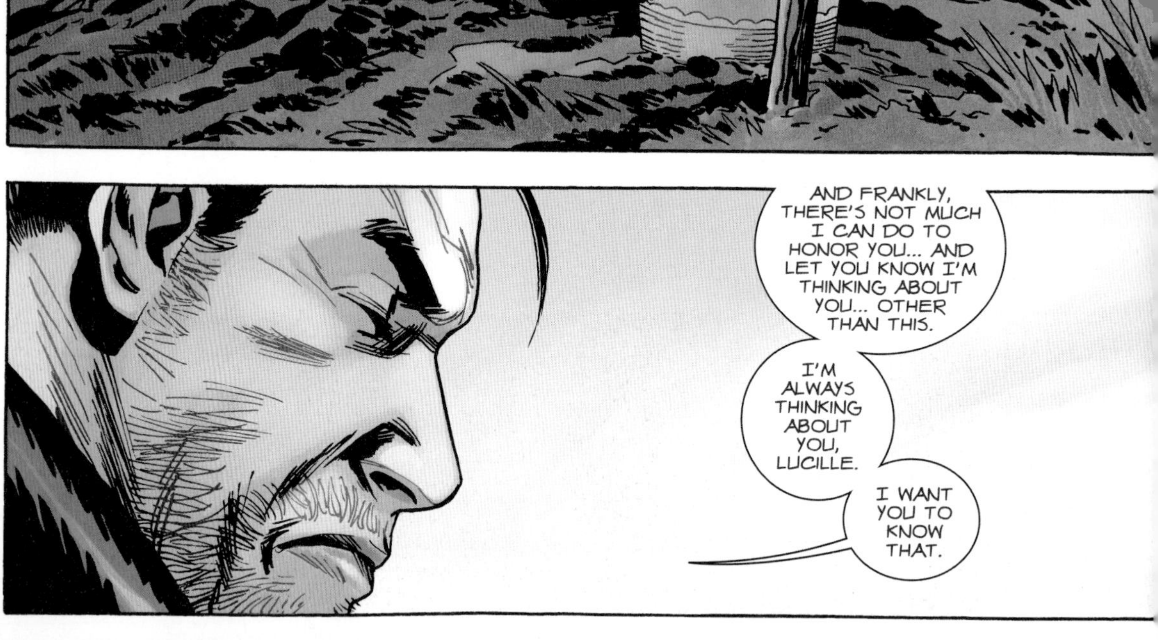
AND FRANKLY, THERE'S NOT MUCH I CAN DO TO HONOR YOU... AND LET YOU KNOW I'M THINKING ABOUT YOU... OTHER THAN THIS.
I'M ALWAYS THINKING ABOUT YOU, LUCILLE.
I WANT YOU TO KNOW THAT.

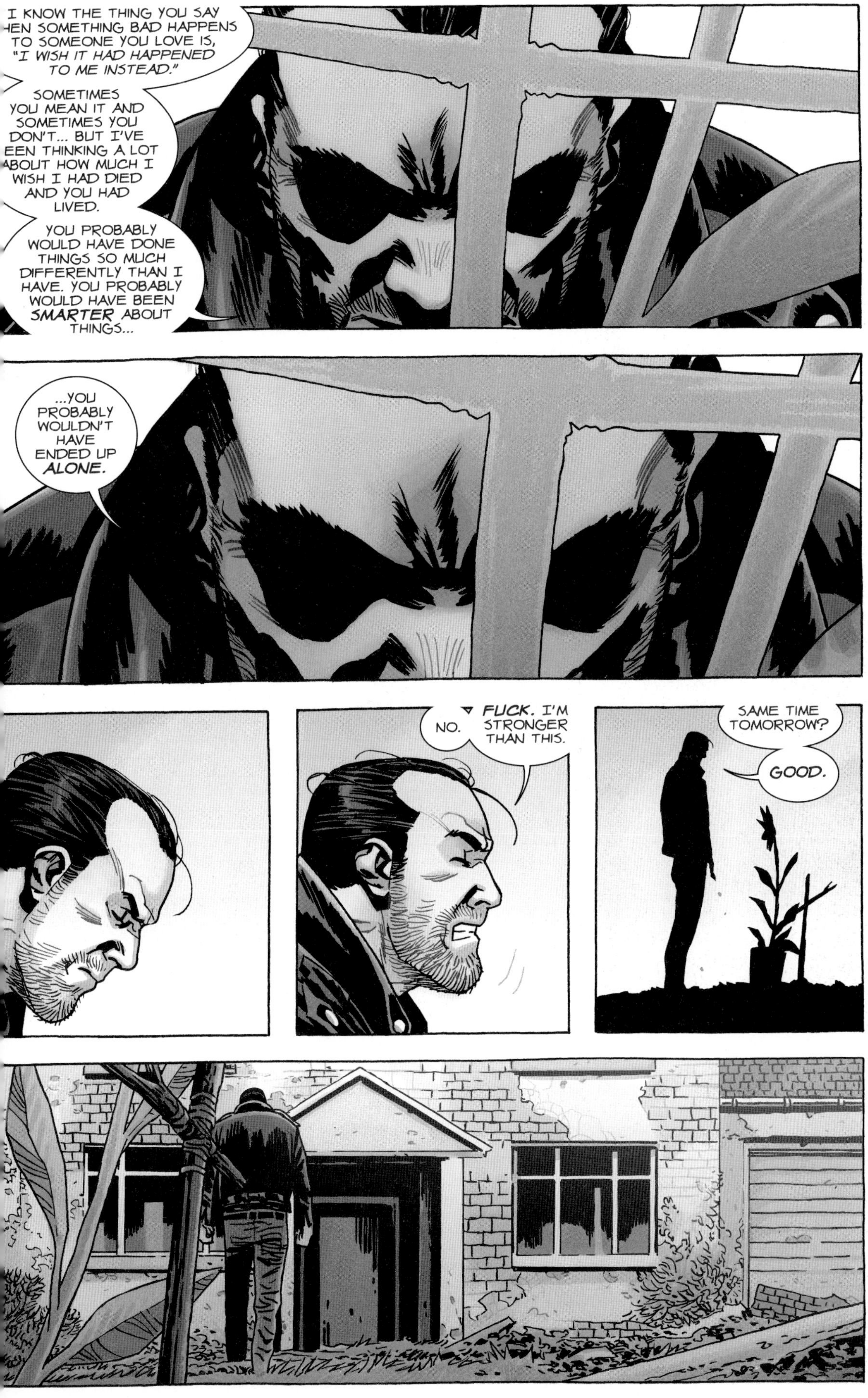
I KNOW THE THING YOU SAY WHEN SOMETHING BAD HAPPENS TO SOMEONE YOU LOVE IS, "I WISH IT HAD HAPPENED TO ME INSTEAD."
SOMETIMES YOU MEAN IT AND SOMETIMES YOU DON'T... BUT I'VE BEEN THINKING A LOT ABOUT HOW MUCH I WISH I HAD DIED AND YOU HAD LIVED.
YOU PROBABLY WOULD HAVE DONE THINGS SO MUCH DIFFERENTLY THAN I HAVE. YOU PROBABLY WOULD HAVE BEEN SMARTER ABOUT THINGS...
...YOU PROBABLY WOULDN'T HAVE ENDED UP ALONE.
NO.
FUCK. I'M STRONGER THAN THIS.
SAME TIME TOMORROW?
GOOD.

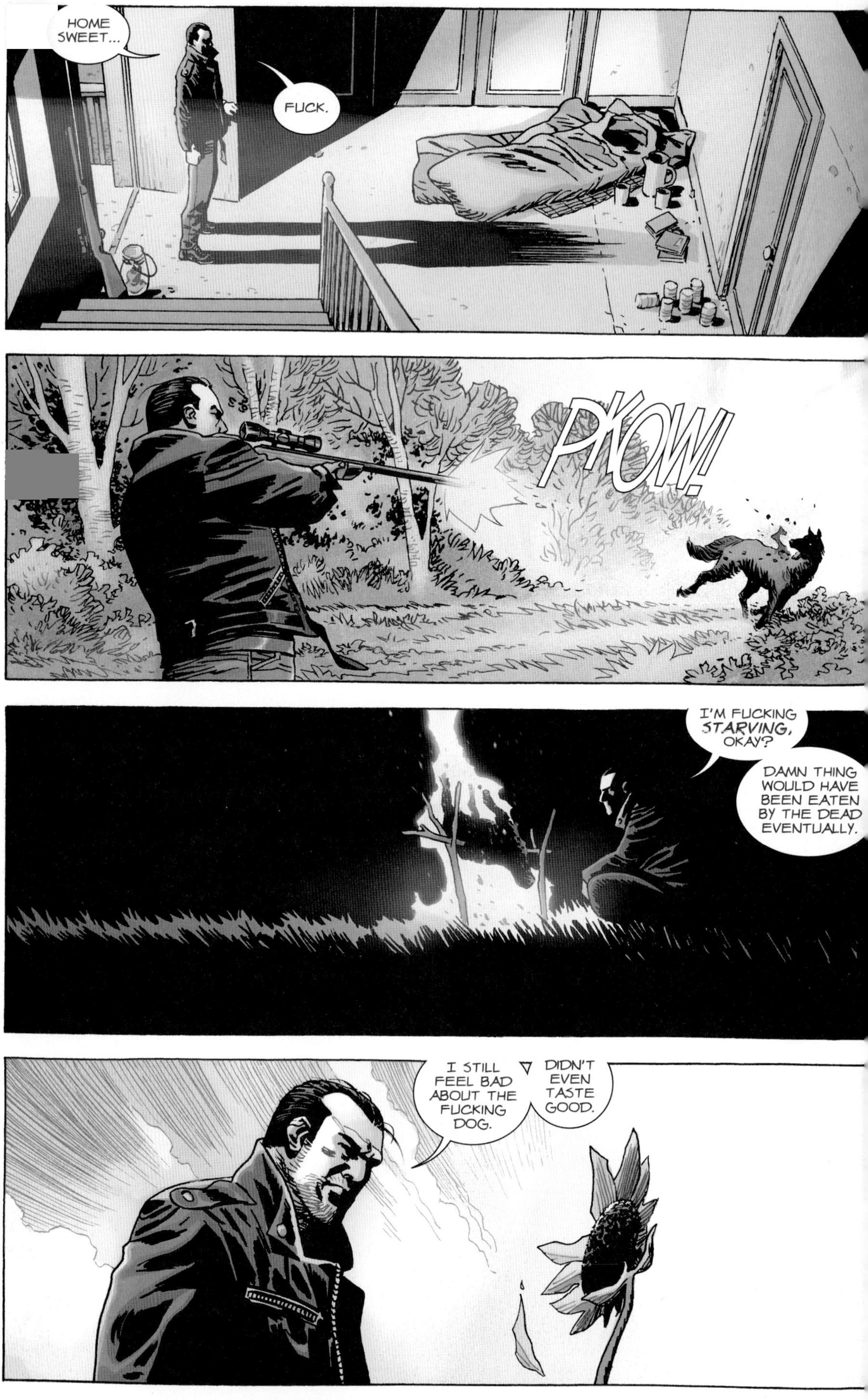
HOME SWEET...
FUCK.
PKOW!
I'M FUCKING STARVING, OKAY?
DAMN THING WOULD HAVE BEEN EATEN BY THE DEAD EVENTUALLY.
I STILL FEEL BAD ABOUT THE FUCKING DOG.
DIDN'T EVEN TASTE GOOD.

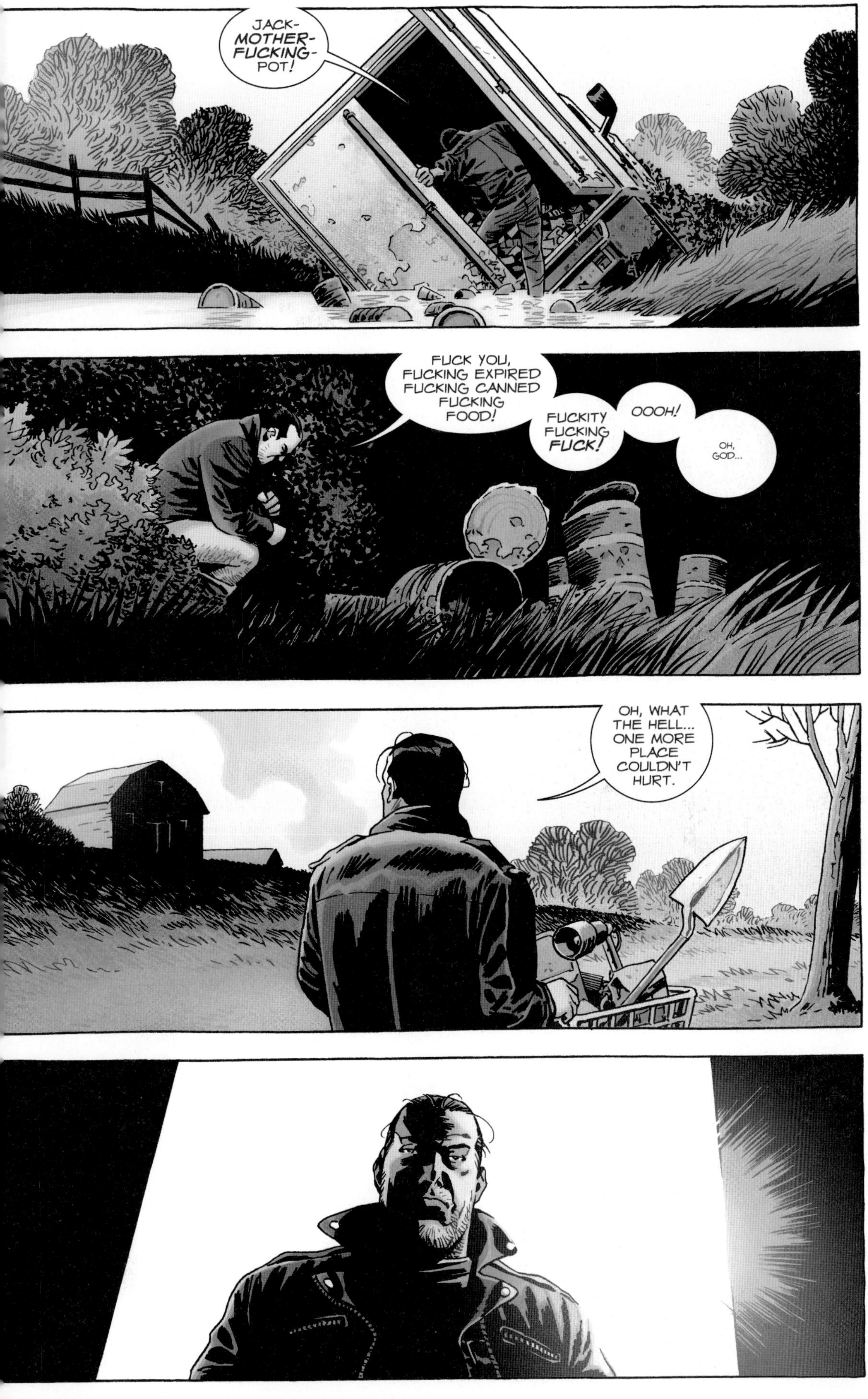
JACK-MOTHER-FUCKING-POT!
FUCK YOU, FUCKING EXPIRED FUCKING CANNED FUCKING FOOD!
FUCKITY FUCKING FUCK!
OOOH!
OH, GOD...
OH, WHAT THE HELL... ONE MORE PLACE COULDN'T HURT.

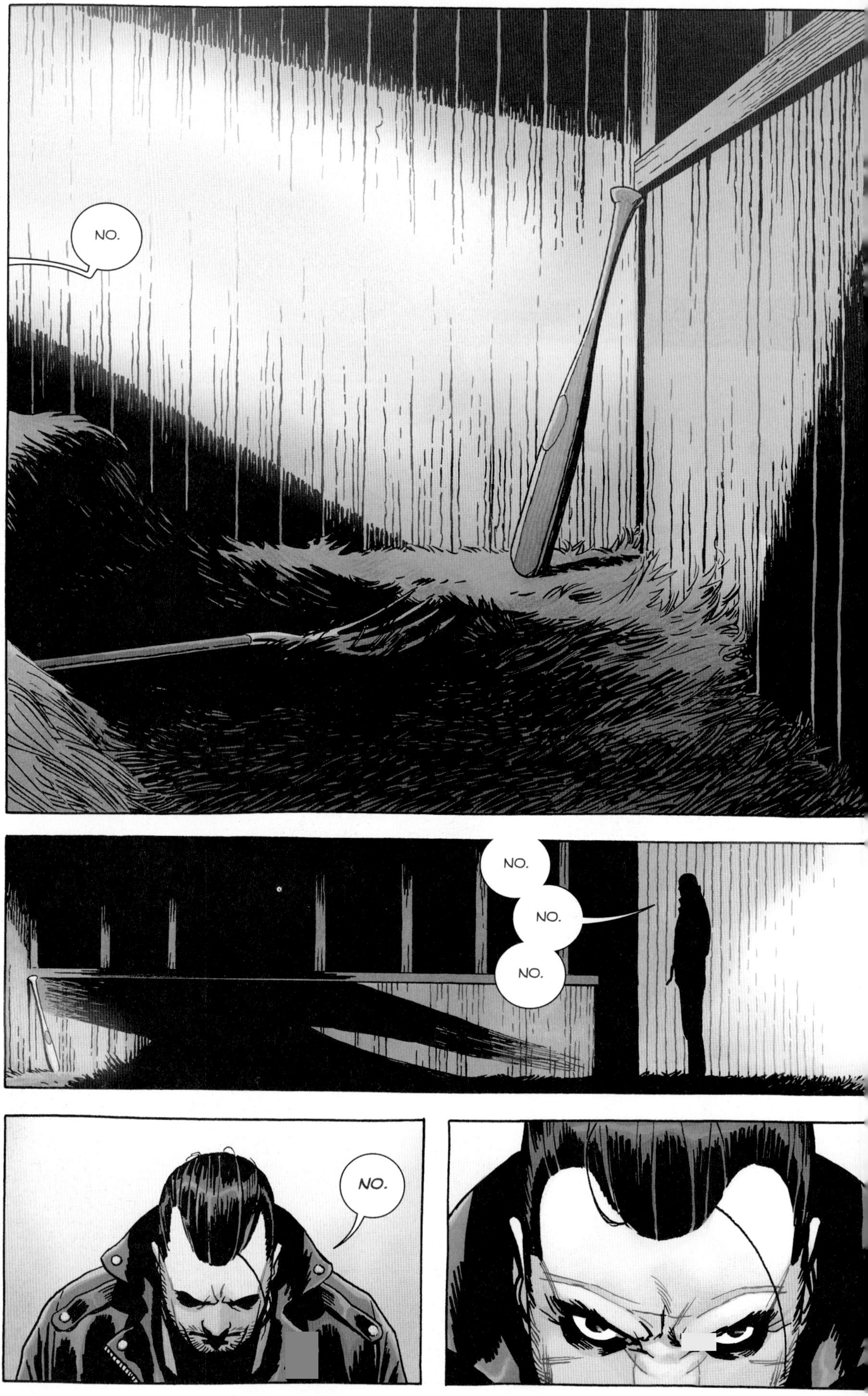
NO.
NO.
NO.
NO.
NO.

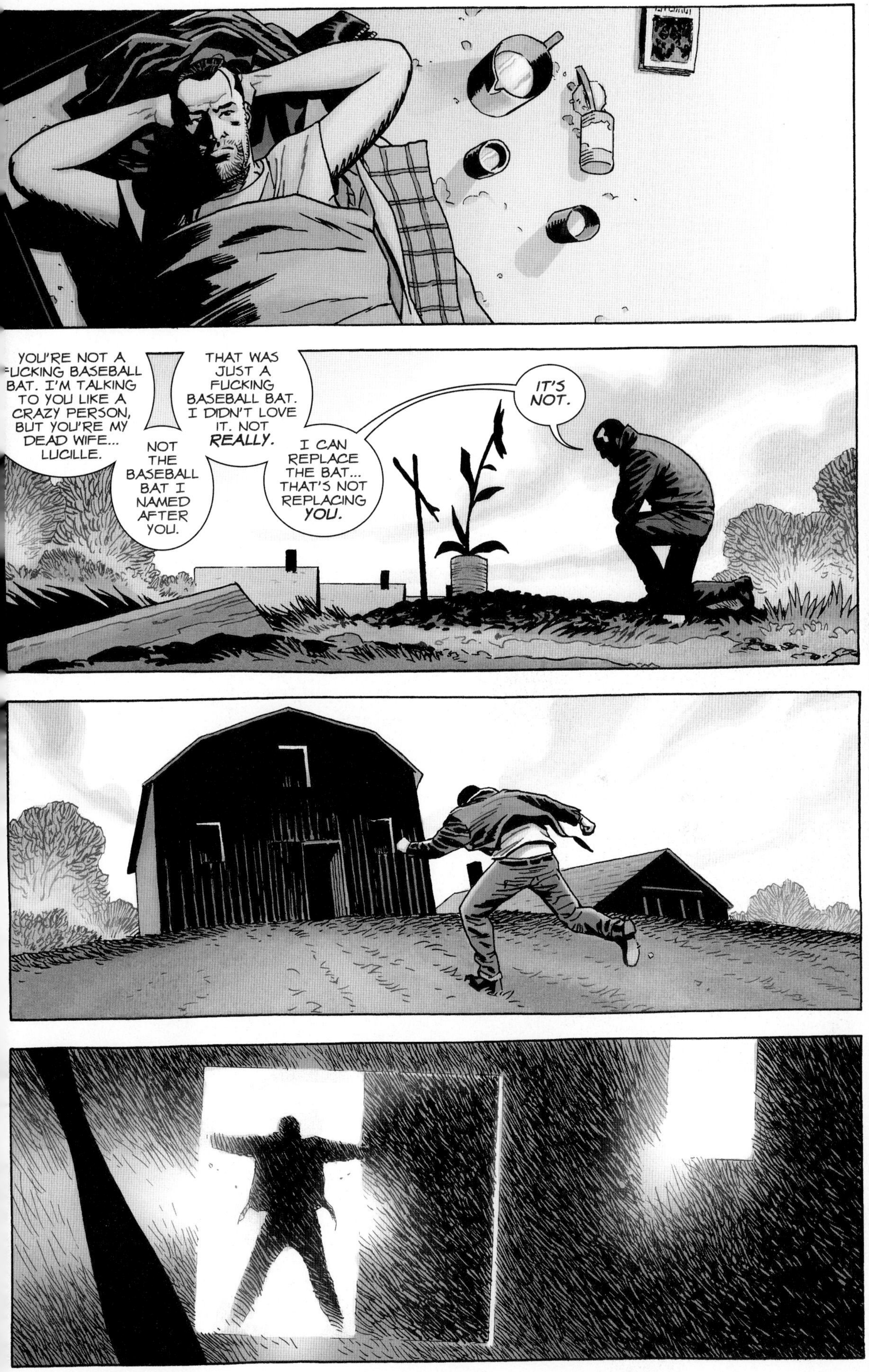
YOU'RE NOT A FUCKING BASEBALL BAT. I'M TALKING TO YOU LIKE A CRAZY PERSON, BUT YOU'RE MY DEAD WIFE... LUCILLE.
NOT THE BASEBALL BAT I NAMED AFTER YOU.
THAT WAS JUST A FUCKING BASEBALL BAT. I DIDN'T LOVE IT. NOT REALLY.
I CAN REPLACE THE BAT... THAT'S NOT REPLACING YOU.
IT'S NOT.

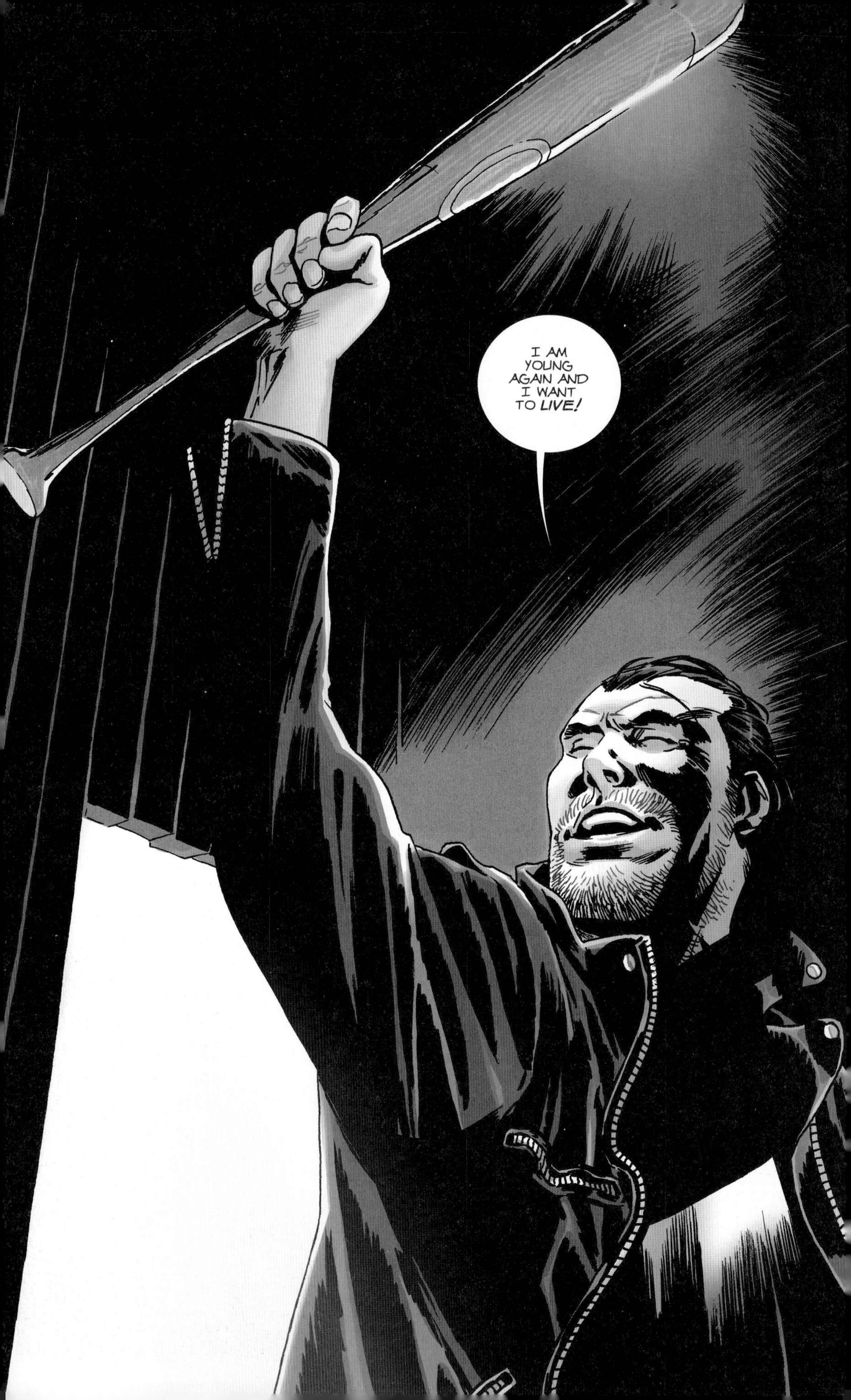
I AM YOUNG AGAIN AND I WANT TO LIVE!

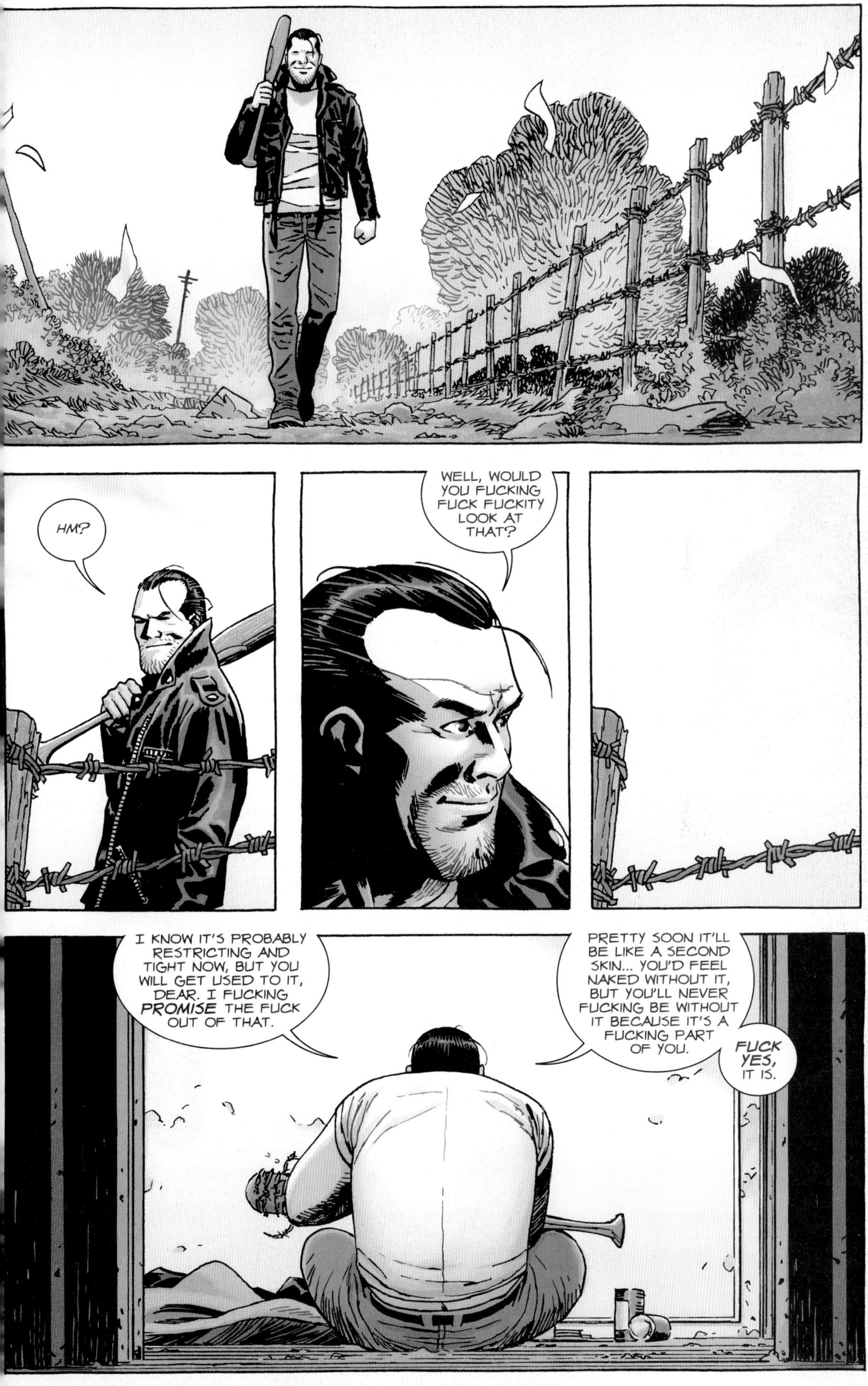
HM?
WELL, WOULD YOU FUCKING FUCK FUCKITY LOOK AT THAT?
I KNOW IT'S PROBABLY RESTRICTING AND TIGHT NOW, BUT YOU WILL GET USED TO IT, DEAR. I FUCKING PROMISE THE FUCK OUT OF THAT.
PRETTY SOON IT'LL BE LIKE A SECOND SKIN... YOU'D FEEL NAKED WITHOUT IT, BUT YOU'LL NEVER FUCKING BE WITHOUT IT BECAUSE IT'S A FUCKING PART OF YOU.
FUCK YES, IT IS.

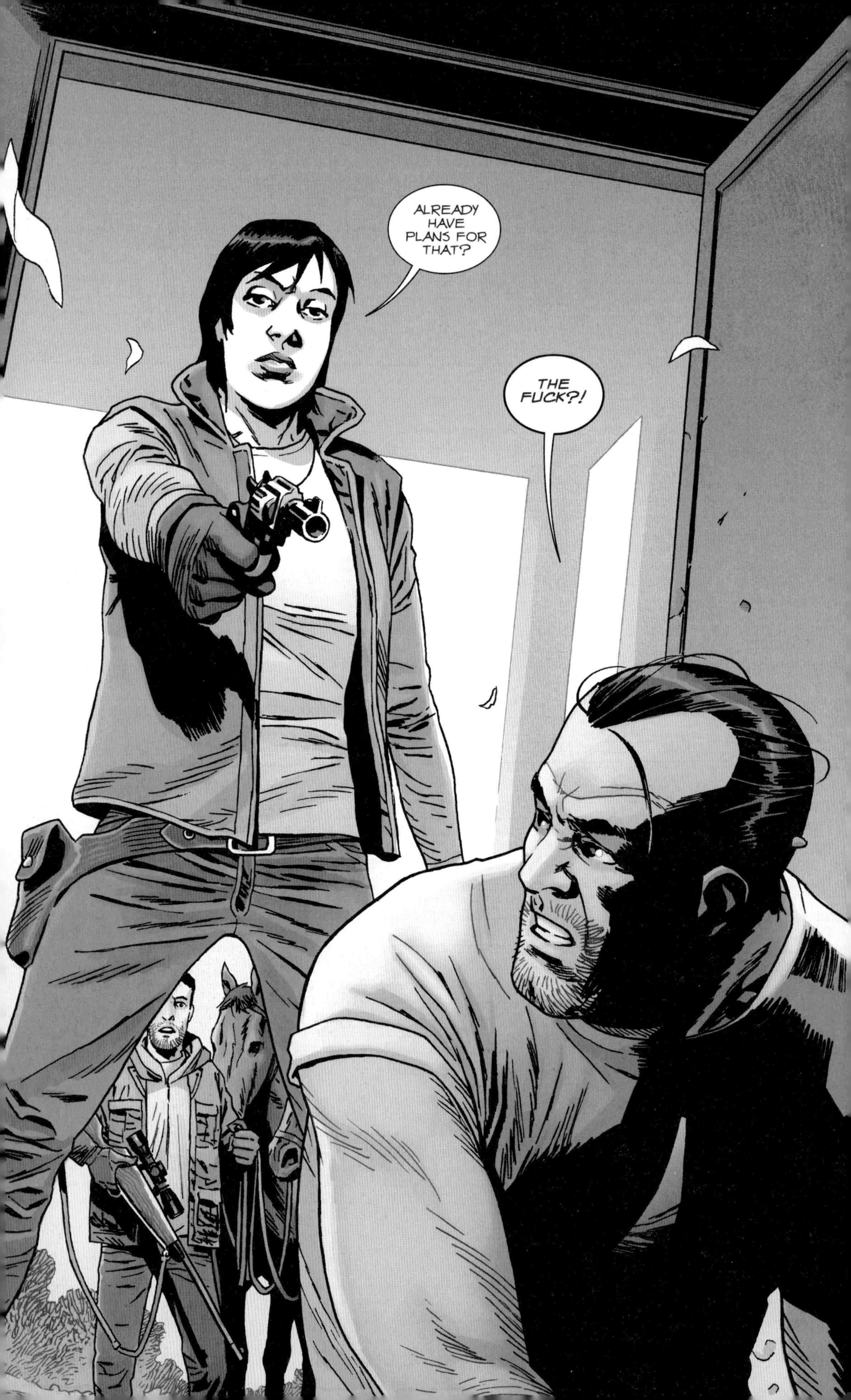
ALREADY HAVE PLANS FOR THAT?
THE FUCK?!

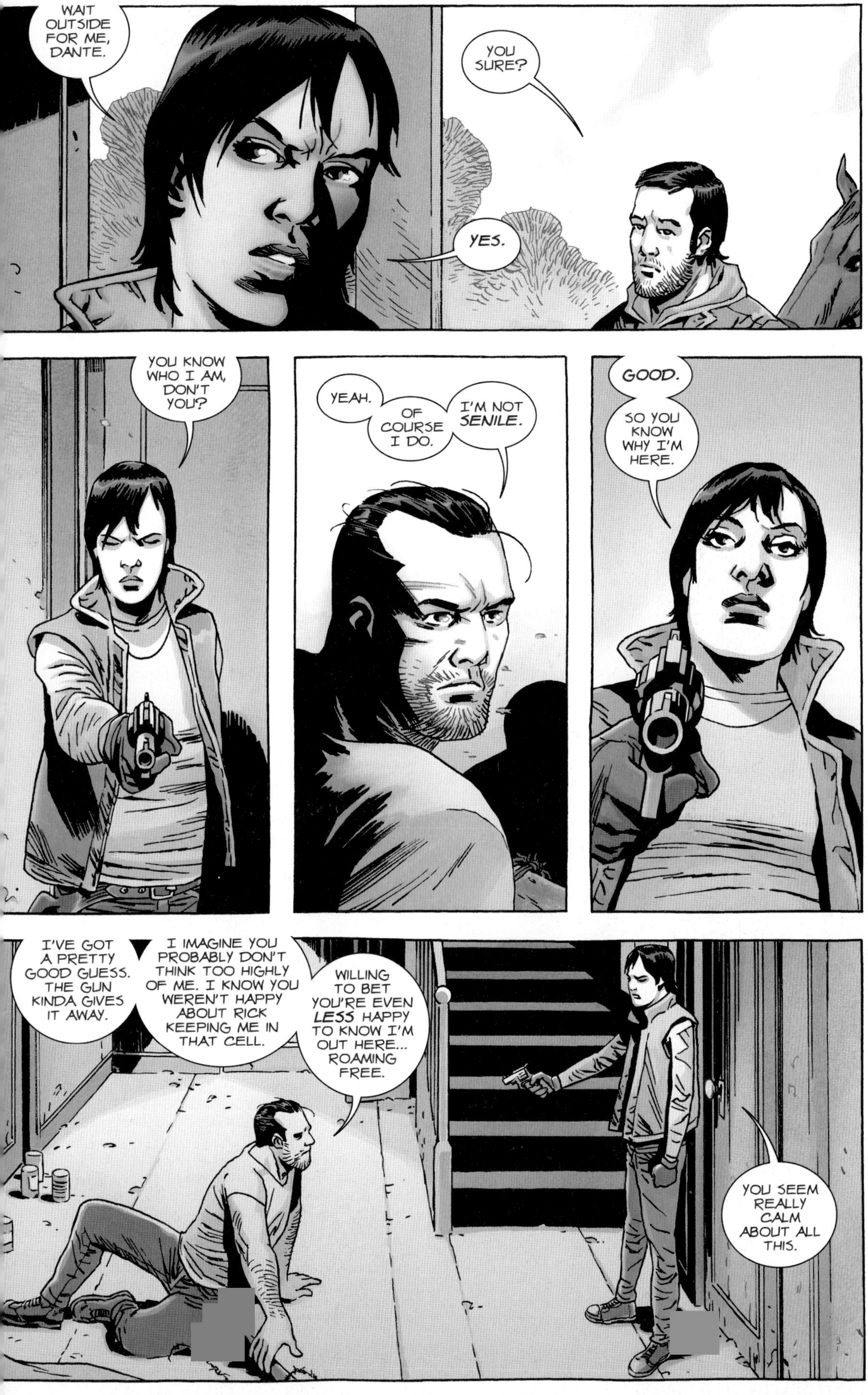
WAIT OUTSIDE FOR ME, DANTE.
YOU SURE?
YES.
YOU KNOW WHO I AM, DON'T YOU?
YEAH.
OF COURSE I DO.
I'M NOT SENILE.
GOOD.
SO YOU KNOW WHY I'M HERE.
I'VE GOT A PRETTY GOOD GUESS. THE GUN KINDA GIVES IT AWAY.
I IMAGINE YOU PROBABLY DON'T THINK TOO HIGHLY OF ME. I KNOW YOU WEREN'T HAPPY ABOUT RICK KEEPING ME IN THAT CELL.
WILLING TO BET YOU'RE EVEN LESS HAPPY TO KNOW I'M OUT HERE... ROAMING FREE.
YOU SEEM REALLY CALM ABOUT ALL THIS.

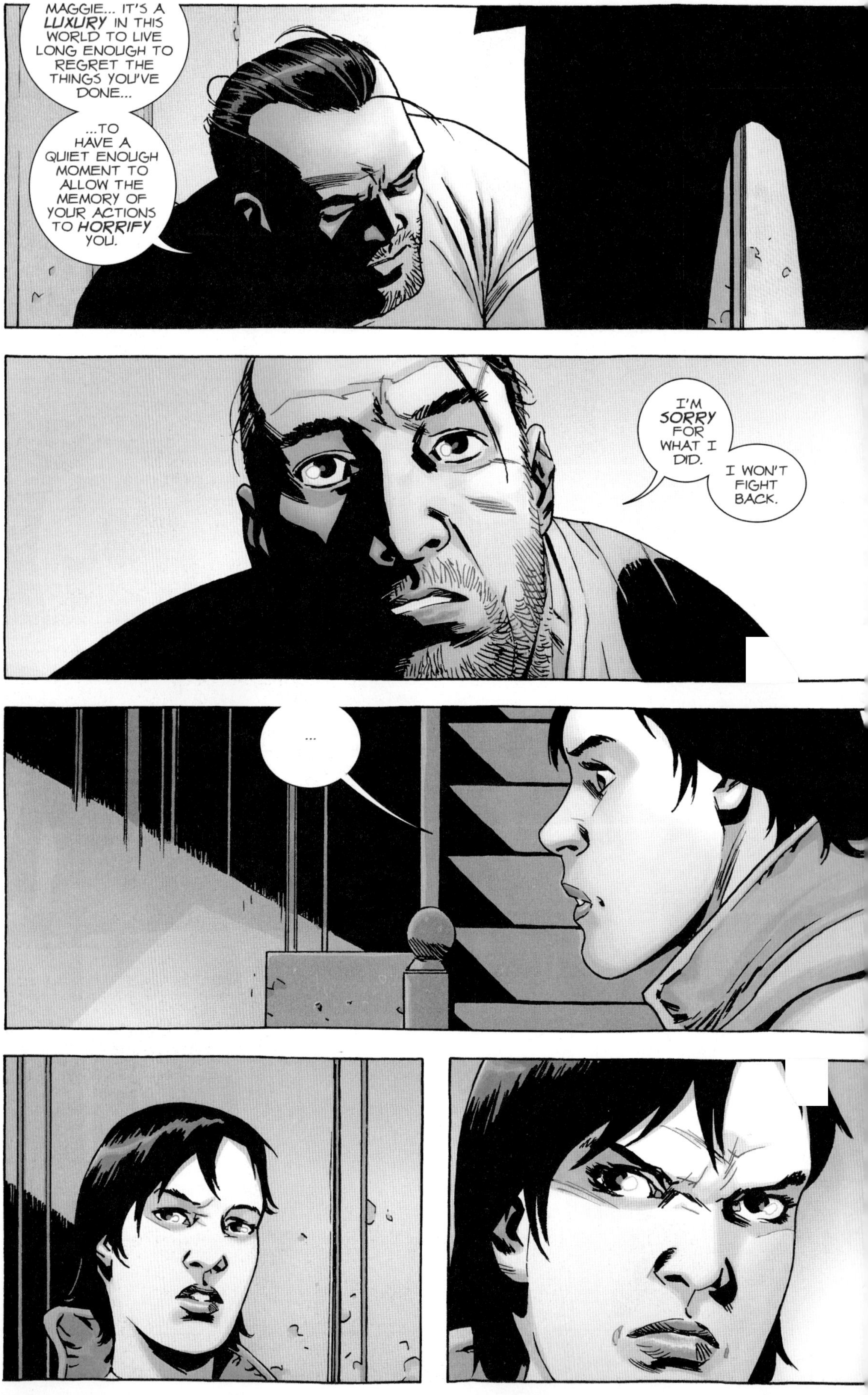
MAGGIE... IT'S A LUXURY IN THIS WORLD TO LIVE LONG ENOUGH TO REGRET THE THINGS YOU'VE DONE...
...TO HAVE A QUIET ENOUGH MOMENT TO ALLOW THE MEMORY OF YOUR ACTIONS TO HORRIFY YOU.
I'M SORRY FOR WHAT I DID.
I WON'T FIGHT BACK.
...

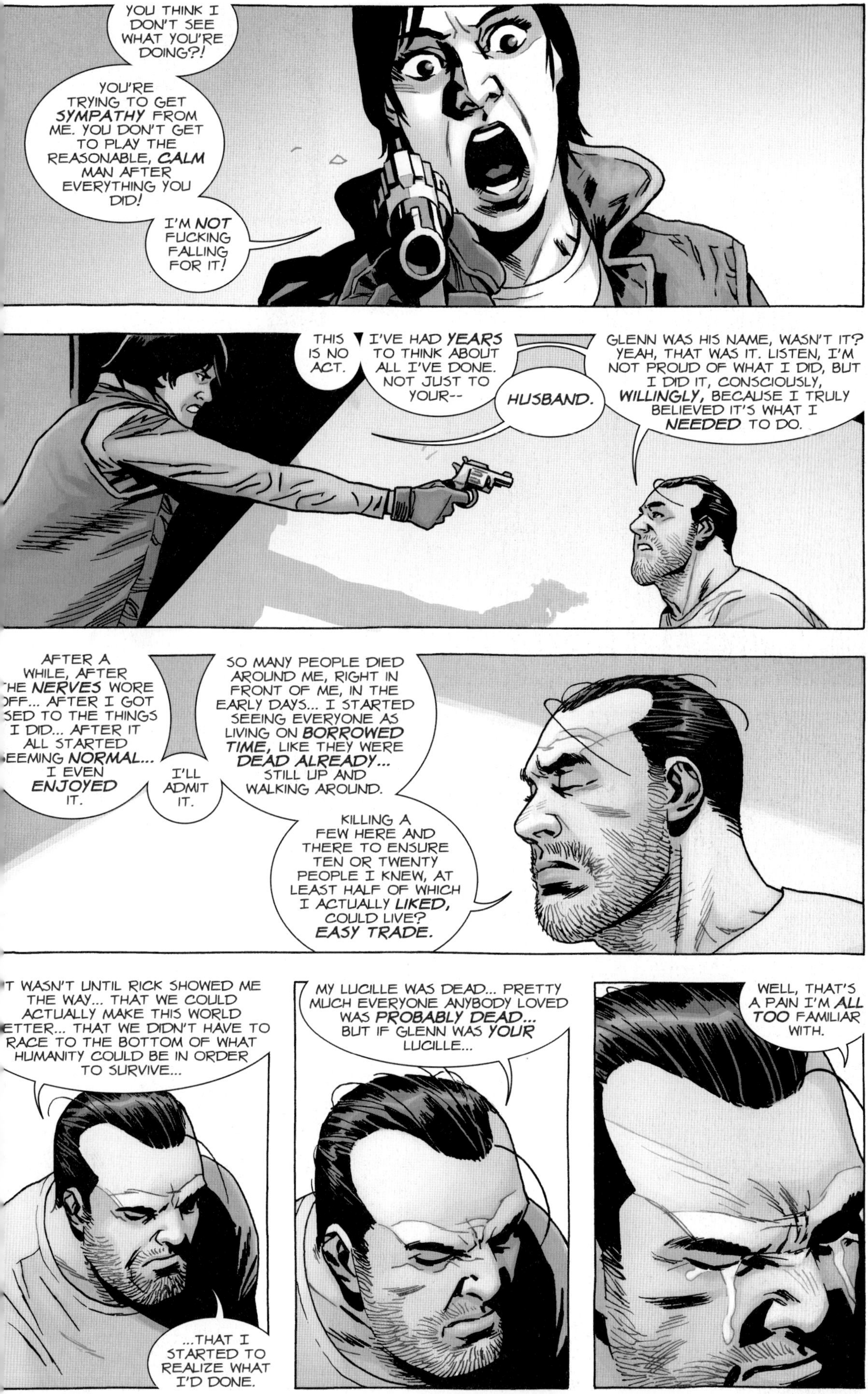

YOU THINK I DON'T SEE WHAT YOU'RE DOING?!
YOU'RE TRYING TO GET SYMPATHY FROM ME. YOU DON'T GET TO PLAY THE REASONABLE, CALM MAN AFTER EVERYTHING YOU DID!
I'M NOT FUCKING FALLING FOR IT!
THIS IS NO ACT.
I'VE HAD YEARS TO THINK ABOUT ALL I'VE DONE. NOT JUST TO YOUR--
HUSBAND.
GLENN WAS HIS NAME, WASN'T IT? YEAH, THAT WAS IT. LISTEN, I'M NOT PROUD OF WHAT I DID, BUT I DID IT, CONSCIOUSLY, WILLINGLY, BECAUSE I TRULY BELIEVED IT'S WHAT I NEEDED TO DO.
AFTER A WHILE, AFTER THE NERVES WORE FF... AFTER I GOT SED TO THE THINGS I DID... AFTER IT ALL STARTED EEMING NORMAL... I EVEN ENJOYED IT.
I'LL ADMIT IT.
SO MANY PEOPLE DIED AROUND ME, RIGHT IN FRONT OF ME, IN THE EARLY DAYS... I STARTED SEEING EVERYONE AS LIVING ON BORROWED TIME, LIKE THEY WERE DEAD ALREADY... STILL UP AND WALKING AROUND.
KILLING A FEW HERE AND THERE TO ENSURE TEN OR TWENTY PEOPLE I KNEW, AT LEAST HALF OF WHICH I ACTUALLY LIKED, COULD LIVE? EASY TRADE.
T WASN'T UNTIL RICK SHOWED ME THE WAY... THAT WE COULD ACTUALLY MAKE THIS WORLD ETTER... THAT WE DIDN'T HAVE TO RACE TO THE BOTTOM OF WHAT HUMANITY COULD BE IN ORDER TO SURVIVE...
...THAT I STARTED TO REALIZE WHAT I'D DONE.
MY LUCILLE WAS DEAD... PRETTY MUCH EVERYONE ANYBODY LOVED WAS PROBABLY DEAD... BUT IF GLENN WAS YOUR LUCILLE...
WELL, THAT'S A PAIN I'M ALL TOO FAMILIAR WITH.

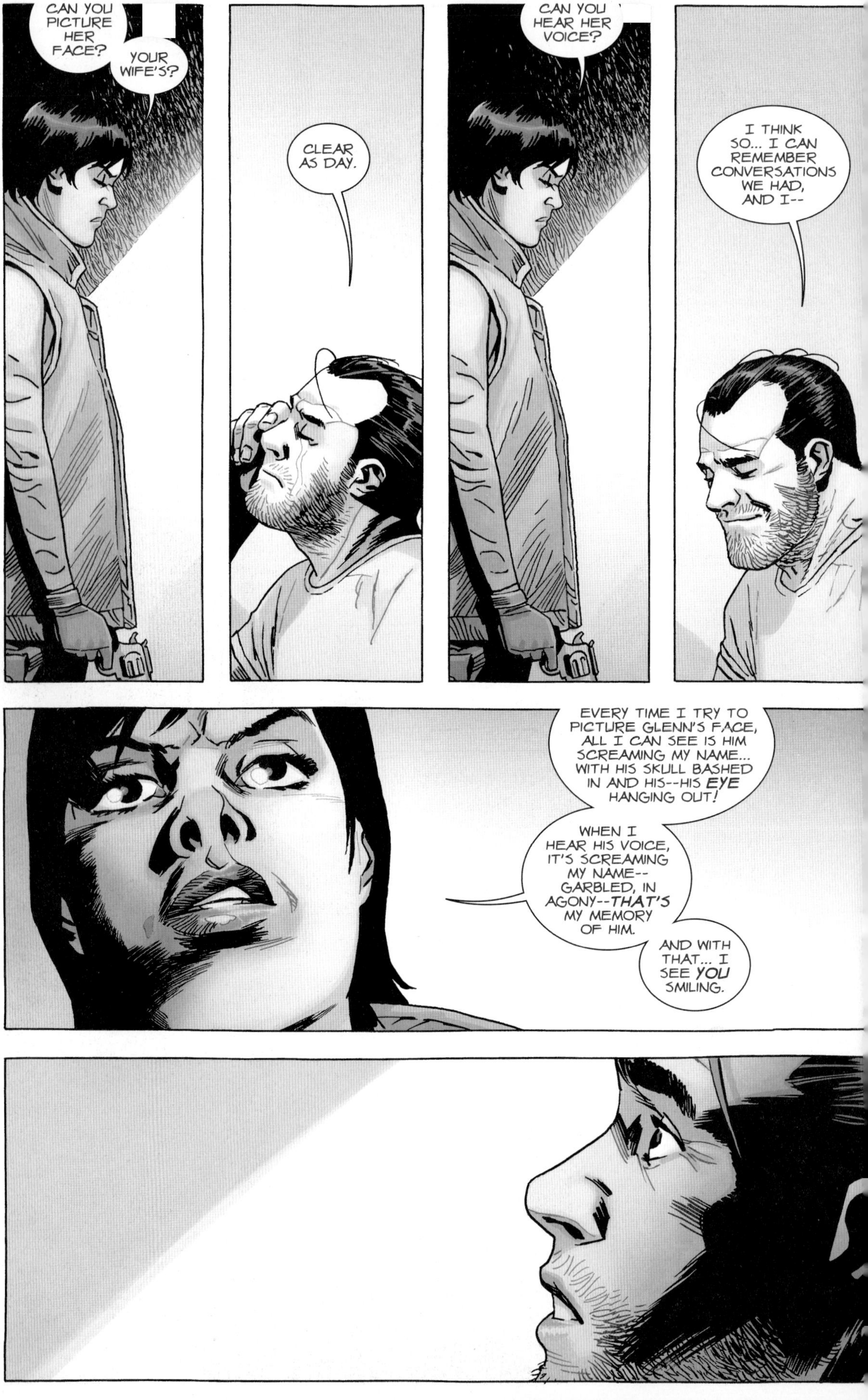
CAN YOU PICTURE HER FACE?
YOUR WIFE'S?
CLEAR AS DAY.
CAN YOU HEAR HER VOICE?
I THINK SO... I CAN REMEMBER CONVERSATIONS WE HAD, AND I--
EVERY TIME I TRY TO PICTURE GLENN'S FACE, ALL I CAN SEE IS HIM SCREAMING MY NAME... WITH HIS SKULL BASHED IN AND HIS--HIS EYE HANGING OUT!
WHEN I HEAR HIS VOICE, IT'S SCREAMING MY NAME--GARBLED, IN AGONY--THAT'S MY MEMORY OF HIM.
AND WITH THAT... I SEE YOU SMILING.

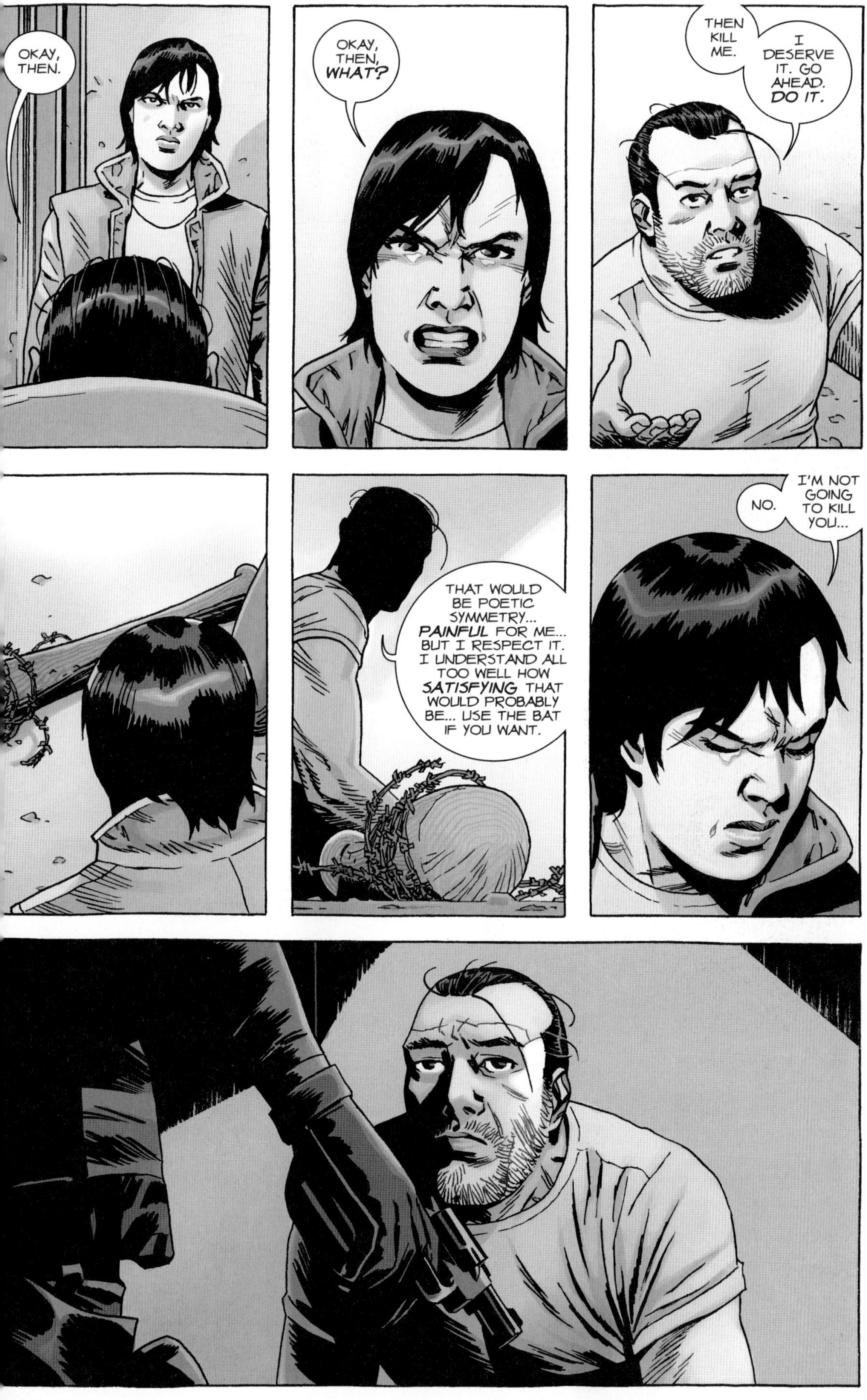

OKAY, THEN.
OKAY, THEN, WHAT?
THEN KILL ME.
I DESERVE IT. GO AHEAD. DO IT.
THAT WOULD BE POETIC SYMMETRY... PAINFUL FOR ME... BUT I RESPECT IT. I UNDERSTAND ALL TOO WELL HOW SATISFYING THAT WOULD PROBABLY BE... USE THE BAT IF YOU WANT.
NO.
I'M NOT GOING TO KILL YOU...

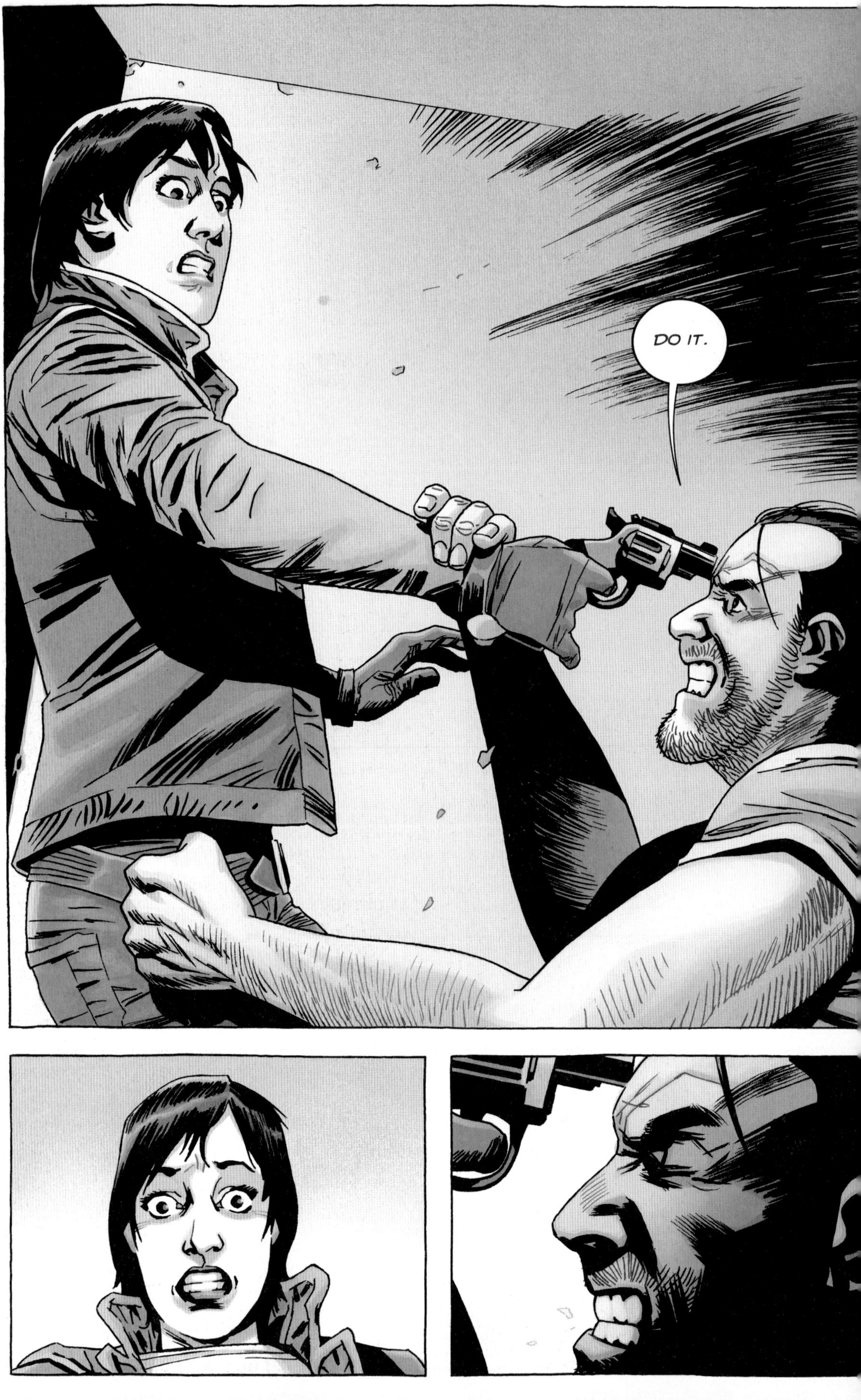
DO IT.

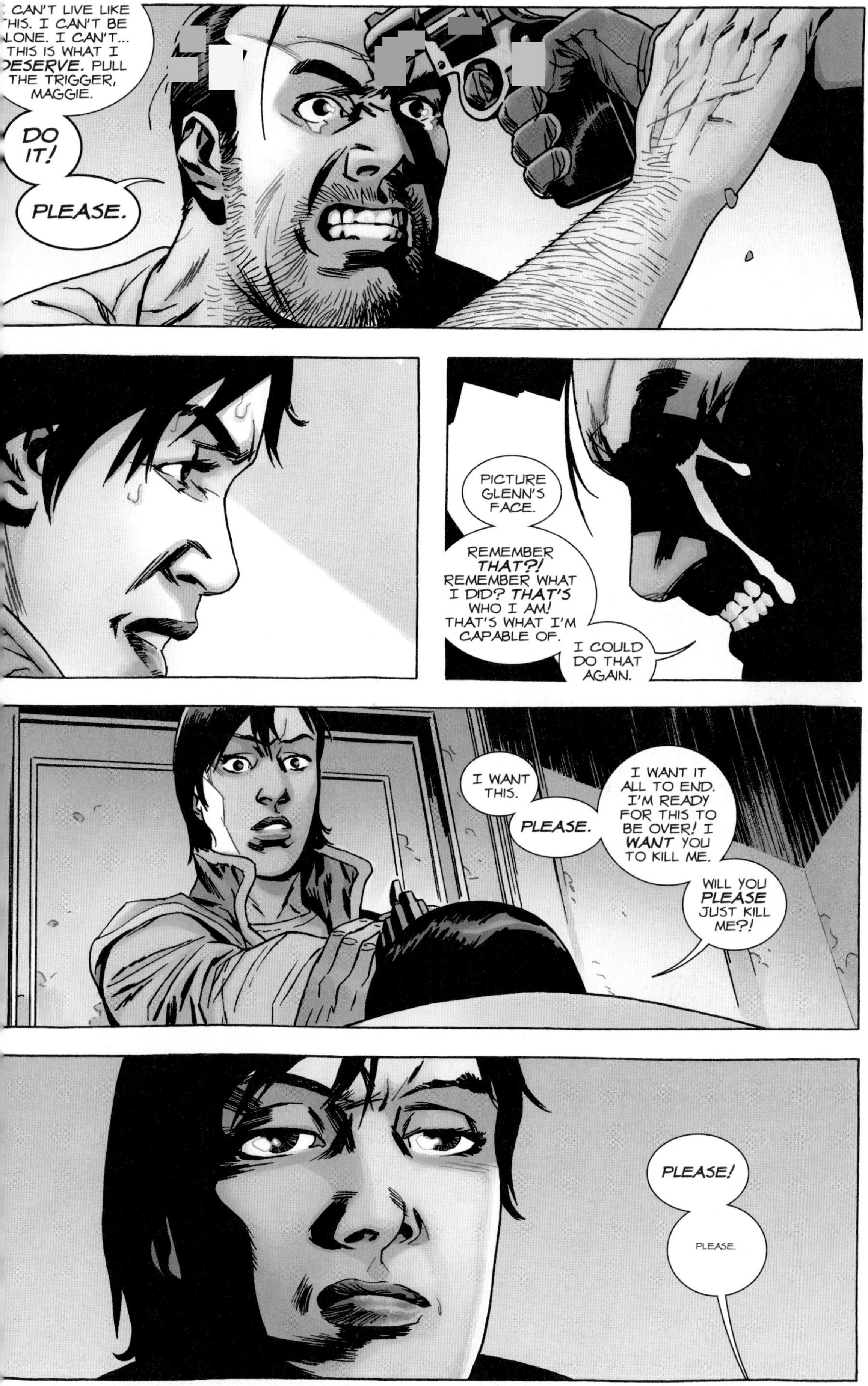
CAN'T LIVE LIKE HIS. I CAN'T BE LONE. I CAN'T... THIS IS WHAT I ESERVE. PULL THE TRIGGER, MAGGIE.
DO IT!
PLEASE.
PICTURE GLENN'S FACE.
REMEMBER THAT?! REMEMBER WHAT I DID? THAT'S WHO I AM! THAT'S WHAT I'M CAPABLE OF.
I COULD DO THAT AGAIN.
I WANT THIS.
PLEASE.
I WANT IT ALL TO END. I'M READY FOR THIS TO BE OVER! I WANT YOU TO KILL ME.
WILL YOU PLEASE JUST KILL ME?!
PLEASE!
PLEASE.

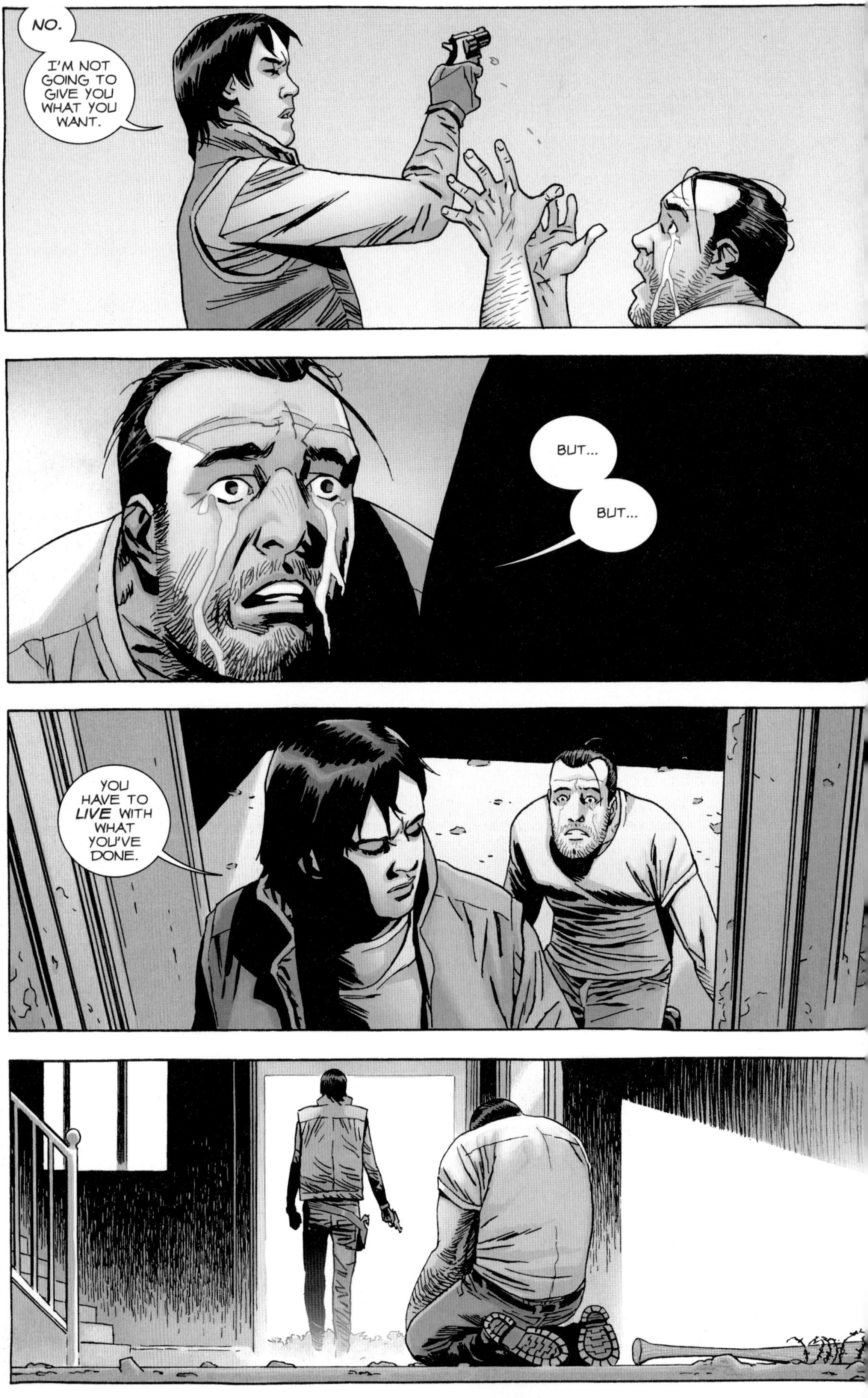
NO.
I'M NOT GOING TO GIVE YOU WHAT YOU WANT.
BUT...
BUT...
YOU HAVE TO *LIVE* WITH WHAT YOU'VE DONE.

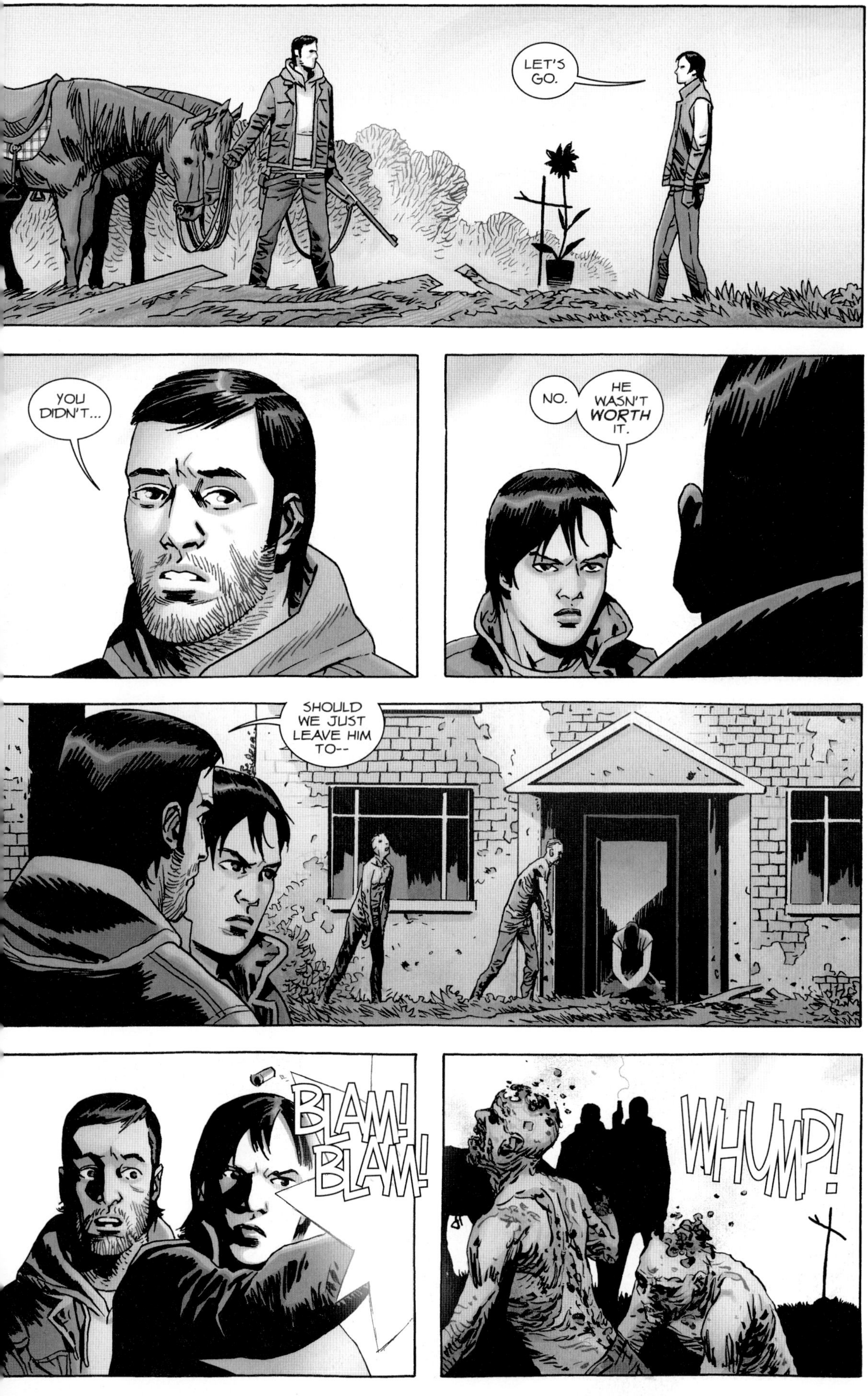
LET'S GO.
YOU DIDN'T...
NO.
HE WASN'T WORTH IT.
SHOULD WE JUST LEAVE HIM TO--
BLAM! BLAM!
WHUMP!

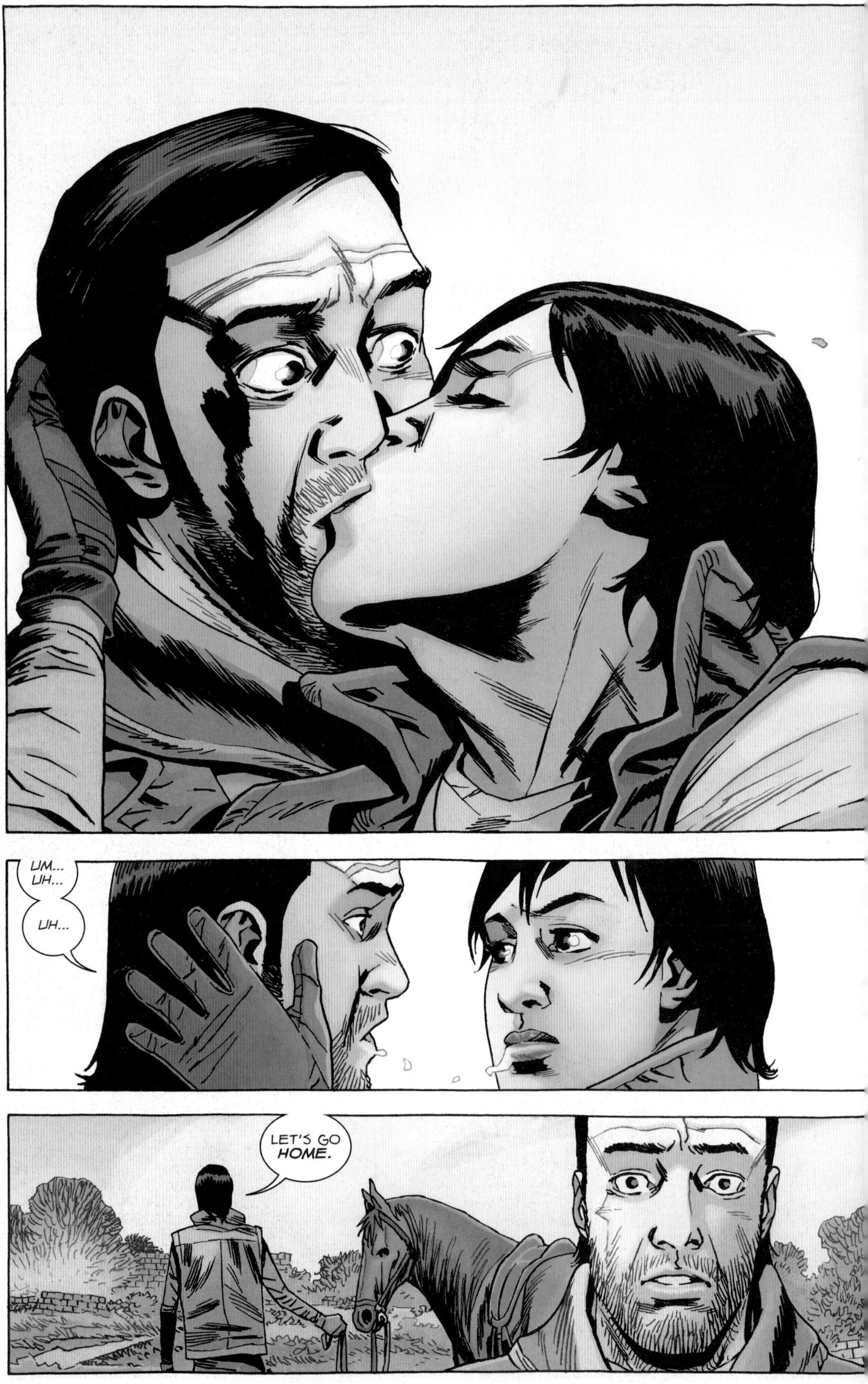
UM...
UH...
UH...
LET'S GO HOME.

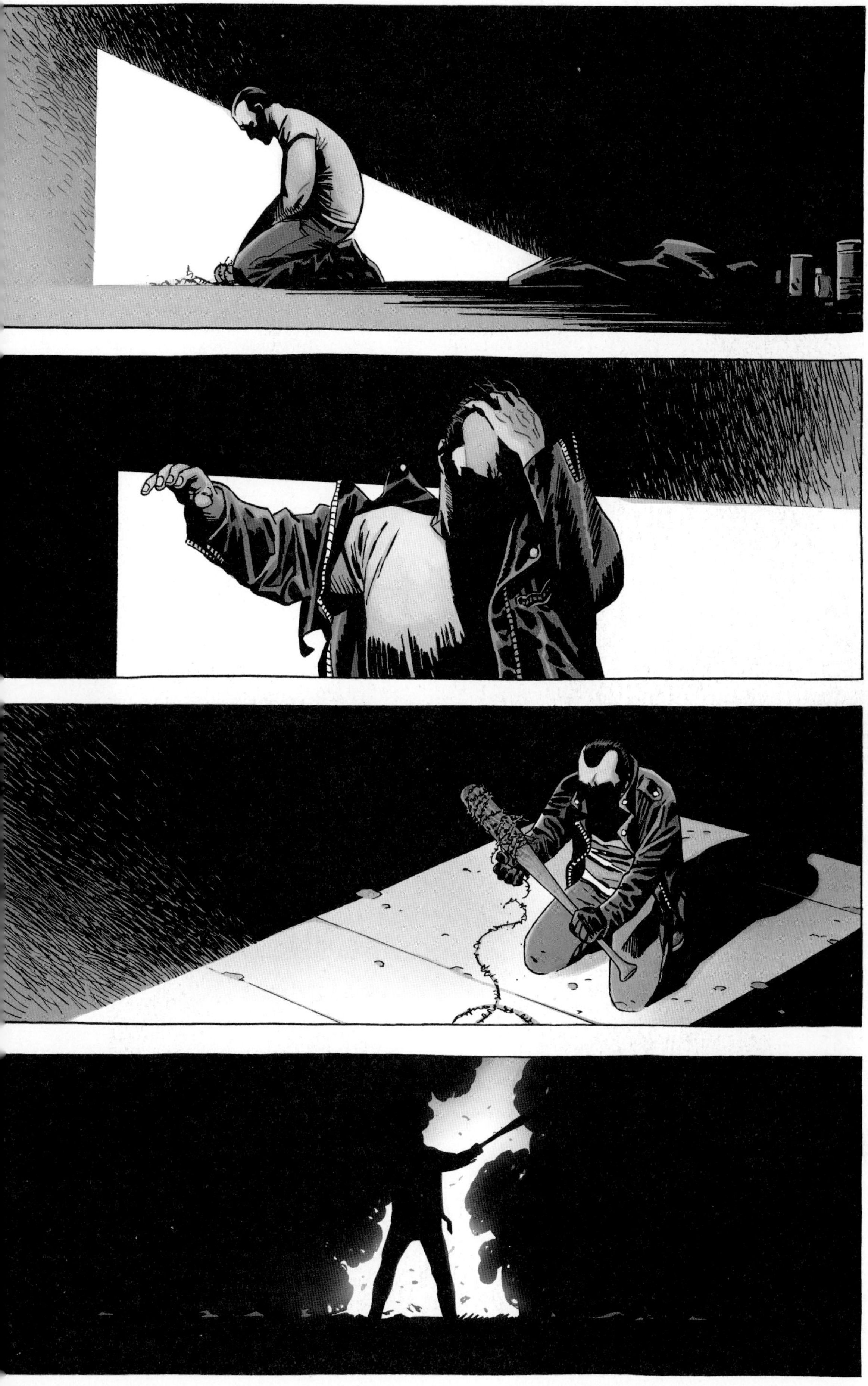

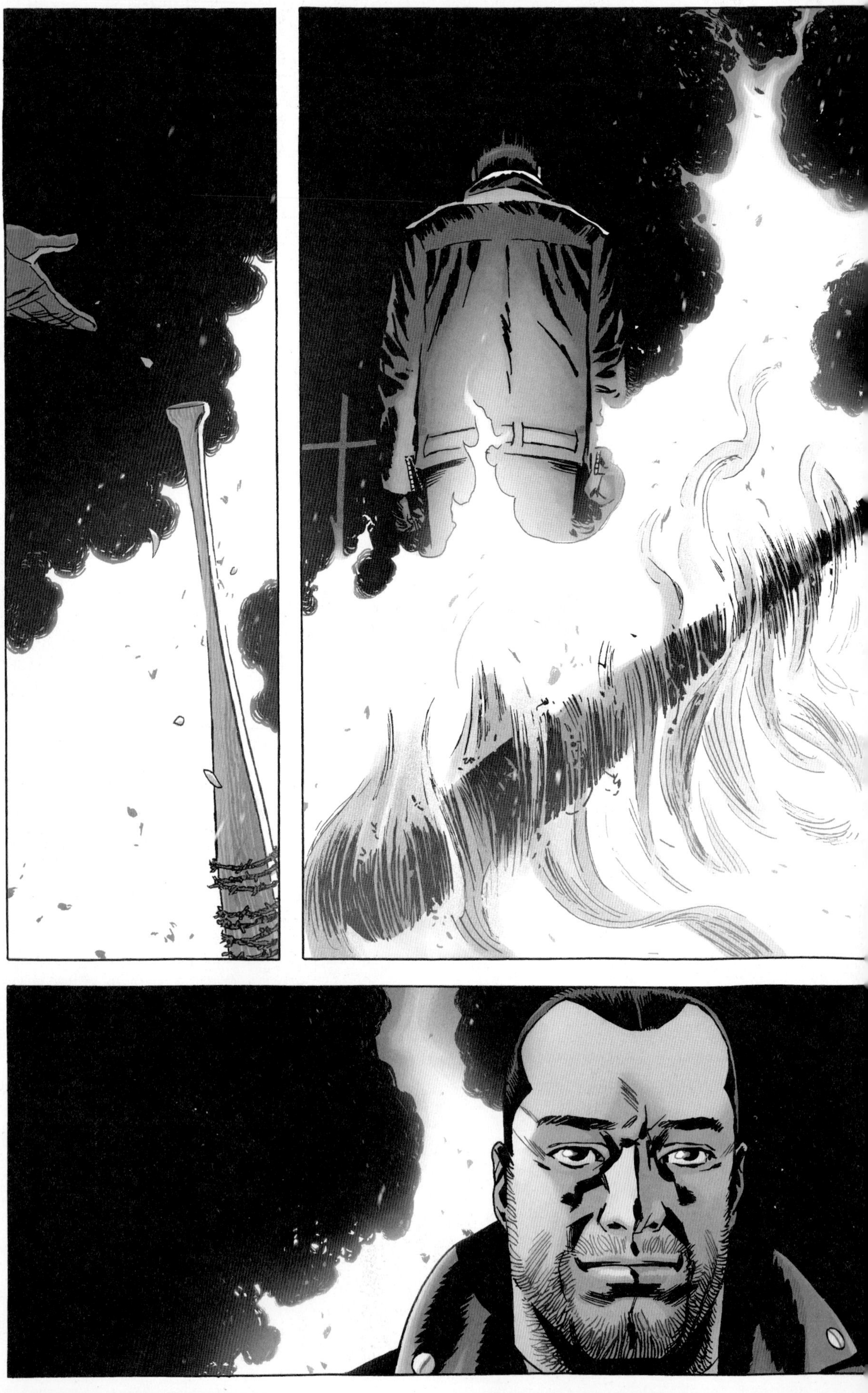